D0152994

LITERARY AND ARTISTIC PATRONAGE
IN ANCIENT ROME

Literary and Artistic Patronage
in Ancient Rome

EDITED BY BARBARA K. GOLD

 University of Texas Press, Austin

First Edition, 1982

Requests for permission to reproduce material from this work
should be sent to Permissions, University of Texas Press, Box
7819, Austin, Texas 78712.

LIBRARY OF CONGRESS CATALOGING IN PUBLICATION DATA
Main entry under title:

Literary and artistic patronage in ancient Rome.

"Essays . . . originally delivered as lectures at a symposium
. . . held in the fall of 1979 at the University of Texas in Aus-
tin"—
    Bibliography: p.
    Contents: Phases in political patronage of literature in Rome
/ Gordon Williams — Pete nobiles amicos / T. P. Wiseman —
Positions for poets in early imperial Rome / Peter White —
[etc.]
    1. Art patronage—Rome—Addresses, essays, lectures.
2. Arts—Rome—Addresses, essays, lectures.
I. Gold, Barbara K., 1945–   .
NX705.5.R6L57   700'.937   81-15964
ISBN 0-292-74631-8   'AACR2

Seven years, my lord, have now passed since I waited in your outward rooms or was repulsed from your door, during which time I have been pushing on my work through difficulties of which it is useless to complain, and have brought it at last to the verge of publication, without one act of assistance, one word of encouragement, or one smile of favor. Such treatment I did not expect, for I had never had a patron before.

—Samuel Johnson,
"Letter to the Earl of Chesterfield,"
February 7, 1755

Contents

Acknowledgments

The essays in this volume were originally delivered as lectures at a symposium on "Artistic and Literary Patronage in Ancient Rome" held in the fall of 1979 at the University of Texas at Austin. I would like to thank the College of Liberal Arts for making this symposium possible and my colleagues in the Department of Classics who joined me in entertaining the visiting scholars. I am also indebted to the Graduate School for a grant which facilitated the preparation of this book and to the support of the Mellon Foundation. Finally, I would like to express my gratitude to William Levitan, who handled with aplomb the many tedious details accompanying a publication of this kind.

Introduction

Although patronage has endured for as long as literature and art have existed, it appears in changing forms in different types of societies, and the nature of its influence on the literature and art has varied considerably. In ancient Greece, the itinerant bards made their living by singing heroic songs at the courts of rich and powerful men. In the Roman republic, political figures like Scipio and Pompey enabled poorer Romans and foreigners to better their financial and social position by supporting their literary and artistic endeavors. In the empire, the Roman emperor became the patron of last resort, who eclipsed all other *principes* and on whom all literature and art was ultimately focused. In sixteenth-century Italy, Benvenuto Cellini revealed the importance of the patronage given to him by various wealthy families and by the pope. He claimed that the lords "sent me such a very liberal present, that I was well content; indeed, there grew in me so great a spirit to do well, that to this event I attribute what will afterwards be related of my progress."[1]

In Elizabethan England, Spenser lamented that "Mecoenas is yclad in claye, / And great Augustus long ygoe is dead."[2] In *The Rape of Lucrece* Shakespeare made unashamed pleas for support to patrons such as the Earl of Southampton, and in *Timon of Athens* he explored the problems created by patronage. This comes up again in his sonnets. In the nineteenth and early twentieth centuries, patronage was frequently replaced by literary circles gathered around a central artistic or literary figure like Gertrude Stein. In recent decades, patronage has taken an interesting turn away from the individual and personal form in which it appeared for so long and has become strangely depersonalized and institutionalized. No longer does a single, wealthy patron seek out a writer of talent who might extol the patron's virtues and career and lend a heroic aura. People of means now submerge their money in a foundation which is then administered by a second person who, in turn, chooses a third person to discover worthy recipients. The recipients are not expected to laud the virtues of the sources of their income; rarely do writers even give thought to the source of the largesse. This book, for example, is published with the help and encouragement of the Paul Mellon Foundation and the University of Texas. Although some acknowledgment of this support is expected from the author or editor out of courtesy, few would think to laud the name and accomplishments of a Mr. Mellon and fewer would do so. If the individual philanthropist gains any fame from generosity, the fame rests on acts of giving, and it is the foundation that disseminates this fame, not the individual author. The personality of the benefactor is subsumed by the foundation or institution that bears the benefactor's name. A university is an even more depersonalized patron: it grants support in order that fame might redound on the institution itself and, in the case of a state-supported university, on the entire state; this fame, in turn, is supposed to attract other scholars to the university. No particular project or individual is singled out, simply a type of person; the recipients are depersonalized. The system has become closed and the goals of the support are now far less practical than they once were; no longer is patronage designed to influence votes, propagate opinions, or provide posthumous fame, as it was in Rome.

In *Timon of Athens*, patronage is called "the magic of bounty" (1.1.6), a curious phrase which succinctly reveals the problems encountered by both the patron and the writer or artist. It is the job of the writer or artist both to appear a person of ease who writes as a pastime and simultaneously to convince a potential patron that there is indeed need for support. In pursuit of this aim, the patron must be praised fulsomely but with sincerity and good taste. The writer or artist must possess both the magic of expression and the material means to parlay this magic into a solid literary or artistic work. The patron also wears two hats. The patron must choose individuals of real ability and talent and convey to them personal wishes and aims without such close guidance that creativity and originality are stifled and unimaginative and dutiful plodders are created.

Certain patrons were highly political men who had specific programs to carry out and who required or desired writers or artists of talent to help them; such was Augustus. But to say that certain patrons, particularly political figures, had programs and plans to be implemented is not the same as saying that they used literary men and artists as a means to this end. As Peter White points out, we must beware of viewing patronage as a deliberate policy of encouraging art and literature and therefore necessarily as a deliberate attempt to promote a broader cultural or political policy.[3] This assumption cannot easily be made. Earlier assessors of Maecenas considered him an instrument of Augustus, a minister of propaganda,[4] and viewed poets as supporters of certain legislative programs because of moral pressures on them.[5] Those who deal with the question of patronage and the arts today are more cautious in their approach. There are three main considerations.

First, it is difficult and dangerous to use works of literature or art, particularly those acknowledged as great works such as the *Aeneid* or the Ara Pacis, as social and historical documents, and to determine from a reading or viewing of them the real attitude of the patron and writer or artist toward each other and toward society. The dilemma of writer or artist, the problem of seeming to produce gracious and unbiased works while in fact being deeply influenced by both an ultimate reward and by the ideas of the patron, creates a problem for the reader as well. The persona created by the poet or artist in a work and the historical person are quite different, yet to the reader they may seem identical and inseparable. Similarly, the persona of the patron as it is presented by the poet and the historical figure meld together in the work and present a third figure, a blend of persona and person, as seen through biased eyes. This makes any discussion of the historical aims of poet or artist and patron taken apart from the literature very difficult.

The second consideration is the changing face of patronage from one age to another and from one society to another. The problems discussed above are common to all ages and societies, but the roles of the patron and writer or artist differ radically from one situation to another. To take just one example, our idea of patronage in the late twentieth century is very different from the Greek or Roman conception of it. Modern patronage, as I have pointed out above, most often emanates from an institution, not an individual, and is not concerned with promoting any specific cultural, political, or moral ideal. Furthermore, the writer or artist is usually supported solely by the institution for a period of time. He or she is singled out by the supporter as somehow different from and superior to people who gain money from standard kinds of employment and is allowed freedom of expression. In contrast, a Roman writer or artist received money from an individual who was usually concerned with having himself praised or his ideas disseminated. This individual supported many people at once and the support took the form of infrequent and irregular gifts in most cases. In addition, the Roman writer or artist often was not singled out for special consideration but was treated as a dependent similar to hangers-on of lower social status. In Greece, artists were regarded as manual laborers along with doctors and architects. Rarely did these men have freedom in choosing themes, styles, and materials. In the late Roman republic, writers and artists of note were allowed much, perhaps total, freedom, but here again we are on unsure ground.

The final general consideration is the difference between the patronage of art and the patronage of literature, which I have thus far treated as one. Seen from a general historical perspective, the two are not far apart on such questions as freedom, propaganda, and the role of the patron and writer or artist. We can point to periods when both artists and writers had great or little freedom. Eleanor Winsor Leach and Gordon Williams address themselves to this point. But naturally there are major differences both between art and literature and between public and private art. In art, we deal with a concrete, tangible object, and we have before us the actual product of patronage. In public art, a piece was often commissioned by a political figure who wished to make a political or social statement. The patron in public art is often known; the artist, rarely. In private art, as in Pompeian wall paintings for example, neither patron nor painter is known and there are few individual or original details from which we might guess the identity of the painter. However, Eleanor Winsor Leach believes that by the mid first century A.D. the wishes and personality of the patron were revealed, and the painter had the freedom to execute the wishes of the patron in his own unique manner. In literature, on the other hand, we have a document which reveals the name of both patron and writer but obscures the aim and purpose of both in a tangle of words.

Opinion differs about the importance of viewing literary patronage from a sociohistorical perspective. Hugh Trevor-Roper makes the following claim: "History which ignores art or literature is jejune history, just as a society without art or literature is a jejune society, and, conversely, art and literature which are studied in detachment from history are only half understood."[6] Some of the contributors to this volume would agree. Williams, Wiseman, White, and Baldwin believe that an awareness of the bare facts of the historical situation is essential to any understanding of patronage. T. P. Wiseman's method is to "look hard at the evidence and ask practical questions—who does what, and when, and where?" Peter White also takes a no-nonsense approach and discusses "the working lives of poets at Rome without raising any consideration that has to do with the quality of their poems." The other contributors deal to a greater or lesser extent with the poetry itself, not with the historical context or hard facts of patronage. James Zetzel, for example, not only avoids treating texts as social documents rather than literary works but says that although "to determine the nature of literary patronage ought to be crucial to our understanding of Roman poetry . . . a good case can be made for denying utterly the importance of patronage to Latin poetry."

These are the major considerations in the essays. The question of patronage is approached by the contributors from every angle— historical, literary, artistic—and both generally and in close detail. In the first essay, "Phases in Political Patronage of Literature in Rome," Gordon Williams surveys patronage from the beginning of Roman literary activity in the mid third century B.C. down to the Flavians. Williams concerns himself with an overall picture of the different phases of literary patronage rather than with the literary merits of the works. His examination is limited to political patronage, that is, patronage aimed at influencing voters, enhancing the reputation of the patron, or disseminating political policies. In each section of his essay, Williams discusses the development of patronage in a particular period of the Roman republic or empire. The changes involve type of patron, type of literature, and reaction of the writer. Williams begins with a discussion of drama, which was supported mainly by *nobiles*, prominent Roman aristocrats. This gave way to epic and oratory, which was less popularized and more acceptable to the elite. The next stage occurred in the second century B.C., when Lucilius became the first to make the writing of poetry a respectable way of life for the Roman *nobilis*. In this period, Greeks were more prominent, particularly in the writing of panegyric. Next, patronage was taken over by the *principes*, great and magnetic men like Pompey and Caesar, who tried to attract writers who would foster a particular "climate of opinion." There followed the era of Maecenas, *the* patron, who allowed great poets like Horace and Virgil to move from "isolation and despair to optimism and reliance" and to deal with important political and social issues through a public persona. The next transition marked a major change in both history and patronage: the advent of the emperor Augustus, who became the "patron of first resort." Williams claims that from this point on the poets were concerned with presenting only one side of an issue and with manipulating panegyric theme and technique. This led to a gradual decline in freedom of expression and to the final paradox under the Julio-Claudians: literature needed imperial patronage to survive but at the same time was suffocated by it.

The next three papers treat patronage from a sociohistorical point of view and ask practical questions about the poets, patrons, and circumstances of the poetry. T. P. Wiseman, in *"Pete nobiles amicos*: Poets and Patrons in Late Republican Rome," discusses in detail three writers in particular. Through Archias, Lucretius, and Catullus, Wiseman examines the *beneficia* and *officia* of client and patron, the problem of dependency of the writer upon his patron, and the differences both between Greek and Roman clients and among Roman clients of varying social ranks. Archias stands out as a man more dependent on his patron because he was Greek, but Wiseman concludes that poets cannot be considered as a class apart but only on an individual basis. Wiseman and White agree that a poet was just as likely to be in a dependent position as a lower-class *cliens*, but usually required different types of favors. One *beneficium* mentioned as important by both is the opportunity for publicity among the right people.

Peter White, in "Positions for Poets in Early Imperial Rome," continues the investigation of the question "What did the poets in Rome want?" White points out that poetry was indeed a money-making career and, more important, was regarded as such by the poets themselves. This was true particularly in the early empire, when taking money for writing and speaking was no longer considered demeaning. White dispels the romantic notion that patronage came only in intangible forms such as praise, encouragement, and support. Roman writers desired and sought financial assistance but were not, despite their protestations, a poverty-stricken group. Most were knights or senators with a large enough income to support themselves at least on a minimal level. What they sought was enhancement of their income, and they gained this from rich *amici* or patrons because of their privileged training and position as gentlemen and their skill in an art often practiced by the patrons themselves.

In a more broadly based paper entitled "Literature and Society in the Later Roman Empire," Barry Baldwin considers the position of the writer in society and the literary interests of the emperors, the primary patrons. He also treats the general state of literary activity in a later period of the empire, from Hadrian to Diocletian. Baldwin reaches different conclusions than White does, contending that literature in the second and fourth centuries A.D. was not in total collapse, as is commonly believed, but that conditions in the third century were bad both in Greece and Italy. Baldwin, like Gordon Williams in *Change and Decline*,[7] maintains that Romans from Ovid's father on considered poetry a useless pursuit, and that nobles and emperors themselves rarely engaged in writing, with notable exceptions. Peter White disagrees, but White and Baldwin would concur, I believe, that poets in all periods had to be useful to the patron in question and not simply good at their craft. Baldwin's most important conclusion is that the rise and decline of literature closely followed political fluctuations. He believes that the dilemma of the literati, in the empire at least, was connected directly to social and material causes.

The next three papers examine the question of patronage from within the poetry itself. Just as Wiseman and White forsake the issue of literary merit for more practical questions, James Zetzel abandons the historical side to examine "The Poetics of Patronage in the Late First Century B.C." Zetzel claims that the patron is no more important as a historical figure in the poem than is the poet himself. If we admit a separation between the actual poet and the persona of the poet, then we must do the same for the patron. To confuse these categories is to drain the poem of poetic meaning for the purpose of gaining useless or faulty information. In any given poem, the patron addressed is chosen by the author solely for his connotation, not denotation, and for his importance to the style and subject matter of the poem, not because of his historical position. Zetzel examines the poetic function and context of the direct second-person addressee, particularly Maecenas, and investigates certain corollaries of these: the existence of individual poems outside of a book, the function of the dedication in a poem, and the Muse as patron. This approach at once keeps us within the world of the poem and allows us to include the social reality of patronage by viewing the poetry as a transformation of social ideas into poetic expression. Catullus and the Augustan poets used social relationships as metaphors to assert literary values. In the poetry of the later republic, art not life is both subject and object of the poem, and primacy is given to literary rather than social values, or to social values only as they are absorbed and transformed by literature.

The second of the three literary essays, which I wrote, discusses Propertius 3.9, a poem which Zetzel also treats. In "Propertius 3.9: Maecenas as *eques, dux, fautor*," I am concerned, as is Zetzel, with the poetics of this programmatic dedication to the patron and not with the poem as a historical record. Propertius uses his poems to patrons as vehicles for poetic statements, and molds the image of the patron to fit the ideas that he wishes to transmit. Maecenas, in 3.9, is drawn as a model of moderation and contentment, the two main themes of the poem, and is used as a medium through which Propertius may exemplify and explain these themes. The image of Maecenas in this poem fits both style and subject matter. Maecenas' connection with Augustus raises the diction of the poem to epic levels at times, but the poem as a whole makes a statement in favor of elegiac. The main point of disagreement between Zetzel and myself is that I believe that the choice of Maecenas as addressee and patron was determined by certain historical elements, but that these elements were then altered and adapted by Propertius to fit the style and subject matter of the poem and to create a picture which in the end has nothing to do with historical reality. Propertius creates the central figure of the poem out of a historical reality but uses art and language, not historical fact, to transmit the message of the poem.

The dual questions examined in Zetzel of the poet as a creator of a world rather than as a recorder of reality and of the link between Roman poetry and real life, form the basis of Jasper Griffin's treatment of Virgil's *Aeneid* in "The Creation of Characters in the *Aeneid*." Griffin discusses Virgil's creation of complex characters from models in history and mythology and investigates the importance of this device for the *Aeneid*. Virgil himself is almost a patron in Zetzel's terms, inasmuch as he creates his characters out of many varying models. In the same way, Propertius and Horace "create" the image of the patron that is transmitted through the poem. Griffin points out that, although many critics have tried to see Virgil's method of using historical and mythological models for his characters as a form of biblical typology, there are major differences between typology and the Virgilian method. First, typology tends to view events and characters as simple and unambiguous; Virgil's characters are complex and multilayered. Second, in typology the later characters always exceed and replace the former. Virgil's allusive narrative style allows the reader to see the complexity of characters and situations through his emotional response to the various models. He alone of the Roman poets allows the complexity to remain. His characters exist both in the poem and in history as real people; by this and other devices Virgil connects the life of Roman poetry to the reality of ordinary life.

The final paper in the volume, by Eleanor Winsor Leach, is entitled, "Patrons, Painters, and Patterns: The Anonymity of Romano-Campanian Painting and the Transition from the Second to the Third Style." In it, Leach focuses on the patron's role in choosing subject matter, style, and architectonic detail rather than on the painter's influence on these things. In private art, unlike literature, the main evidence for patron/painter relationships is concrete, mainly Romano-Campanian house paintings, but rarely is the name or background of painter or patron known. According to Leach, however, who offers a new theory about Romano-Campanian painting, the rooms of the villas reveal much about the social standing, rituals, pretensions, and even fantasies of the patron-owner. The assumption heretofore has been that there was a natural evolution of style in Campanian painting, and therefore no room was allowed for the taste of the patron in the change of styles. Most scholars have also assumed that much of the impetus for decorative Roman wall painting came from Greek art and was directly inspired by the Hellenistic stage. There is ancient evidence, however, that particular forms and themes were considered suitable for certain rooms in a Roman villa, and that there was an alteration between the second and third styles which allowed a wider choice for both patron and painter. New evidence for the third style from the Oplontis villa confirms this change and disproves the theory that Roman painters copied material directly from the Greek stage. Rather, the scenes appear to be illusionary views of an ideal Roman villa. Leach suggests that many of the villa owners, the patrons, were wealthy knights from the commercial class who desired their houses to reveal their fantasies and illusions and to match in visual detail the fabled aristocratic houses. The surviving Campanian villas reveal familiar motifs which are appropriate to the particular room and owner. Leach contends that earlier, in the second style, there were competing workshops, offering a limited repertoire, but by the third style the patron was offered a wider choice and an opportunity to reveal his individuality, and the painter had the freedom to adapt to both the space available and the patron's wishes. Especially popular was the *pinacotheca*, or representation of a picture gallery, which held equal appeal for patron and artist and created a new reciprocity between them.

The essays in this volume cover all of the important concerns related to patronage, and they overlap to a surprising degree even when they disagree. No one approach—literary, historical, or artistic—can ignore the others without running the risk of misunderstanding the complexities of patronage, which is both a sociohistorical and a literary issue and as important for the question of art as it is for literature. The apology by several contributors for pursuing only one approach indicates a general realization that, despite individual bias toward one particular approach, in order to fully understand the effect of patronage we must recognize the importance of all its various elements—historical, literary, social, and economic. More work must be done in this area, particularly on the relationship of art patronage to literary patronage, and on the impact of a particular type of patronage or patron on works of art and literature. The broader questions concerned with the relationship of art to life are also central to this topic and may be illuminated by it. For example, did the genius of a Virgil, a Cellini, or a Shakespeare grow in proportion to

the amount or type of patronage he received? Is talent so readily co-
erced and compelled? Questions such as these need not be answered
in order for us to enjoy the art or the poetry, but an answer would add
to our appreciation of them.

Barbara K. Gold
The University of Texas at Austin

NOTES

1. B. Cellini, *The Life of Benvenuto Cellini*, trans. J. A. Symonds, p. 58.

2. E. Spenser, *The Shepherd's Calendar*, "October," 61–62.

3. P. White, "*Amicitia* and the Profession of Poetry in Early Imperial
Rome," *JRS* 68 (1978): 75.

4. See, for example, C. E. Beulé, *Auguste, sa famille et ses amis*, p. 282;
H. J. Rose, *The Eclogues of Virgil*, p. 78; P. Grimal, "Le quatrième livre des
'Elégies' de Properce et la politique d'Auguste," *Comptes Rendus de l'Académie des Inscriptions et Belles-Lettres* (1952): 258–61; and an unpublished paper by P. White, "Maecenas and the Ministry of Propaganda."

5. G. Williams, "Poetry in the Moral Climate of Augustan Rome," *JRS*
52 (1962): 43.

6. H. Trevor-Roper, *Princes and Artists: Patronage and Ideology at
Four Habsburg Courts, 1517–1633*, p. 7.

7. G. Williams, *Change and Decline: Roman Literature in the Early
Empire*, p. 53.

HISTORICAL APPROACH

Phases in Political Patronage of Literature in Rome

GORDON WILLIAMS

By political patronage here is meant patronage whose aim was to obtain political advantage for the patron, often of course by having his qualities and achievements paraded before voters in such a way as to influence the casting of their votes. But that was just one type of political advantage, and it was a characteristic reflection of republican institutions. There were others that ranged from the enhancing of a man's *auctoritas* and *dignitas* to the propagation of his political aims and policies. When republican institutions began to be manipulated by prominent individuals in the last century of the republic, those other types of political advantage began to be exploited and extended by literary patronage. There was a further aspect of such patronage over which Romans—prominently among them Cicero— were apt to wax lyrical.[1] This consisted in the proposition that, since life on this earth is brief, the only stimulus for men to undertake toil and hardship (that is, political and military careers) resides in the prospect of eternal glory, and that is guaranteed by poetry more than by anything else. There was certainly some truth in this; but, just as Cicero fails to lend his eloquence to the more concrete advantages of literary support, so he omits to explain that, given the importance of the family in Roman politics, the continuity of influence that a man could exercise on behalf of his descendants after his death was likely to be greatly increased if he were celebrated in literature destined to be read long after he was gone. To a Roman *nobilis* that was a consideration that carried weight.

My aim in what follows is not so much to examine the detailed working of political patronage or the names and circumstances of the patrons or the literary qualities of the works involved or the circumstances of their authors, but rather to outline certain characteristic phases in the history of such patronage during the period that extends from the beginnings of Roman literature in the third century B.C. to the time of Hadrian, and particularly to analyze the points of transition from one phase to another. For this purpose literature will be treated more or less as a commodity, purveyed to the mutual advantage of both parties involved. That will make questions of merit and appreciation to a large extent irrelevant.

We may begin from the only extensive treatment of such patronage that has come down from the ancient world. In 62 B.C., flushed with the triumph of his consulship and the quelling of Catiline's conspiracy, Cicero defended Aulus Licinius Archias, a Greek poet born in Antioch, on a charge of making false claim to Roman citizenship. The case was a petty incident in the rivalry between Pompeius Magnus and L. Licinius Lucullus, who was Archias' principal patron: Pompey was persecuting Archias in order to attack Lucullus. In the course of his speech Cicero recalls that when Archias came to Rome (102 B.C.) Marius and Catulus were consuls, "one of whom could supply the greatest material for literature, the other both achievements as material and also a cultivated interest in literature" (*Arch.* 5). The meaning of this comment emerges later: "In his youth Archias touched on the Cimbrian campaign [of Marius in 102 B.C.] and made himself acceptable even to Marius, who was clearly somewhat resistant to literary pursuits. But in fact no one is so averse to the Muses that he cannot readily suffer an eternal proclamation of his achievements to be committed to verse" (19). So Archias had shrewdly made it one of his first poetic endeavors after reaching Rome to catch the attention of Marius by celebrating his victory over the Cimbri, perhaps in an epigram. We are not told what he did for Catulus, but some thirty years later he wrote what was probably a short epic poem on the war against Mithridates and celebrated the military achievements of Lucullus.

The kind of activity described here by Cicero goes back almost to the beginning of Roman literature. Naevius, in addition to adapting tragedies and comedies from already existing Greek plays, invented a type of tragedy that took Roman history for its subject matter. One of the *fabulae praetextatae* was called *Clastidium*;[2] this must refer to the battle against the Gauls in 222 B.C. in which M. Claudius Marcellus won the *spolia opima* by defeating Viridomarus, the Gallic leader, in single combat.[3] We know that in or about 204 B.C. Naevius was imprisoned by a clique of aristocratic families and especially the Metelli for constant insults hurled against them from the stage.[4] It is a ready conjecture that the family of the Claudii Marcelli was Naevius' patron and that the *Clastidium* was written and performed to exalt the reputation of that family against political rivals, especially the Metelli. In fact, the iambic senarius which is the only certain example of Naevius' insults ("fato Metelli Romae fiunt consules") may well have come from the *Clastidium*;[5] its point is that the Metelli do not owe their political prominence at Rome to any ability of their own.[6] Naevius had presumably been persuaded by the distinguished M. Claudius Marcellus to attack his rivals from the stage; but Naevius overestimated his patron's political power and the Metelli succeeded in collecting enough influence by family alliances to attack Marcellus, not directly but, as Pompey attacked Lucullus in 62 B.C., through a vulnerable client.

A similar though more fortunate relationship can be seen in the case of Quintus Ennius. He was brought from Sardinia to Rome in 204 B.C. by Cato (an act that Cornelius Nepos applauds as greater than any triumph for a military victory in Sardinia).[7] We learn from *Pro Archia* 22 that Ennius not only lauded the great P. Cornelius Scipio Africanus Maior but also Cato. The laudation of the famous Scipio was not only in Ennius' epic *Annales* but also in a special poem (it may have been a *fabula praetextata*) called *Scipio*. Cato was a difficult personality and Ennius found a more suitable patron in M. Fulvius Nobilior, who took him on his campaign in Ambracia in 189 B.C. This was celebrated by Ennius in the *fabula praetextata* called *Ambracia* and also in the *Annales*. Ennius' reward came in 185 B.C. when the general's son, Quintus Fulvius Nobilior, used his membership of a colonial commission to make Ennius a full Roman citizen.[8]

Later examples of the same type of literary patronage can also be seen. Ennius' nephew Pacuvius wrote a *fabula praetextata* entitled *Paullus* that celebrated the victory of L. Aemilius Paullus at Pydna in 168 B.C. The great tragic poet of the next generation was Accius; his patron was D. Junius Brutus Callaicus, and it was certainly in his honor that Accius composed the *fabula praetextata* entitled *Brutus*, celebrating his patron's most distinguished ancestor.[9] He also composed an inscription that was carved over the entrance to the temple of Mars, built by Brutus to celebrate his victory in Spain over the Callaici. That inscription was in Saturnians,[10] a fact that well accords with the antiquarian and scholarly interests of Accius, which certainly did not miss the mark with a family eager to recall its past glories.

The advantage of the *fabula praetextata*—and this may have been the motive for its invention—was that what happened on the stage could be made immediately relevant to Roman political life; that was not possible with the mythological material of Greek tragedy. Its crippling disadvantage, however, was that it disastrously curbed the imaginative freedom of the poet.[11] But its usefulness remained as long as drama was vigorously alive in Rome—and that survived because the occasions of dramatic performances in Rome were also political occasions. The curule aediles who for the most part were in charge of the entertainment on these public holidays were young men at the beginning of political careers, and not only did they want to show all possible favor to their superiors actually in higher office or aspiring to it, but each performance was a mass meeting of potential voters and they wanted their names remembered as efficient administrators who provided memorable entertainment. It was in the interest of dramatists to cooperate: typical of the conditions under which they worked is the fact that Terence wrote his *Adelphi* for the *ludi funebres* of L. Aemilius Paullus in 160 B.C. In the prologue Terence makes skillful use of an accusation (whether real or invented for the purpose) that certain *homines nobiles* helped him write the play (15). The games were put on by Q. Fabius Maximus and P. Cornelius Scipio Africanus the younger, two major political figures of the time; Terence uses the accusation to remind his audience about men who are popular with them and on whose efforts both in peace and in war the state relies (19–21). No one is named, but the audience will have had no doubt about who was meant nor hesitation in showing their tumultuous agreement with such worthy sentiments. This recalls a number of passages in plays of Plautus that appeal to patriotic sentiment and joy at military victories.[12] There is no need to inquire anxiously whether such sentiments were officially inspired or whether they came naturally to the dramatist's instinct for getting an audience on his side. Both motives happily coincided on such occasions: the same sentiments satisfied both political interests and the dramatist's convenience. In these circumstances it is easy to conjecture that Plautus' sympathetic reference to Naevius' imprisonment in *Miles gloriosus* (210–12) had the encouragement of patrons who were unhappy with the success of the Metelli but who could go no further than to arouse a modicum of sympathy for the persecuted poet.[13] It would be interesting to know the names of the curule aediles who arranged that performance of the *Miles gloriosus*.

Here an important feature of dramatic performances of this period in Rome needs notice. The audience provided a broad spectrum of the population extending from senators and their wives at one end to slaves at the other; that is, the political coverage was good. But it was also temporary: plays were not regarded as works of literature. They remained the property of the managers who produced them and were not published as texts to be read.[14] "The eternal proclamation of a man's fame" (to use Cicero's words) needed a different vehicle if it were really to be eternal. Accius first began the scholarly work of collecting copies of plays and making editions of them—though he found it difficult to discover even the authorship of plays, since managers attributed plays to popular playwrights wherever deception was possible. But by then drama was coming to an end as a living art and by the beginning of the first century B.C. was virtually confined to revivals of plays written a century or more earlier. The reason for this was that a widening gap had been making itself felt between popular entertainment (which of political necessity had to be a prime consideration with the curule aediles) and the literary interests of the upper classes, who were increasingly familiar with the great achievements of Greek literature.[15] The new social forces are seen particularly clearly in the prologues to Terence's *Hecyra*: two attempts to produce the play had to be abandoned because of the rival attractions of rope dancers and boxers. Soon there were to be added gladiatorial shows and combats with animals, not to mention mimes and farces. This meant that the weight of political patronage had to be shifted to works intended to be read, like the epics of Naevius and Ennius. These in the short run were directed to a very restricted audience—though an important one—of the great man's peers; but the eternity of a man's fame was more solidly guaranteed by such works. The immediate political impact, however, of drama had to be surrendered, though the loss was offset by the increase not only in the importance of oratory as a political force but also of its expertise in the second century B.C. Thenceforward the great—and even the competent—orator could pay all sorts of debts and acquire all sorts of obligations by the exercise of his art.

All of the writers so far mentioned were of inferior social status, starting as slaves like Livius Andronicus or Terence or being *libertini* like Accius or simply not possessing citizenship like Naevius and Ennius. They acquired social status in virtue of their usefulness as poets, and their celebration of great men was naturally in return for appropriate help of all sorts—a reciprocity that was of course not anxiously weighed or examined; both sides had tact and a proper sense of obligation and good manners.[16] The relationship is well expressed by Cicero at the beginning of *Pro Archia*, where he alleges that he owes his whole basic training and encouragement to Archias and that he is now using that talent in return on Archias' behalf; here Cicero uses that concept of reciprocity in the way that will set his client in the best possible light. Social inferiority created a useful vacuum in writers that could be filled to mutual benefit by men with political ambition. That happy balance was upset only when that social inferiority disappeared.

A totally different situation was created when Lucilius invented a type of poetry that was accommodated to the character and outlook of aristocrats.[17] Previously, the upper classes in Rome had regarded poetry as an adornment of life to be provided, like the paintings, statuary, and decorations that enhanced their houses, by artisan specialists. The only literature that they allowed themselves to indulge in was of the kind that enabled them to confer the benefits of their own experience upon the rest of the world; they confined themselves to technical manuals on subjects such as farming and jurisprudence and especially historiography (since after all they made history). Lucilius' satire, with its strong autobiographical mode and its concentration on the unique status of the individual, made the writing of poetry available to this aristocratic point of view. Lucilius explicitly disavows anything approaching panegyric, no matter how deserving the person and his achievements, and asserts the centrality of his own personality and his unique identity.[18] For the first time in Rome poetry became a way of life with Lucilius—so far as we know he was like Catullus in taking no active part in politics (as distinct from expressing many pungent opinions on the subject). A direct line of poetic tradition descends from the inventive genius of Lucilius through Catullus to Propertius and Tibullus and of course to Horace. There is as little panegyrical element in Catullus as in Lucilius (though that will need a slight modification later); but what will happen will be that the independence of high social status will later be modified by an intensification of civil war in which promising Roman poets, by being on the wrong side, will become subjects for patronage through losing estates and assets. Meanwhile there is little sign of political patronage in the enigmatic Lucretius. Memmius is treated as the (distinguished) pupil of the poet throughout the *De rerum natura* apart from a brief reference to him as essential to the safety of the state (1.41–43). That political puff for Memmius is neatly accommodated to its context: the poet prays to Venus for peace, since otherwise Memmius will be needed by the state and will not have the time to listen to the poet. This reads like an obligatory bow to a patron who is needed as an addressee in a didactic poem.

It is time here to return to the *Pro Archia*, for it was in this period (the first third or so of the last century B.C.) that Archias—and Greeks generally—provided an alternative to and a replacement for Romans dependent on benefactors. It was not that there totally ceased to be Roman writers who needed patronage, but that the new poetry, with its interest (starting with Lucilius) in the difficult and sophisticated Alexandrian tradition,[19] needed a degree both of education and of leisure that was unusual below the class of the *equites*— apart, that is, from Greeks, who started *ex hypothesi* from an inferior social level. Such Greeks needed patronage—and earned it. Cicero not only tells his audience of the way in which Archias celebrated the achievements of Marius and Lucullus, he also recalls for them how Theophanes is at the moment heralding the great deeds of Pompey—a shrewd hit at the man who instituted the charge against the misjudged Archias (*Arch.* 24). And he reserves the climactic virtue of Archias to the latest section of his speech: Archias is actually preparing to celebrate Cicero's own consulship. One can well imagine the speaker compelled to pause quite a time for spontaneous applause at that piece of good news (28).

Slightly earlier Cicero had met a possibly disturbing thought that could well have occurred to at least some of the jury: Archias and Greeks like him were writing in Greek, not in Latin. Cicero therefore explains that anyone who thinks Greek verse less valuable than Latin is wrong, for Greek is read all over the world, Latin only within narrow boundaries (23). Allowance must be made here for Cicero's desire to enhance his client, yet the point, made in these terms, has validity if it is directed to the sort of literature required for political patronage. These Greeks not only supplied a need, they were role models for writers of the type needed by great men looking for political advantage from literary support. Greeks had had practice in panegyric since the end of the fourth century B.C., and had built up not only a technique but a readily available body of thematic material.[20]

Such poets had other advantages too. Cicero describes Archias performing before company in a great house: "How often, gentlemen of the jury, have I seen Archias, without having written down a single letter, recite a very large number of excellent verses about current affairs on the spur of the moment. And how often have I seen him also encored and then, with change of words and expressions, recite on exactly the same subject matter" (18). There are important features in the portrait of this happy type of occasion. The first is the subject matter—current affairs ("de iis ipsis rebus quae tum agerentur"): the political value of the tactful handling of such topics in distinguished company needs no stressing, and it will not have been lessened by elegantly varied repetition. The second is directly relevant to that: these Greeks were well practiced in public poetic recitation, which had for long been a feature of Hellenistic literary culture. The habit was Romanized only much later by Asinius Pollio.[21]

This gave Greeks a distinct advantage in the eyes of Romans looking for political benefit. Third, such poets were entertaining; they were skilled in rendering enjoyable occasions that could be made to have some political value. They became members of the family and were on close terms with its adherents: Cicero recalls that Archias lived with the Luculli and was close friends with Metellus and his son, with Aemilius and Catulus, Lucius Crassus, Drusus, the Octavii, Cato, and Hortensius (6). If one were to make a brief roll call of important and influential men throughout this period, it would include all those names.

Men like Archias will also have encouraged the poetic talents of their friends such as Cicero and helped with the education of their children. We can see all of this happening slightly later in the case of Philodemus and his friend and host L. Calpurnius Piso.[22] There is extant a flattering and apologetic invitation in the form of an epigram from Philodemus to Piso in which he hints very broadly at his hope for practical favors from the great man.[23] It became a widespread practice in this period for politically prominent Romans to attach literary Greeks to their households. Such Greeks were adept at providing exemplary service of whatever kind was needed by their patrons—who responded in an equally exemplary way. The pattern had long been set by the time Juvenal sharpened his wit on it in *Satire* 3.

What was characteristic of this period was that as poetry became a respectable activity for Romans of the upper classes Greeks took over that function of poetry that was of political advantage to prominent Romans. This meant, however, that poetic celebration was confined to certain traditional fields, mainly military exploits, and that current political and social problems were still a subject unsuited to poetry. We can assume that if Archias really had undertaken to celebrate Cicero's consulship he would have treated it as a battle against a common enemy threatening the state. He may have delivered an epigram on that inspiring topic; if so it was inadequate to the conception of its hero, and it was left to Cicero to concoct his own "eternal proclamation of his achievements" in a notorious poem of his own on his consulship.

A new period begins (though its essential features had been visible sporadically since the dictatorship of Sulla) when a single individual of magnetic personality, unrivaled talent, and magnificent achievement (or the appearance of these qualities) succeeded in persuading Romans to regard him as the only means of salvation from continued civil war. It would be an oversimplification to portray

Julius Caesar thus, but it would be true to emphasize his preeminence and his capacity to identify and to attract the right men to his side. He was also not only a considerable literary figure in his own right, but he had a shrewd sense of the value of literary support to a man of vast political ambition who could manipulate it with skill. It is highly probable that not only did Caesar, marching south in 49 B.C., send letters setting out his case to the chiefs of all the relevant Italian communities (Cass. Dio 41.10.2), but that he had also made a strategic distribution of his own *Bellum Gallicum*, published two years earlier, to ensure a favorable reception for one who had achieved so much and merited so well of the Roman state (*BCiv.* 1.13.15).[24] What he did for himself he could also encourage others to do for him. So the earliest work of Varro of Atax was an epic poem entitled *Bellum Sequanicum* and concerned with Caesar's campaign of 58 B.C., the first in his conquest of Gaul.[25] There is no evidence that Varro was interested in a political career. Nor was Catullus, and yet after a series of lampoons against Caesar (despite his status as a family friend) Catullus wrote in what seems to be one of his latest poems "Caesaris visens monimenta magni," speaking of Gaul and the famous though dangerous places in the world that a brave man might be eager to visit (11.10). The words are a modest panegyric of Caesar and there is no reasonable possibility of irony in them that is directed at Caesar. Nor can we leave out of account the extraordinary poem 34, written in choriambic meters, a lyric poem designed to be sung by a choir. It is the only poem of Catullus that has a purpose not made clear in the poem itself. It ends:

> sis quocumque tibi placet
> sancta nomine, Romulique,
> antique ut solita es, bona
>   sospites ope gentem.
>   [34.21–24]

> Be blessed by whatever name pleases you, and, as you have been accustomed to do since long ago, rescue with your saving power the people of Romulus.

When this is interpreted in the light of Horace's imitation of it (*Odes* 1.21), rather than label it a literary exercise as is often done and so feel able to dismiss it as an anomaly, it is more logical to regard it as a hymn written for a specific occasion. If so, one thinks of the ceremonies of 217 B.C.[26] and 207 B.C.[27] and 200 B.C.[28] when, at times of crisis, the senate consulted the Sibylline Books and found directions for a lyric hymn in Greek fashion to be sung throughout Rome by a choir of boys and girls. In the last two cases the poets were Livius Andronicus and P. Licinius Tegula respectively. It seems to me a reasonable conjecture that Catullus was persuaded by adherents of Caesar to compose this hymn after the news of the Parthian disaster, with the slaughter of Crassus and his sons and the destruction of some four legions, reached Rome in 53 B.C. If so, Catullus late in his poetic career was persuaded to take note of political themes in his poetry, and the persuasion came from Julius Caesar.

In this he would have been like M. Furius Bibaculus to some extent: he proceeded also from lampoons against Caesar to an epic poem, the *Annales*, in at least eleven books on Caesar's Gallic wars (though, at a later stage, he seems to have returned to lampoons—against Octavian).[29] This is paralleled by the fact that notable members of Catullus' circle like Q. Cornificius, C. Helvius Cinna, and C. Licinius Calvus Macer also came to support Caesar. One can think further of Hirtius the historian, of Q. Hortensius Hortalus the orator, of Quintus Cicero, and even of Marcus Cicero's asserting that Britain would make a wonderful subject for an epic poem (*QFr.* 2.16.4–5). Some of these men were certainly interested in a political career and saw in Caesar their best hope for advancement. They were not wrong, nor presumably was C. Cornelius Gallus, the most interesting of these literary adherents. Gallus, about whom we know very little, was probably significantly older than Virgil (though the biographies of Virgil understandably connect them in age too), and he was possibly already a literary partisan of Caesar in the fifties. His partisanship has become clear in recently discovered fragments and, as with the other Caesarians, it concentrates on Caesar's military achievements—here either the wars of conquest in Gaul or a projected Parthian war.[30] In all this he was like C. Asinius Pollio, born in 76 B.C., who was also an adherent of Caesar;[31] Gallus continued to be a friend of Pollio, and the instinct for independence which that friendship signifies was perhaps one element in his catastrophic downfall in 26 B.C.[32]

What is clear from all this is that Julius Caesar deliberately gathered the most distinguished writers of his time around him to foster a climate of opinion that would benefit him politically. He was assassinated too soon for us to be able to see how that political patronage functioned. But that is not the only difficulty: most of the work of these writers has either perished completely or exists in wretchedly meager fragments. However, what clearly differentiates this phase of political patronage is the fact that a single preeminent man concentrated literary attention on himself with the design of having himself identified with the state and his will with the best interests of the state. What that meant—or, rather, would have meant—can be seen in practice in the case of Augustus.

The civil wars that followed the assassination of Julius Caesar brought an important change. Caesar had to rely on his *auctoritas*, his *dignitas*, and his political power and influence to attract writers to him—he could help them in their careers by obtaining offices and promotions for them, but if they were uninterested in a political career there was a limit to what he could offer them. However, after 44 B.C. a deliberate policy of penal confiscation of assets and estates was instituted on a very wide scale designed to punish those who were found on the wrong side.[33] That policy, among a whole series of other effects, produced a number of poets who needed patronage to help them regain their fortunes and status; among them were the greatest of Roman poets, Virgil, Horace, and Propertius. Octavian (Augustus from 27 B.C.) was lucky in finding Maecenas to manage that patronage, for he not only had good literary taste and judgment (except when it came to his own writing),[34] but he had a tact and personality that appealed to such poets, as can be seen from the way they address him.

There is a significant change that mirrors the impact of that patronage, and it is to be seen in the work of all three poets. It is a movement from isolation and despair to optimism and reliance on a unique individual. In the *Eclogues* of Virgil the figures are those of C. Asinius Pollio, Cornelius Gallus, and the distinguished jurist from north Italy, P. Alfenus Varus. Octavian, the distant young god of *Eclogues* 1, produces no solution, only an arbitrary alleviation of one individual's suffering. He is not even mentioned by name, and there is no good reason to accept the suggestion made in the ancient world and still being revived that he is addressed in *Eclogues* 8.[35] That is Pollio once again. The optimism of *Eclogues* 4 is also centered on Pollio, and the strategy of the poem depends on a carefully preserved neutrality between Antony and Octavian, that is, no living individual is seen as the savior—the end of civil war depends on the agreement engineered by Pollio at Brundisium. But the *Eclogues* do not leave an impression of optimism; they are dominated by the despair of the first and ninth.

So it is also with the early *Epodes* of Horace. In *Epodes* 7 ("quo quo scelesti ruitis?") and *Epodes* 16 ("altera iam teritur bellis civilibus aetas"), the poet himself speaks to the citizen body and sees no possible solution to the insanity of civil war except in an evacuation of the best citizens to a far-off imaginary land of bliss. The tone is one of despair. In the same way the first book of Propertius ends with two grimly despairing poems on the stage of the civil war that involved his own family—the fierce war that broke out in central Italy in 41 B.C. because of a complex series of factors, including land confiscation. The effect of giving prominence to those two striking poems is to end the book on a note of despair, unrelieved by any sense of a solution to the condition that gave rise to it.

But a dramatic change can be seen within the *Epodes* themselves (which span a much longer period than the *Eclogues*). The opening poem and the ninth are both about the battle of Actium in 31 B.C. and both point firmly to a solution in the single figure of Octavian. Both poems are addressed to Maecenas. Virgil's *Georgics* are similarly addressed to Maecenas, and the poem moves from a tone that resumes something of the despair of the *Eclogues* to the sense that a savior has been found for the state in the figure of Octavian. The second book of Propertius starts with a poem addressed to Maecenas that takes up the despair of Perusia from the end of book 1 and transforms it into an optimism that is again concentrated on the figure of Octavian.

The key personality here is that of Maecenas. It is through him that political optimism is channeled and focused indirectly on the figure of Octavian. That sets the tone for the poetry of the twenties. No poet directly addresses Augustus, but in addressing Maecenas each can concern himself poetically with the problems for whose solution all men look to Augustus. Horace is the most explicit, directly dealing with a series of contemporary political issues. Virgil uses epic poetry in a novel way to analyze the present. Propertius finds an ingenious way of reflecting on political themes that does not compromise his presentation of himself as a devoted lover, unconcerned with the troubles and ambitions of the great world of Rome.[36]

What Maecenas had to work on was the fact that the situation of these poets (a situation of sudden comparative, if genteel, poverty) could readily be seen by them to be the direct result of the social and political evils that had to be the prime concern of anyone who aspired to, or held, power. Their own personal interests coincided with those of the state in the solution of those problems. What needed to be done for these poets, apart from alleviating their practical difficulties, was to convince them that Augustus—and Augustus alone—had both the insight and the capacity to solve the problems. That was the function of Maecenas. We cannot tell how that was done because we cannot distinguish in any of these poets the real private individual from the persona that he adopted. It is significant, however, that in Horace's *Satires* and *Epistles* where there is the least distinction between the real personality and the poetic persona there is also the least reflection on political issues; those are the particular theme of the *Odes*, for which the poet adopted the highly specialized persona of the *vates*, the voice that speaks with an authority that comes from outside itself and that carries a weight far greater than that of any private individual. It was precisely the fact that, to a large extent, the real personal interests of these poets coincided with those of the state as a whole that compelled them to adopt personae that would insulate them from the sense of speaking with a merely private voice and from the sort of sneer represented by this modern quotation: "It was not the glorious battle of Actium and the defeat of the greatest soldier of the day that called forth the shrillest jubilation from the victors, but the death of the foreign queen, the 'fatale monstrum.' 'Nunc est bibendum' sang the poet Horace, safe and subsidized in Rome."[37] The danger was the appearance of panegyric and the punctual praises of authority that Greeks had long since become adept at dispensing.[38] What needed to be expressed was that the same authority that had rescued these poets was also the authority best suited to save the state. All these poets concurred in presenting the battle of Actium as a battle won primarily over a foreign enemy; there was a truth in this and it also happened to be a useful truth. The truth was that Antony's close involvement with Cleopatra and the forces of Egypt was deeply repugnant to Roman sentiment: conquered Egypt could not be allowed to threaten her conqueror, Rome, and that cause itself provided a stimulus to national feeling that was independent of the partisanship of civil war (an opportunity not missed in propaganda of the thirties).[39] The usefulness of that truth was parallel to the usefulness of the concept of a crusade against the Parthians which was presented in the twenties as an expiation for civil war and a means of unifying national sentiment behind the Augustan regime.[40] The sneer quoted above deliberately ignores the distinction carefully devised by the poet between his existence as a private individual and his persona as an inspired critic of his own society. That persona provided a means for him to escape the stigma of a paid hack dutifully rehearsing a dictated line by allowing him to take a detached point of view in which events were judged not in their immediate context but by their long-term effects. Virgil achieved the same end by appearing to concentrate on the beginning of Roman history but setting that decade after the fall of Troy within the context of the whole sweep of history from the twelfth century to his own present day.

There is no mistaking the freedom of judgment that this technique permitted, nor the importance of that freedom to these poets.

It is clear in their constant use of the poetic form of the *recusatio*,[41] which they adapted to establish a gap either between their own individuality as real persons and the poetic personae they adopted, or between that adopted persona and another that they wished for one reason or another to reject. A constant distinction is made between what they want to do and what they feel they ought to allow themselves to do: that gap is like one between a subsidized parrot and a poet freely inspired with a vision of society. The freedom was precious and preserved. Propertius actually rejoices over the rejection of Augustus' marriage legislation in 28 B.C. (2.7), and he constantly asserts the distinction between the values that he as poet-lover cherishes and those that he sees to be beneficial to Roman society as a whole. That is a form of indirection by which the poet preserves the integrity of his poetic persona. Virgil and Horace invented other forms of indirection through figures of thought by means of which much more was suggested than was actually said. These poets all fully exploited the advantages of meaning more than they actually said.[42] They took care not to be the creatures of a patron, however much their views coincided with his.

What is most remarkable in this period is the poetic examination and treatment of a whole range of contemporary political and social problems. On occasions we can even see that the poet has been the recipient of privileged information, as, for instance, when in *Odes* 1.12 Horace treats the marriage of Julia and Marcellus as Augustus' means of attempting to ensure some kind of orderly succession to himself—a concept that was without forms of expression in the terms of the Roman constitution.[43] The death of Marcellus evoked *laudationes* expressing that point of view from Virgil (*Aen.* 6.854–86) and from Propertius (3.18). But Horace is most remarkable in treating not just this but a whole range of issues of contemporary politics in his poetry.

A new phase in political patronage of literature must be marked from the time Augustus took over control of patronage from Maecenas.[44] This happened soon after 20 B.C. and it is signaled by the disappearance of Maecenas from Horace's writings after *Epistles* I (published in 19 B.C.). Not only had every earlier work been dedicated to Maecenas, but many poems in each work were also addressed to him and mentioned his name. After 19 B.C. there is only one third-person reference to him (*Odes* 4.11.19). The change can be seen in the fourth book of Propertius too: he virtually abandons his persona of love poet and all that it had meant for the viewpoint he had devised for himself on political themes.

The change can be expressed in the form of a contrast. Before 19 B.C.—or perhaps 17 B.C., the date of Horace's *Carmen saeculare*, would be a better marker—the important political issues are still unresolved, still open to discussion, however much the solutions to them may be clear and even prescribed. The issues are social, moral, and political: of land-tenure and social justice, of public and private morality, of social values and priorities, of military dangers and external enemies, above all of a society divided tragically against itself in civil war. But after 17 B.C. the strong impression one gets is that the business of poets has changed: it is now their task to celebrate the solution of all problems—the one ever-recurring exception being that of the military conquest of Rome's enemies, as the armies pushed back the frontiers farther and farther. It is the time when, from the *Carmen saeculare* on, Horace invents an unparalleled formula for the treatment of political themes—a bare factual list, often even using technical language, of the solutions that have been devised to alleviate Rome's social problems.[45] Propertius celebrates military conquest, composes a panegyric on the battle of Actium (4.6), and finds moving expression (in 4.11) for the marriage ideals inherent in Augustus' moral legislation, passed in 18 B.C. (the very legislation whose earlier defeat he had celebrated in 2.7). Thus poetry on political themes inexorably tended to move into panegyric, for the poet's mind was no longer engaged in wrestling with real problems; it was focused on the ingenious manipulation of themes of praise and panegyric for achievements already gained and issues now happily laid to rest.

Parallel with this, the various techniques of indirection that characterized the poetry of the twenties were abandoned; it is much less true of the poetry of this phase that it means more than it says. Poetry increasingly tends to exhaust ideas rather than to suggest or leave areas dimly visible, to be apprehended by the reader. One reason for this is that for the first time not only is Augustus addressed directly (by Horace in response to direct requests from Augustus),[46] but the full consequences of something that was partially visible earlier are now realized. The effect of focusing on a single preeminent individual when considering political issues was to move toward making the great man and the state coterminous, that is, to tend to identify the will of the *princeps* with the best interests of the state. The political conditions in which that could be a possibility had simply not existed in Rome (as distinct from many Hellenistic kingdoms) before the preeminence of Julius Caesar. At first the effect was good, since it encouraged serious political reflection by opening up the whole range of contemporary political issues for po-

etic discussion. However, once the issues had to be regarded as settled, the focus on the *princeps* not only tended toward panegyric but
also, together with the practice of direct address to him and his taking over patronage of literature, provided him with the possibility of
exercising control over literature at the same time as it aroused that
desire in him.

It is not clear that this happened in the case of Propertius and
there is no sign that it happened in the case of Horace—the flattery
of receiving direct invitations from the *princeps* to write on certain
topics did not inhibit his poetic genius. The danger was acute with
poets who not only did not have the instinct for political themes as
material for poetry but who had not grown up amid the miseries that
existed before the Augustan solutions. Ovid is the outstanding case
in point. For instance, the *leges Juliae* of 18 B.C. virtually closed off a
favorite thematic area for him, the erotic relationships between married persons; such liaisons became increasingly dangerous after 18
B.C., and Ovid could only enter that area by modifying his approach.
So, after *Amores*, which lies well within the area of danger, he wrote
Heroides, which takes refuge in the safe topics of Greek mythical
men and women. In *Ars amatoria* and *Remedia amoris*, both published by about A.D. 2, he modified his approach with constant, and
unfortunately unconvincing, explanations that his erotic advice was
certainly not intended for respectable *matronae*: the area of married
bliss was to be considered totally outside his field.

What now happened could easily have been foreseen in the success with which Julius Caesar gathered important writers around
him: the *princeps* became the literary patron of first resort. This was
just a reflection of a general social condition. As Augustus continued
in power society became more pyramidal in form, with the *princeps*
at the top; eventually all patronage originated with him, and the
longer he lasted the greater the proportion of the citizen body that
relied on his patronage. There were other patrons of course. Out-
standingly there was M. Valerius Messalla Corvinus.[47] This gifted
aristocrat had the useful capacity to remain on good terms with men
of all kinds and of all shades of political opinion—with the intran-
sigent Pollio as well as with Augustus, and with the elite circles that
certainly opposed the moral legislation and among whom originated
many fine jokes against it.[48] He was a master orator and also a writer
both of prose and of verse, including erotic poetry. He gathered a circle of poets around him, the most distinguished of whom in the twenties was Tibullus.[49] Here a comparison is interesting, for Tibullus
never treats political issues as such nor does he mention Augustus;
he celebrates the military achievements of his patron and the ap-

pointment of his patron's son as a *quindecemvir* (2.5). The latter is
the only poem in which he looks at contemporary Rome to some extent as a political entity. The reason for his ignoring Augustus and
his political concerns was not, as has been variously suggested, that
he was hostile to Augustus. The reason was that it was only in the
circle of Maecenas that political themes could be treated in such a
way as to avoid panegyric; partly this must have been due to Maecenas himself and the way in which he presented political issues, but
it will have been equally due to the nature and circumstances of the
three poets, all of whom had suffered personally from the conditions
(especially that of civil war) on which the burning political issues
were concentrated. Also all three had been writing of those conditions before they came under the influence of Maecenas.

In the circle of Messalla, on the other hand, there were no
means for avoiding panegyric on political themes. This can be seen
perfectly in the case of Ovid, who joined the group around Messalla
about 20 B.C. When Ovid treats political themes he writes panegyric.
It is hard to resist the impression that his treatment of such themes
was at the urging of the astute Messalla, who could easily see the
danger ahead for Ovid. But panegyric was characteristic of that circle
and of the times: of the circle for the reasons stated above; of the
times because of the tendency toward panegyric when political issues were seen as settled and because of the adoption from the
Greeks of public recitals of poetry.[50] The various devices of indirection used by poets in the twenties became impossible when poetry
had to make an immediate impact on an audience.

But this only recalls the fact that Greek poets and writers had
been active in Rome during all this time.[51] They found many Roman
patrons, but the fact that the *princeps* had become the patron of first
resort is clear in the way in which they sometimes look past their
immediate patron towards the *princeps*. That is something that
Tibullus never does and the reason for this given above is confirmed
by the fact that the technique of these Greeks is invariably that of
panegyric, with formulas worked out over centuries of practice in
Hellenistic kingdoms.[52]

In fact, for this reason Greek writers clearly became more satisfactory in the eyes of Augustus. So, once again they began to play the
congenial part of role models. There were various other reasons for
this. Greeks were not Romans (even when they were accorded citizenship), and so they did not feel personally affected by Roman political and social issues; also they did not normally become closely
involved with undesirable (generally aristocratic) elements in Roman society. They were not subversive, however temperamental

they might very occasionally be.[53] They admired the best contemporary Roman writers and took themes from them.[54] Most of all, they showed a satisfactory sense of their proper place; they were respectful to their patrons and, when they looked beyond them, it was to the *princeps* and the members of the imperial family.[55] There is something symbolic in the story of the Greek poet who tried to present an epigram to Augustus; instead, Augustus gave the Greek an extempore epigram of his own, whereupon the Greek gave him a few denarii and got handsomely paid himself in return.[56] Such Greeks were adept at panegyric in which they were the beneficiaries of a long tradition and they did not inquire too anxiously into the exact truth of their poetic fantasies. Ovid learned a lot from them, but only partially and too late.

The ever-increasing authority of the *princeps* added a dangerous new element in the situation. This change was manifested in many ways. In 18 B.C., for example, Augustus had to propose the moral legislation himself, lending it the authority of his own name; in A.D. 9, a large extension of that legislation could safely be left to the consuls of the year. At least by the turn of the century Augustus had acquired a sufficient range of legal and quasi-legal authority to coerce writers who needed persuasion of that kind. Several instances of this are known and no doubt there were many more. In A.D. 6 the senate was prevailed upon, allegedly by enemies of the man, to pass a decree ordering that the books of Titus Labienus be collected and publicly burned. Titus Labienus was an orator and historian who wrote on triumviral times, was an admirer of Pompey, and had the unwise habit during public readings of quickly passing over passages of his work, with the remark that they should be read after his death. His books were burned.[57] Then, in A.D. 12, Augustus ordered a widespread search made for libelous writings intended to defame certain individuals, no doubt, prominent supporters of his; when found they were to be burned, in the city of Rome by the aediles, elsewhere by local magistrates.[58] Cassius Severus may have been caught in this sweep (it may have been intended especially for that purpose), for his works were certainly burned,[59] but he was also punished in addition with the harshest form of exile. The senatorial decrees by which these burnings were ordered were certainly inspired, at whatever remove, by Augustus himself. The worst case, however, was that of Ovid, exiled in A.D. 8 to Tomis on the Black Sea, the exile being imposed personally by Augustus on his sole authority and Ovid's books being banned from public libraries. This latter measure, like the burning of books, was intended to disgrace the author rather than destroy his works. Augustus succeeded in connecting Ovid in some way as an accomplice in the adultery of the younger Julia, but the main reason for the exile was the publication of *Ars amatoria* eight years earlier. It availed Ovid not at all to have included large elements of panegyric in his *Metamorphoses* and *Fasti* and to rise to new levels of poetic fantasy in panegyric of Augustus in his *Tristia* and *Epistulae ex Ponto*.[60]

The mark of this phase of political patronage is therefore the increased necessity for suppression of writers and literature on the one hand and the increasing fantasy that was acceptable, if not obligatory, in political panegyric: truth was no longer a criterion. Yet another mark is that the *princeps* becomes of necessity the literary patron of first resort. With some variations from time to time, this phase set the general pattern for political patronage of literature, for as long as it lasted, under the empire.

The period of Tiberius emphasized an aspect that was to prove important. The lesson of Augustus' vicissitudes as a literary patron was not lost on the aristocratic Tiberius. His observation of Augustus seems to have convinced him that literary support was dispensable and could easily cause more trouble than it was worth. He seems, therefore, to have given no support to Roman poets, and so Ovid, when his *Fasti* was still only half complete when Augustus died in A.D. 14, rededicated it not to Tiberius but to Germanicus, nephew and adopted son of Tiberius. It is significant that Phaedrus, something of a minor genius in the unusual genre of verse fable, who succeeds in some political and social reflection, had to beg for gifts from patrons and received no recognition.[61] His status as a freedman of Augustus cannot have helped in an era of social snobbery, but earlier times would have recognized his worth. More to Tiberius' taste was the solid moralizing and prosaic worthiness of a Valerius Maximus, flatteringly obsequious in his dedication, or a Velleius Paterculus with a revisionist history showing that Tiberius had always been the real genius. He accepted such tributes; one imagines that he did nothing, however, to extort them.[62] Instead, it would seem that to Tiberius literature was essentially something trivial, a passing entertainment of leisure hours; hence his gifts to Apollonides of Nicaea for his commentary on the perverse ingenuity of the *Silloi* of Timon, which was dedicated to Tiberius,[63] or the two hundred thousand sesterces given to Asellius Sabinus for a dialogue between a truffle, a figpecker, an oyster, and a thrush.[64] Tiberius was also something of a gastronome.

Nothing was more debilitating to literature than an attitude of contemptuous and amused tolerance. Only occasionally did Tiberius feel moved to repression: seven speeches published by the orator Scaurus, who was severely criticized by the elder Seneca, were burned by decree of the senate (Sen. *Controv.* 10 *praef.* 1−3); the tragedies of an unnamed poet were also burned, his offence being that of criticizing Agamemnon (Suet. *Tib.* 61.3), a similar case to that of Mamercus Aemilius Scaurus who, in A.D. 34, in the period of Tiberius' paranoia after the treason of Sejanus, was compelled to commit suicide for his tragedy *Atreus*, in which Tiberius thought he detected a portrait of himself;[65] finally there was the notorious case in A.D. 25 of Cremutius Cordus, who praised Brutus and Cassius and whose histories too were burned by decree of the senate.[66] It is clear that Tiberius, like Augustus, felt more at ease with Greek epigrammatists, a number of whom addressed flattering poems to him.[67]

This pattern was briefly broken by Nero, who was inspired with the desire to re-create the Augustan ideal of the golden age. The atmosphere in the early years of his reign was that of the twenties under Augustus, but though he considered literature important, Nero had no Maecenas and was forced to be the patron of literature himself. In this situation, however, that essential freedom of discussion of political issues which was the mark of the early age of Augustus could not be revived. The reason was not only that to have the emperor himself as patron was oppressive, it was also that *ex hypothesi* the problems had already been solved, and those that were an inherited legacy from the reign of Nero's predecessor Claudius had to be regarded as solved simply by the accession of Nero itself and the consequent return to the ideals of Augustus. That point was made strongly enough in Seneca's *De clementia*, presented to Nero soon after his accession. But the concept of a golden age was an agreeable and safe topic: it is found in Seneca's *Apocolocyntosis*, and in his *De clementia*, in the anonymous *Einsiedeln Eclogues*, in the *Eclogues* of Calpurnius Siculus, and in the *Bellum civile* (1.33−66) of Lucan, where it is associated with the ideal of a universal world peace that goes far beyond the restricted ideal of the *pax Augusta*.[68] We can see even Petronius taking the concept of the golden age and transposing it into the low-life milieu of vulgar and amusing upstarts.

The essential weakness of the ideal can be seen in Calpurnius Siculus' dim grasp on reality; he attempts to imitate the freedom of discussion of political issues that characterized the twenties under Augustus by feebly referring now and again to trivial but real events of contemporary life.[69] But he gives away his own sense of inferiority by imitating the habit of Greek writers who look past their own patrons toward the emperor.[70]

Nero's most imaginative move was to institute literary festivals both to mark the importance of literature and also to create for it a fixed place of honor in the national life. In that way he ought to have been able to achieve two important goals—those of encouraging literature and at the same time controlling it.[71] The supreme political patron could not hope for more. But he failed, largely because he was a practitioner as well as a patron; so, paradoxically, the more successful the patron was, the more the practitioner found himself a failure. The history of his relations with Lucan is a perfect example of the tragic working of the paradox. What Nero's reign did show, however, with perfect clarity was that literature in Rome needed not just patronage but, under the conditions of the empire, imperial patronage. Yet it could not survive such patronage because if Roman literature received the emperor's patronage it became important; if it became important it needed control, and so it lost its essential freedom.[72] The solution was simple, although it was not attained till the reign of Trajan: literature was politically unimportant. The attitude of Tiberius was simple and pragmatic and made good political sense: give political encouragement to writers and they want freedom; ignore them and they cause no trouble. It is a nice paradox that it was under Trajan that the great constellation of Tacitus, Pliny, and Juvenal wrote. But all of them had been silenced under Domitian who, also paradoxically, had wanted to be an Augustus and a Nero and encourage literature yet ended up repressing it. That repression was sufficient inspiration to Tacitus, Pliny, and Juvenal to reflect in their writing on their own society.

Essentially what happened was that when the Julio-Claudian line ended with Nero there ended too the kind of imperial patronage that came from a genuine understanding and appreciation of literature. It was only revived from time to time by the backward-looking imitations of emperors like Domitian and Hadrian.[73] It would be largely true to say that with Trajan the emperor ceased to be the literary patron of first resort, though in that respect he had been anticipated to some extent by Tiberius and rather more by the pragmatic Vespasian.[74] So when Juvenal rejoices that the accession of Hadrian portended hope of literary patronage (*Sat.* 7.1–7), he seems seriously to have misjudged, although he was, of course, giving the emperor a broad hint rather than expressing a sincerely held opinion.[75] Literature had become an innocent source of diversion for the bored upper classes; it no longer took a passionate interest in political and social problems that could be embarrassing or even dangerous to authority, and imperial interests saw it as mere entertainment.

NOTES

1. Cic. *Arch.* 26–30.
2. Varro *Ling.* 9.78.
3. Plut. *Marc.* 6–8; Polyb. 2.34.
4. Gell. *NA* 3.3.15 with Paulus Festi s.v. *barbari* and Plaut. *Mil. Glor.* 210–12.
5. Pseudo-Asconius on Cic. *Verr.* 1.29 (p. 140 Orelli).
6. As Cicero's use of the barbed witticism in *Verr.* 1.29 shows.
7. Cornelius Nepos *Cato* 1.4.
8. Livy 39.44.10 and Cic. *Brut.* 79.
9. Cic. *Div.* 1.44.
10. Cic. *Arch.* 27 and the *Schol. Bob.* ad loc. (p. 359 Orelli).
11. See G. Williams, *Tradition and Originality in Roman Poetry*, p. 294.
12. See especially Plaut. *Cist.* 197–202 and *Capt.* 67–68, 888.
13. The clue that Naevius is meant comes from Paulus Festi s.v. *barbari*: "Plautus Naevium poetam Latinum barbarum dixit."
14. On the textual history of plays in this period see especially F. Leo, *Plautinische Forschungen*, chap. 1.
15. The most striking evidence of the nature of that gap comes from the prologues to the comedies of Terence (and especially those to *Hecyra*) as contrasted with the way in which Plautus addresses his audience, but just the nature of those prologues shows an appeal to a narrow band of the population.
16. On the rewards of writing see P. White, "*Amicitia* and the Profession of Poetry in Early Imperial Rome," *JRS* 68 (1978): 74–92.
17. See Williams, *Tradition and Originality*, pp. 446–52 and *Change and Decline: Roman Literature in the Early Empire*, pp. 106–7.
18. Williams, *Tradition and Originality*, p. 449.
19. See especially M. Puelma Piwonka, *Lucilius und Kallimachos: Zur Geschichte einer Gattung der hellenistisch-römischen Poesie* together with I. Mariotti, *Studi Luciliani*, pp. 3–92.
20. A collection and review in E. Doblhofer, *Die Augustuspanegyrik des Horaz in formalhistorischer Sicht*.
21. Sen. *Controv.* 4 *Praef.* 2. See Williams, *Change and Decline*, p. 303.
22. Cic. *Pis.* 68–72 and the commentary on this speech by R. G. M. Nisbet, *M. Tulli Ciceronis in L. Calpurnium Pisonem*, pp. 183–88. Allowance must be made throughout for Cicero's malicious wit at Piso's expense.
23. *Anth. Pal.* 11.44. On this type of poem see Williams, *Tradition and Originality*, pp. 124–29.
24. E. Badian reviewing M. Gelzer, *Kleine Schriften* in *JRS* 57 (1967): 221.
25. This was too long a work to be an epyllion, for Priscian (Keil, *Gramm. Lat.* 2, p. 497, 10–12) quotes from book 2. Atax was in the province of Gallia Narbonensis and Caesar may have spotted his talent there.

26. M. Laelius, *augur*, quoted by Macrob. *Sat.* 1.6.13–14; Livy 22.1.14–18.

27. Livy 27.37.7 with Festus s.v. *scribas*.

28. Livy 31.12.5–6.

29. Tac. *Ann.* 4.34.8. Macrob. *Sat.* 6.1.34 quotes from book 11 of the epic. It is sometimes thought that two poets may be involved. See H. Bardon, *La littérature latine inconnue*, vol. 1, pp. 347–54.

30. R. D. Anderson, P. J. Parsons and R. G. M. Nisbet, "Elegiacs by Gallus from Qaṣr Ibrîm," *JRS* 69 (1979): 125–55. The editors have there decided on a reference to Caesar's abortive Parthian campaign, and do not discuss the Gallic wars. From the way Virgil addresses him, Gallus could have been at least five years older, and could therefore have been writing in the late fifties. It is useless to try to reconstruct a history of the love life of Volumnia Cytheris as H. J. Rose does in *The Eclogues of Virgil*, pp. 109–10, 243 n. 44, and the editors, loc. cit., pp. 152–53. Roman love elegy, whatever the realities, is posited on the freedom of women to engage in multiple liaisons, and we know far too little of the social conventions to exclude the possibility of simultaneous affairs with an important man like Antony as well as with an obscure poet. Her age and status in the late fifties are unknown and irrelevant; she could certainly have retained enough of her charms from the fifties to be still appreciated about 39 B.C. (*Ecl.* 10). The editors regard the fragments as epigrams, but they seem oddly incomplete for complete poems. The possibility should be considered that what we have is not a sheet from a volume of poetry but some sort of index, listing either poems or beginnings and ends of books, by means of quatrains rather than first lines or couplets. An anthology of favorite passages seems unlikely. The importance of the Gallic wars to Caesar's propaganda, together with Gallus' obscurity in the late fifties, would account for his pose of looking forward to reading inscriptions recording the triumph; that was certainly the time when Caesar was in real need of support. He was not able to celebrate a Gallic triumph until 46 B.C.

31. For Pollio see R. Syme, *The Roman Revolution*, Index s.v. Asinius Pollio, C.

32. Ibid., pp. 309–10.

33. Ibid., chap. 14.

34. A hostile review by Sen. *Ep.* 114.

35. See Williams, *Change and Decline*, p. 130.

36. For the technique see Williams, *Tradition and Originality*, pp. 56–57, 557–59.

37. Syme, *The Roman Revolution*, p. 299.

38. See Doblhofer, *Die Augustuspanegyrik*.

39. Syme, *The Roman Revolution*, pp. 270–71.

40. See G. Williams, *Figures of Thought in Roman Poetry*, pp. 13, 118–19, 160, 237.

41. On this see W. Wimmel, *Kallimachos in Rom*, and, for example, Williams, *Tradition and Originality*, Index s.v. *recusatio*.

42. These techniques are examined extensively in Williams, *Figures of Thought*.

43. See G. Williams, "Horace *Odes* 1.12 and the Succession to Augustus," *Hermathena* 118 (1974): 147–55.

44. See Williams, *Tradition and Originality*, pp. 86–88; *Change and Decline*, pp. 56–58.

45. See Williams, *Tradition and Originality*, pp. 58–61, 78, 100, 162.

46. See E. Fraenkel, *Horace*, pp. 364–65, 383.

47. For a characterization, see Williams, *Change and Decline*, pp. 65–70.

48. They are largely collected in Macrob. *Sat.* 2.1–6.

49. On his circle see R. Hanslik, "Der Dichterkreis des Messalla," *Anzeiger der österreichische Akad. d. Wiss.: Phil.-Hist. Kl.* 89 (1953): 22–38, and C. Davies, "Poetry in the 'Circle' of Messalla," *Greece and Rome* 20 (1973): 25–35.

50. See Williams, *Change and Decline*, pp. 303–6.

51. On these writers see especially G. W. Bowersock, *Augustus and the Greek World*, chap. 10.

52. See Doblhofer, *Die Augustuspanegyrik*.

53. The quarrel of Timagenes with Augustus is exceptional: Sen. *Controv.* 10.5.22; Sen. *De ira* 3.23. He retired in a huff to the house of Pollio after burning his panegyric on Augustus.

54. See Williams, *Change and Decline*, pp. 124–32.

55. See, for example, the epigram of Antipater of Thessalonica: *Anth. Pal.* 10.25; and Williams, *Change and Decline*, pp. 134–35.

56. Macrob. *Sat.* 2.4.31.

57. Sen. *Controv.* 10 *praef.* 4–8.

58. Cass. Dio 56.27.1.

59. Suet. *Calig.* 16.1.

60. See Williams, *Change and Decline*, chap. 2. For the idea that Ovid was really attacking Augustus, see R. Marache, "La révolte d'Ovide exilé contre Auguste," *Ovidiana*, ed. N. I. Herescu, pp. 412–19; and to a lesser extent R. Syme, *History in Ovid*, pp. 222–25.

61. See especially the prologue to book 3.

62. On Tiberius' literary tastes, see Williams, *Change and Decline*, pp. 129, 298–99.

63. Diog. Laert. 9.12.109; and see A. Hillscher, "Hominum litteratorum Graecorum ante Tiberii mortem in urbe Roma commoratorum historia critica," *Jahrb. f. cl. Phil. Suppl.* 18 (1892): 387–88.

64. Suet. *Tib.* 42.

65. Cass. Dio 58.24.3–5.

66. Tac. *Ann.* 4.34–35.

67. *Anth. Plan.* 61 (Crinagoras); *Anth. Pal.* 9.178 (Antiphilus), 9.287 (Apollonides), 9.219 (Diodorus).

68. See Williams, *Change and Decline*, pp. 160–65.

69. I am unconvinced by the arguments of E. Champlin, "The Life and Times of Calpurnius Siculus," *JRS* 68 (1978): 95–110, that the works of Cal-

purnius Siculus are at least equally suited to the time of Severus Alexander. The problem is too extensive to handle here; but, for instance, the words in *Ecl.* 1.45, "maternis causam qui vicit Iulis," seem to me typical of a type of phrase making by Calpurnius whereby he takes a linguistic idea from Virgil and "improves" on it by adding point. The point here resides in the use of *Iuli* to mean "Trojans" (a surprise since one would naturally take it to mean "descendants of Iulus," i.e., the *gens Iulia*) together with the concrete reference to Nero's speech on behalf of the Trojans (Tac. *Ann.* 12.58.1 and Suet. *Ner.* 7.2). That pointed combination, so typical of the period as well as of the poet, cannot be accidental. The fundamental examination of the evidence is still A. Momigliano, "Literary Chronology of the Neronian Age," *CQ* 38 (1944): 97–99.

70. In Calp., *Ecl.* 1.92–94 and 4.152–63, the speaker looks past his patron, who appears under the guise of Meliboeus, to the possibility of his poems reaching the ears of Nero.

71. See Momigliano, "Literary Chronology," p. 100.

72. Williams, *Change and Decline*, pp. 299–300.

73. Ibid., pp. 274, 298, 300–3.

74. Ibid., p. 300.

75. Ibid., p. 298.

Pete nobiles amicos:
Poets and Patrons in Late Republican Rome

T. P. WISEMAN

What exactly do we mean by patronage? It is perilously easy to be misled by false analogies and anachronistic preconceptions. As with all questions of social history, the only way to proceed is to look hard at the evidence and ask practical questions—who does what, and when, and where. Some literary scholars, I think, regard that level of discourse as beneath their intellectual dignity, but to ignore it is to cut ourselves off from the society for which the literature we study was written.

And so I begin in a context as untheoretical as I can find: in a Roman street, outside a great house. The door of the house does not open straight onto the street, as do those of the small-town worthies of Pompeii, but is set back in such a way as to leave a substantial rectangular area outside, open to the street but not public property.[1] This is the *vestibulum*, reached by a flight of steps if the house is on a hill and perhaps with a loggia (*ambulacrum*) flanking the door on each side.[2] If the owner is a *triumphator* or the descendant of *triumphatores*, the walls are hung with armor and trophies, the spoils of war;[3] if he is a praetor or a consul, his lictors with their fasces are stationed here.[4] Long before dawn the *vestibulum* starts to fill up with those who have come to perform their *officium salutandi* to the master of the house; it was from their standing waiting for the door to be opened that the Romans derived the etymology of the word *ve-stibulum*.[5]

The moment when the doors are opened is the one chosen by Virgil in *Georgics* 2 (461–63) to sum up the grandeur of wealthy city life, from which the *fortunatus agricola* is so mercifully free. The open doors vomit a flood of *salutantes* into the atrium, gaping at the tortoiseshell inlay and the Corinthian bronzes. For some it is just the one word *ave* and the daily kiss of greeting;[6] others have real business with the great man as he sits in his chair of state or strolls round the atrium.[7] (That, incidentally, is what lies behind Livy's pretty story of the taking of Rome by the Gauls: M. Papirius and his fellow patricians were sitting on ivory thrones behind the open doors of their houses because that is what they did every day, waiting for their dependents to call on them. Plutarch got it wrong and had them sitting on curule chairs in the Forum.[8]) What do the clients want? Legal help, perhaps, or a loan, or advice about property or the betrothal of a daughter; but Cicero and Horace, who give us these examples, use them to illustrate ancestral custom rather than that of their own day.[9] No doubt such questions did still come up from time to time, but our evidence for the late republic itself suggests a slightly different picture of the relationship between the great man and his *tenuiores amici*.

Quintus Cicero[10] divides them into three categories in ascending order of honorific activity: *salutatores*, who come in the morning to pay their respects but may make many other calls as well;[11] *deductores*, who stay on to escort the great man as he proceeds down to the Forum and perhaps remain with him for one length of the basilica before going about their business;[12] and *adsectatores*, whose devotion or obligation is to one patron only and who therefore stay at his side all day, clearing the way for him and making themselves useful however they can.[13] (*bodies?*)

The *locus classicus* for this last and humblest category is Cic. *Mur.* 70–73. Dismissing the prosecution's allegation that Murena had hired *adsectatores* for pay, Cicero dwells on the mutual and therefore honorable nature of the *officium*. How else, he says, can our friends of humbler station repay us for what we do for them? They cannot speak on our behalf, they cannot stand security for us, they cannot invite us to their homes; but that is what they ask of *us*, and in return all they can offer is their service. The word he uses is *opera*,[14] which is regularly used of a freedman's obligation to his patron; in this context we should remember Clodius' *adsectatores*, doing him what service they could by beating up his enemies.[15] Three characteristic *beneficia* of the patron are suggested: to speak on the client's behalf in a lawsuit, as Cicero did for Q. Roscius the actor; to stand security for him in a financial venture, as D. Brutus did for P. Iunius in the contract for restoring the temple of Castor;[16] and to invite him to his house for dinner, as L. Philippus did for Volteius Mena the *praeco* in Horace's story.[17] Another that was mentioned in the Murena trial was to get the client a place at the Circus to watch the games or in the Forum to watch the gladiators, as Clodius did for his new clients from Sicily.[18] Finally, a favored client might enjoy the more substantial benefit of free lodging. Ulpian in the *Digest*, discussing liability for things thrown out of apartment windows, says that the patron is responsible if he has given *gratuitae habitationes* to clients of freedmen of himself or his wife; since Cicero's friend Trebatius is cited on this question, the practice must have been a common one in the late republic.[19]

Invitations to dinner call to mind the parasites of Roman comedy. Under that name they are merely stock stage characters,[20] but in Roman society, as in Athenian, they no doubt represented a type of person that really existed. Their *operae* in return for being fed at the patron's table evidently included going to the *macellum* to buy provisions, arranging with the *leno* for a girl for the young master, and telling jokes and making fools of themselves to make the dinner party go well.[21] We may perhaps define them as a specialized subclass of *adsectatores*.

Adsectatio could be a full-time occupation,[22] and those who performed it were presumably under the protection of one patron only. The *salutatores*, the first of Q. Cicero's categories, were on the other hand less committed. His description of them as "magis vulgares" is reminiscent of Tacitus' distinction between the "plebs sordida" and that part of the populace which was "integra et magnis domibus adnexa."[23] No doubt permanent attachment to a single patron was regarded as highly desirable, but for every lucky man like Horace, whom Maecenas told to consider himself "in amicorum numero,"[24] there must have been dozens who aspired to such a position and spent their waking hours pursuing it by the zealous cultivation of every potential patron in sight.

That too was a full-time occupation, though an insecure one, and those who lived by it were called *ardeliones*.[25] Orion the hunter, who gives quick wits and untiring legs, is the sign the *ardelio* should be born under; he must be all over town at once—from a *salutatio* to a funeral, from a betrothal to a lawsuit, escorting a litter or even carrying it.[26] He is in fact a familiar character in Latin literature. We meet him, in negative image, at the Porta Capena in Juvenal *Satires* 3, where Umbricius asks "Quid Romae faciam?" and lists all the things he cannot do; a century earlier we meet him in the Sacra Via in determined conversation with Maecenas' friend, listing his qualifications and angling for an invitation to the great man; in the late republic we meet him in the Forum, always ready to push himself forward when he thinks a great noble family may need a job done, like bearing false witness against their enemy in court.[27]

"Out of all this crowd," said Cicero to the jury in the trial of Caelius, "how many do you think there are who, when they think something is required of them by men of power and influence, regularly offer their services of their own accord and devote their ener-

gies to them [*operam navare*]?" That was not just an advocate's exaggeration; in a casual aside in a letter to Ap. Claudius, Cicero says
people are always calling on Appius to ask if they can do anything
for him.[28] It was *observantia*, the offer of *officia*, the hope of *beneficia*[29]—the reality, that is, of the patron-client relationship.

Now, where does the poet fit into this Hogarthian picture? The
answer depends on what kind of poet we mean. Let us consider three
representative examples—A. Licinius Archias, T. Lucretius, and C.
Valerius Catullus.

Archias first came to Rome, his defense counsel tells us, in 102
B.C. He was still a very young man but already with a considerable
reputation in his native Antioch and in the Greek cities of Asia
Minor, Greece proper, and south Italy, through which he had passed
on his way.[30] In a famous passage Cicero lists the noble Romans with
whom Archias came in contact:

> Erat temporibus illis iucundus Q. Metello illi Numidico et
> eius Pio filio, audiebatur a M. Aemilio [sc. Scauro], vivebat
> cum Q. Catulo et patre et filio, a L. Crasso colebatur, Lucullos
> vero et Drusum et Octavios et Catonem et totam Hortensi-
> orum domum devinctam consuetudine cum teneret, afficie-
> batur summo honore.   [*Arch.* 6]

As Susan Treggiari points out, Cicero's phraseology in this passage
exemplifies "the range of situations open to a client intellectual:
being liked by, lecturing or reading his works to, living with, or being
on visiting terms with his patrons."[31] It is worth considering each of
these in turn.

What exactly does Cicero mean when he says that Archias was
iucundus to Metellus Numidicus and Metellus Pius? He uses the
same phrase elsewhere about Archias and Marius: "nam et Cimbri-
cas res adulescens attigit, et ipsi illi C. Mario, qui durior ad haec studia videbatur, iucundus fuit."[32] Since it is hardly credible that Marius could be described as a *familiarissimus* of Archias, which is
what Cicero twice calls Metellus Pius,[33] the phrase *iucundus fuit* is
clearly a vague one. I suspect it means no more than that Marius
found Archias an agreeably sycophantic *Graeculus*, perhaps worth
a dinner invitation on the strength of his poem about the defeat of
the Cimbri. As Gordon Williams has recently suggested, the poem
Cicero refers to was probably just a flattering epigram, like those of
Alcaeus and Polystratus earlier on the victories of Flamininus and
Mummius respectively and Crinagoras later on those of Tiberius and
Germanicus;[34] when Cicero refers to the large-scale poem on the

Mithridatic war that Archias wrote for the Luculli (on which more in a moment), he uses quite different phraseology.[35] Perhaps Archias came with it one morning to Marius' *salutatio* or else sent it up *de populo* when Marius was accessible in public, at a *contio*, for instance, like the occasion when Sulla rewarded a poet who had written an epigram in his honor.[36]

Next, "audiebatur a M. Aemilio." Where would he have read his works to Scaurus? Probably not at a dinner party, where reading for the guests was the job of a slave *lector*.[37] The verb may suggest a more formal *acroasis*, like the reading Atticus arranged for Tyrannio's book on Homeric prosody in May 45.[38] For a Roman noble to come to such a reading, given by a *Graeculus* for a Greek-speaking audience, would be a notable mark of honor. Cicero, who was an untypical philhellene, clearly enjoyed them:[39] he was sorry to have missed Tyrannio's and, if we are to believe his forensic enthusiasm, had been to at least one or two of Archias', where he had seen him encored and applauded.[40] For the young Archias to have had the *princeps senatus* in his audience, however, must have been a considerable triumph.

He "lived with" Q. Catulus, father and son. That is slightly odd, since Cicero has just told us that the Luculli had received Archias into *their* house. Perhaps he was lent to the Catuli from time to time, as we find Atticus' learned freedman Dionysius at Cicero's Tusculan villa in 55 B.C., reading Greek literature with his patron's friend.[41] (Dionysius, incidentally, had the citizen name M. Pomponius Dionysius, taking Cicero's praenomen with Atticus' *gentilicium*. Archias, enfranchised thanks to M. Lucullus, has the praenomen Aulus attached to his patron's *gentilicium*; perhaps A. Terentius Varro, into whose family Lucullus was later adopted, was another of Archias' noble friends.[42] If so, the memory of a disgraceful case of judicial corruption in the seventies may account for the omission of the name in the *Pro Archia*.[43]) At any rate, to live in the patron's house, as Philodemus did in the house of L. Piso, was the height of success, just as it was for Lucian's friends eight generations later:

> "Happy men!" some enthusiast has cried. "The elite of Rome are their friends. They dine sumptuously, and call for no reckoning. They are lodged splendidly, and travel comfortably— nay, luxuriously—with cushions at their backs, and as often as not a fine pair of creams in front of them. . . ."[44]

What did Archias do for his hosts? The elder Catulus was a profoundly Hellenized Roman, a very unusual phenomenon for his generation, Cicero observed, and his literary work reflected it.[45] His political memoirs were written in the style of Xenophon,[46] his epigrams imitated Callimachus,[47] and he probably also wrote antiquarian "history" linking the origins and antiquities of Rome with Greek mythology.[48] He dedicated his memoirs to a poet, A. Furius, and was evidently on close terms with the Greek epigrammatist Antipater of Sidon, whose work like Archias' own was anthologized by Meleager for his *Garland*.[49] It is likely enough that Archias and Antipater, along with Catulus' learned freedman Daphnis, helped him with these works in much the same way that Tiro helped Cicero.[50]

The Luculli were a different matter. When L. Lucullus wrote Greek, he made sure his readers knew it was written by a Roman.[51] For him Archias wrote an extended historical poem on the Mithridatic war, which was finished by 61 B.C. at least and probably in time for Lucullus' triumph in 63 B.C.[52] It has recently been suggested by T. W. Hillard, in a detailed argument which I hope will one day be generally available, that Archias' poem was one of Plutarch's main sources in his life of Lucullus.[53] The epic battle of Tigranocerta in Plutarch's chapters 27–28 could well have been Archias' culminating set piece, and the repeated portents, visions, and divine interventions seem to betray the poet behind the biographer.[54] After Lucullus' own "battle of the Granicus," where three hundred thousand were supposed to have been killed, and his dramatic relief of Cyzicus, he went to the Troad and spent the night at Ilion in the temple of Aphrodite; warned by the goddess (Aeneas' mother, of course), he sailed out of the "harbor of the Achaeans" in time to intercept a squadron of Mithridates' fleet. In this episode, resonant with echoes of Homer and Alexander, we may even have a line from Archias' poem itself, in the hexameter spoken by Aphrodite: τί κνώσσεις, μεγάθυμε λέον; νεβροὶ δέ τοι ἐγγύς.[55]

The next item in Cicero's list is a surprise—"a L. Crasso colebatur." The verb expresses something a dependent *Graeculus* might be expected to do for his patron, not vice versa.[56] But Crassus was not only a friend of Greek culture,[57] he was also a genial man—"omnium venustissimus et urbanissimus"—who did not stand on his dignity and may well be imagined calling on Archias himself instead of waiting for a call at his own house as stricter protocol might expect.[58] Whether the *consuetudo* of Archias with the Luculli, M. Drusus, the Octavii, M. Cato, and "the whole house of the Hortensii" was as informal as that, it is impossible to say.

It was, of course, in the interests of Cicero's case to emphasize the closeness of Archias' personal relationship with these great men. We must not allow his forensic evidence to blind us to the social reality: Archias lived at their expense and wrote what they required. When Cicero wanted some couplets written for the statue bases in the Amaltheum of his villa at Arpinum, Archias was one of the two poets he turned to. Neither he nor Thyillus, as it turned out, was prepared to do the job, but that was probably because Cicero had offended some of their aristocratic patrons by his feud with Clodius; under normal circumstances it was just what they might be expected to provide.[59]

The poems of the *Greek Anthology* give us a very clear idea of how the poet could apply his skill for the needs of his patrons, both in the Hellenistic world and in the Hellenized society of late republican Rome. Gravestones, dedications in temples, deluxe copies of books, paintings, reliefs, statues, fountains, shrines—all these things needed elegantly composed elegiac inscriptions, and most of the *Anthology* consists of examples which seemed worth preserving. It is based on the garlands of Meleager and Philippus, compiled probably in the nineties B.C. and the forties A.D. respectively. Philippus' *Garland* contains many examples of the client Greek's everyday work for his Roman patron, mostly from poets of the Augustan period, particularly Antipater of Thessalonica and Crinagoras of Mytilene, but essentially the same conditions applied for Archias in the previous generation.[60] We have Antipater's praise of the master's cupbearer, his epitaph for the lady Pompeia's African slave girl, his lines on Piso's statue of Dionysus, Piso's sword, and Piso's helmet, and his little poem to accompany a splendid present to Piso from a certain Theogenes as well as those to go with much humbler presents from the poet himself. We have Apollonides praising the consul Laelius' poetic gifts, inscribing the shrine of Aphrodite at Postumus' seaside villa, and celebrating young Gaius' first shave. Most characteristic of all, we have Crinagoras' complimentary address to Sallustius Crispus, "whose aim is the infinite prosperity of his friends."[61] When even the distinguished Crinagoras, whose work for the imperial family made him little short of a court poet, has to make his financial dependence as clear as that, we can see beyond doubt what the reality of Archias' situation was.[62]

With Greek poets at Rome, the question of social definition is comparatively straightforward, since dependent status was inherent in their very Greekness. With Roman poets it is not so easy.

D. Brutus, the consul of 138 B.C., had his triumphal *monumenta* (including the temple of Mars) inscribed with verses by L. Accius the tragedian.[63] Accius also wrote *praetextae*, including one entitled *Brutus* which celebrated his noble friend's legendary ancestor.[64] We must remember that in the second century B.C. poets and actors shared a professional guild, housed in the temple of the patroness of artisans,[65] and that both categories of artists served by their skills the needs of an aristocratic society, particularly at the *nobilium ludi* that were put on at triumphs and funerals.[66] But the straightforward relationship of a tradesman with his aristocratic customers could not remain unchanged when the aristocrat himself began to value and practice the tradesman's skills. D. Brutus and Accius are described by Cicero as *amicissimi*, and by the nineties B.C. we find a patrician playwright frequenting the *collegium poetarum* and causing awkward problems of protocol.[67] For the Hellenized society of the first century B.C., all we can do is to look hard at the work of the surviving poets and see what inferences we can make about the social realities of their position.

Take Lucretius. Some years ago I tried to pick out from the argument of the *De rerum natura* those illustrations which might reflect the poet's own experience.[68] What seemed to emerge was a man familiar with manual work and life at the street level in Rome and at the same time with the luxurious house and expensive life style that one would more naturally associate with C. Memmius, his addressee.[69] My argument was that this inconsistency corresponds to another, in the aim of Lucretius' message: his great crusade against the fear of the gods and the fear of death seems more appropriately aimed at the man in the street, and is essentially separate from the sermon against ambition from which Memmius was presumably meant to profit. A possible solution, I suggested, is that Lucretius started life as a comparatively humble citizen and then, when already launched on his great Epicurean evangel, successfully applied to Memmius for the benefits of his friendship and wrote much of his work in the comfort of Memmius' household.

The essay appealed to some critics more than others.[70] I still stand by it, with the repeated proviso that inference from such very uncertain evidence can never be more than an informed guess. Without going into the whole question again, there are just two points on which I should like to add something here.

First, the critical phrase "sperata voluptas suavis amicitiae" (1.140 f.). In arguing that this does not, as some think, refer to *amicitia* in the technical Epicurean sense,[71] I referred to Walter Allen's article on the passage, which concludes after a survey of the use of the words *amicus* and *amicitia* that "Lucretius was looking for a patron, a man of importance with literary inclinations and a taste for philosophy. Memmius met these requirements."[72] Since then, Peter White's fundamental discussion of *amicitia* and the profession of

noble families in Livy.)

poetry has put the matter beyond question. Although he does not cite Lucretius' lines, they are, I think, a perfect illustration of his main point: "Whether a man is superior, equal, or inferior in standing to another, both are called *amici* and the relationship itself is *amicitia*. . . . *Amici* rarely could be and rarely considered themselves as peers"—and that applied as much to poets as to any other dependents.[73] Lucretius, I think, hoped for Memmius' friendship much as Horace hoped for that of Maecenas.

Second, and perhaps more important, the question of poetry and the man in the street. E. J. Kenney is probably not alone in finding "extremely implausible" the idea that Lucretius may have been of comparatively humble origin and hoped that his poetry would reach the *vulgus* as well as men like Memmius.[74] But the Roman populace listened, or had the opportunity to listen, to a lot more poetry than we think. The evidence is unobtrusive and therefore usually disregarded, but it exists and to ignore it is to misunderstand the profession of letters in Rome.

In his discussion of *decorum* in the first book of the *De officiis*, Cicero mentions casually that poets like to try their work out on the *vulgus* before committing themselves to the final version.[75] It is precisely the casualness of the observation that makes it important; Cicero was illustrating a point in his argument on the correction of faults, and could only do so by appeal to something that was common knowledge to his readers. Horace confirms it when he contrasts his own habit of reading his poems only to friends with the more general custom of reciting them in the Forum, the baths, or the theater.[76] Rome's first permanent theater dates only from 55 B.C., though we do not know how long the aediles allowed the temporary wooden theaters erected for the annual *ludi scaenici* to stay in place. The terraced steps of the Comitium, however, had always provided an auditorium in the Forum, and since about 80 B.C. there had also been the Gradus Aurelii, which Cicero expressly likens to a theater.[77] Moreover, the public porticoes incorporated *scholae* and *exedrae* which were designed for just such performances; Eumolpus in Petronius' novel recites his *Troiae Halosis* in a portico.[78]

Now ever since the mid second century, according to Suetonius, public readings of the Roman poets had been regularly held, sometimes drawing great crowds as when Q. Vargunteius gave his recitals of Ennius' *Annales*.[79] Philosophers too sought a public audience for their moral preaching, like Stertinius the Stoic, who gave the bankrupt Damasippus something to live for in Horace's satire,[80] though according to Cicero the Stoics, with their austere definition of virtue, were "left deserted in their *scholae*" and it was the Epicureans

who drew the crowds.[81] It is therefore not impossible to imagine Lucretius as a "man in the crowd," getting both his Epicurean convic-
tions and his poetic and philosophical learning without the necessity of an expensive education or an expensive library. He would
have needed obsessive commitment, high intelligence, and a first-
rate memory, but there is no reason to think he did not possess all
three.

In the same way, both his evangelical message of deliverance
from fear and his proud ambition to win fame and the Muses' crown
as Ennius had make better sense if we think of Lucretius as writing
with a big public audience in mind.[82] That brings me back to his relationship with Memmius. In my earlier essay I suggested that the
main things Lucretius wanted from Memmius, apart from "the pleasure of sweet friendship," were good working conditions and a library. I now think that publicity, the provision of an audience, may
have been just as important.

Once more I refer to Peter White's essay: "In the pyramid of
Roman society, wealthy men with a large following were uniquely
placed to publicize the work of their poet friends."[83] He quotes two
passages of Martial which are particularly interesting for our purposes. In 12.2, the poet's book is sent to Rome—either to the Palatine library or else to L. Arruntius Stella, who will "give it to be
read" not only to knights and senators but also to the people. In 7.97,
the *liber* is sent to Caesius Sabinus of Sassina, who will make it
famous: banquets will resound with it, and so will the Forum, temples, crossroads, porticoes, and shops.[84] In each case the great man is
expected to publicize the book both to his own friends and to social
equals by having it read at dinner parties, as Atticus publicized
Cicero's *De gloria*,[85] and to the population at large by having it read
in public places, as Regulus had the eulogy of his son recited in
public.[86]

The fact that Martial includes crossroads (*compita*) is especially
interesting in view of Juvenal's disparaging reference to a *carmen
triviale* and Menalcas' sneer at Damoetas in *Eclogues* 3:

> non tu in *triviis*, indocte, solebas
> stridenti miserum stipula disperdere carmen?[87]

When Propertius thinks of *compita* he thinks of *mimae* dancing and
singing.[88] This association of crossroads with entertainment is presumably due to the *ludi compitalicii*, which were held in the various wards of the city at the end of December or the beginning of Jan-
uary each year;[89] on the other days of the year the open space where
they were held by the altar of the Lares at each *compitum* was pre-

sumably available for private performers to take advantage of the crowds of loungers and gossipers who were normally to be found there.[90]

The *Lares compitalicii* were under the control of *magistri*, sometimes freedmen but persons of consequence within their sphere,[91] whose permission would presumably have to be obtained before the recital could take place. For the more prestigious auditoria mentioned by Horace, higher authorities would have to be approached, the aediles no doubt for the theater and the praetors for the Forum.[92] As for the baths, they were all privately owned before Agrippa's time (Cicero mentions the *balneae Saeniae* and *Pallacinae*[93]) and the owner would doubtless be able to prevent anything more ambitious than a snatch of echoing song. In each of these cases, an ordinary humble poet might well find difficulty in setting up the public recital he needed to give his work general currency. With a powerful friend, on the other hand, he could expect the relevant authorities to be much more accommodating.

Even in a wholly public place, the small man without powerful friends would find it hard to get a hearing. Eumolpus had only done sixty-five lines before the passersby stoned him out of the portico, and that was in a country town in south Italy.[94] The Roman populace was an even more difficult audience: it whistled and threw stones at the greatest dignitaries, and it made even Pliny nervous when he got up to speak in the centumviral court.[95] If Lucretius was hoping to get a hearing for six substantial volumes on Epicurean atomic theory, it may well be that he needed some of Memmius' clients and freedmen, not only to applaud at the appropriate places but to keep order at the back of the audience.

Third and last, Catullus. It is impossible to imagine *him* reading his works to the Forum crowd. What the populace enjoyed was turgid stuff like Volusius' *Annales*, and he despised their taste just as his master Callimachus had.[96] There is in fact nothing in Catullus about reading poetry aloud; we may imagine some of the shorter poems being recited for his friends by Catullus himself *in ioco atque vino*, but that is just guesswork on our part. Whenever Catullus talks of poetry, whether his own or his friends' or his enemies', he has written works in mind, either *pugillaria* and *tabelli*, on which presumably they were first distributed, or *libelli* and *volumina*, in which form they were found on the booksellers' shelves.[97]

One reason no doubt is that he and his friends prided themselves on Callimachean λεπτότης[98]—even their most ambitious works were *parva monumenta* (95.9)—and slender verse was easily accommodated on wax tablets or in conveniently sized volumes. Another, I think, is that they could afford to pay for scribes to write out editions of their work, and their sophisticated readers could afford to buy the written copies from the *scrinia librariorum.* Publication in our sense, the reproduction and distribution of written work, was a rich man's luxury, and so was buying books.[99]

Our external evidence on Catullus is lamentably inadequate but still enough to place his social and financial position with a fair degree of certainty. Caesar habitually stayed with Catullus' father, and the peninsula of Sirmio is the finest villa site in north Italy.[100] The Valerii Catulli were a favored senatorial family under Augustus and of consular rank under Tiberius.[101] The natural inference is that in the late republic they were wealthy *domi nobiles* and that Catullus' father was one of the *principes viri* of Verona.

The internal evidence is consistent with that conclusion. The *fundus* in the Sabine or Tiburtine territory is mentioned casually as the excuse for a poem; there is no sign that it meant to Catullus what the Sabine farm meant to Horace. True, he speaks of cobwebs in his purse (13.8), but even if that is more than genre convention[102] it can no more be taken as evidence for his socioeconomic status than can Cicero's comment to Sestius in 62 B.C. that after buying his house he is so much in debt that he will join a conspiracy if anyone will have him.[103] True, Catullus had not brought eight strong litter bearers back from Bithynia, but it is equally significant that the company at Varus' girl-friend's house took it for granted that he could have done (10.14–16). We do not find in Catullus' poetry any requests for financial assistance; on the contrary we hear about what other people had cadged from him, or tried to.[104] Just as his friend the orator Calvus is a man of standing whose client may send him a respectful present at the Saturnalia,[105] so too the picture we get of Catullus is of a man at the upper end of the Roman social scale, more likely to be the source of patronage in a small way than in any need of a patron for himself.[106]

Theodor Bergk thought otherwise. Assuming that Cornelius Nepos had made a generous mention of Catullus in his *Chronica,* Bergk went on to read *patroni ut ergo* instead of *patrona virgo* in the penultimate line of the dedication poem.[107] Catullus would thus be asking Nepos to have his little book so that *because of its patron* it may last for centuries. This reading has itself lasted well into its second *saeculum;* it passes my comprehension why scholars whose judgment deserves respect—Munro in the last century, and Fordyce, Goold, and Sandy in our own day[108]—should prefer it to the simple, elegant, and comprehensible reading of the manuscripts.[109] Palmer rejected it for good reasons in 1879, and I have tried to bring his argument up to date a century later,[110] the crux being that if the book's *patronus* is supposed to be the author's as well, as Goold, for instance, explicitly avers,[111] then the emendation introduces an element quite alien to Catullus' situation.

Both Munro and Goold were, I think, misled by the supposed parallel with Martial. Just because Martial admired Catullus' sparrow poems and used him as a precedent to justify obscenity,[112] it does not follow that they had anything else in common, either poetically or socially. Catullus did not have a patron and did not need one—and we may add that if he had had one he would not have called him *patronus*.[113] The word implies a humility and dependence which a man even in Martial's position would not have found it necessary to express. It is, however, a quite appropriate expression for the relationship between a poet and the goddess of poetry. As a learned author had observed in Catullus' youth, all writers and poets were in the Muses' *clientela*.[114]

Much more interesting, from the point of view of social relations between mortals, is poem 47:

> Porci et Socration, duae sinistrae
> Pisonis, scabies famesque mundi,
> vos Veraniolo meo et Fabullo
> verpus praeposuit Priapus ille?
> vos convivia lauta sumptuose
> de die facitis, mei sodales
> quaerunt in trivio vocationes?

Veranius and Fabullus seem to be on the same social level as Catullus himself: they go with Piso to Spain[115] just as he goes with Memmius to Bithynia; his references to them seem to reflect a relationship of equals, and the Veranii at least advanced first to senatorial and then to consular rank at about the same rate as the Valerii Catulli.[116] Porcius and Socration, on the other hand, "the itch and hunger of the world," are hangers-on of Piso's who do his jobs for him.[117] What excites Catullus' indignation is the reversal of roles: it is the young gentlemen who ought to be enjoying the smart dinner party and the itchy-fingered parasites who ought to be hanging about the crossroads hoping to strike up an acquaintance with their betters, as Horace's unwelcome companion was intending to do with Maecenas.[118] We are reminded of Catullus' feud over Juventius with Aurelius, "pater esuritionum," and Furius, "cui neque servus est nec arca": the boy was too good for the likes of them.[119]

It would be dangerous to take this poem as evidence that Veranius and Fabullus were literally cadging invitations on the street corner. But it is not inconceivable. We have been at these crossroads already with the poet who was looking for an audience; one conspicuous category among the crowd he hoped to interest there was that of idle young men with their dirty jokes, malicious talk, and gossip about other people's love lives—*convicium scurrarum*, as Cicero put it.[120]

Now, what exactly was a *scurra*? For Cicero as for Plautus he was a wealthy playboy, witty in a libelous sort of way and the very soul, at least in his own estimation, of *urbanitas*.[121] There is one perfect example in Catullus—perfect, that is, except for one flaw. Suffenus in poem 22 is "homo venustus et dicax et urbanus," he is rich enough to afford deluxe volumes for his disastrous poetry, and he is a *scurra*,—"or whatever can be more witty than that." Sixty years later, however, by the time of Verrius Flaccus, a *scurra* was a parasite, *tenuioris fortunae homo*, and his name derived from *sequi*.[122] Horace's usage is transitional: his *scurrae* include wealthy gamblers and spendthrifts in the late republican style, but also the slave-born buffoon Sarmentus who entertained the company on the way to Brundisium.[123] The common factor that applies from the top to the bottom of this scale is that the *scurra* is found at dinner parties.[124] Of the company at Nasidienus' banquet in Horace's satire, the *scurrae* by the later definition are Porcius and Nomentanus, whose job is to flatter the host and not drink too much; the *scurrae* in the earlier sense are Vibidius and Balatro: "Unless we drink him bankrupt we shall have lived in vain."[125] Transposed into late republican terms, the two equivalent pairs at Piso's dinner table might be respectively Porcius and Socration, and Veranius and Fabullus.

The mere angling for a dinner invitation is not in itself evidence for social dependence on the host. There is a famous and quite credible story in Plutarch of Cicero and Pompey deliberately getting themselves invited to dinner with Lucullus. And when Catullus tries to get an invitation to Sestius' table, and succeeds only at the expense of having to read Sestius' awful speech *In Antium petitorem*, that does not make him in any sense a parasite.[126] Probably Cicero would have called Catullus, Fabullus, and Veranius *scurrae*, but all that means is that they were men about town, racy talkers with plenty of *sal* and *lepor*, and therefore of good value at a dinner party. They would hardly have been human if they had not known that value and exploited it.

Finally, we come to poem 28 and the phrase I have used in my title. Here and only here, in the special circumstances of the provincial governor's *cohors amicorum*, do we find Catullus and his two friends cultivating their social superiors with a view to direct financial advantage. The *beneficium* they are looking for is a share in the exploitation of Rome's empire, a much greater prize than any aimed at by a client in the ordinary sense of the term.

How did Catullus get his potentially profitable position with Memmius in Bithynia? Or Veranius and Fabullus theirs with Piso in Spain? Or for that matter Caelius Rufus his five years earlier with Q. Pompeius in Africa? [127] No doubt it took more than a casual meeting at the *trivium*; attendance at the great man's *salutatio* would surely have been necessary. But if Catullus met Archias or Lucretius in the *vestibulum* of Memmius' house in 58 B.C., as he may easily have done, it would have been about business very different from theirs. All three could have said "peto nobilem amicum," but only two of them would have hoped to interest their noble friend in their abilities as poets.

NOTES

1. C. Aelius Gallus ap. Gell. *NA* 16.5.3 and Macrob. *Sat.* 6.8.16; Varro *Ling.* 7.81 ("quod est ante domum"), Paulus *Dig.* 10.3.19.1, Serv. *Aen.* 4.507. *Vestibulum* later came to mean the first room in the house itself (e.g., Ov. *Fast.* 6.302 f., Suet. *Aug.* 100.2, Macrob. *Sat.* 6.8.15), but Fiechter ("Römisches Haus," *RE* 1A [1914]: 983 f.) is wrong to assert that the change took place in the second century B.C.: see B. Tamm, *Auditorium and Palatium*, pp. 94–101.

2. Plaut. *Mostell.* 817, "viden vestibulum ante aedis hoc et ambulacrum quoiusmodi?" Steps: Sen. *Ep.* 84.12.

3. Cic. *Phil.* 2.68 (Pompey's *rostra*), Livy 10.7.9, Aug. *RG* 34.2, Pliny *HN* 35.7, etc.

4. *Vir. ill.* 20.1.

5. Cic. *Att.* 4.3.5, Vitr. *De Arch.* 6.5.1–2, Sen. *Ad Marc.* 10.1. Etymology: Gell. *NA* 16.5.8–10, Macrob. *Sat.* 6.8.19–20 (con. Serv. *Aen.* 6.273).

6. Manilius 5.65 ("unum verbum"), Sen. *Ben.* 6.34.3, Mart. 1.108.10, 7.39.2, 9.7.2. Kiss: Suet. *Tib.* 34.2.

7. *Sedens in solio*: Cic. *Leg.* 1.10, *De Or.* 2.143, 3.133. *Inambulare domi*: Cic. *Att.* 6.2.5.

8. Livy 5.41.2 and 7–8 ("patentibus atriis"), Val. Max. 3.2.7 ("apertis ianuis"); cf. Plut. *Cam.* 22.

9. Hor. *Epist.* 2.1.102–7, Cic. *De Or.* 3.133.

10. *Comment. Pet.* 34–8. I still think (cf. T. P. Wiseman, "The Census in the First Century B.C.," *JRS* 59 [1969]: 66 f.) that the essay is probably authentic; see now J. S. Richardson, "The 'Commentariolum Petitionis,'" *Historia* 20 (1971): 436–42, R. E. A. Palmer, "Tre lettere in cerca di storico,"

RFIC 99 (1971): 385–93, Claude Nicolet, "*Amicissimi Catilinae*: A propos du *Commentariolum petitionis*," *REL* 50 (1972): 163–86.

11. *Comment. Pet.* 35; Cic. *Fam.* 9.20.3; Manilius 5.65 f., "limina pervolitans . . . per omnia . . . communis amicus."

12. *Comment. Pet.* 36; Cic. *Att.* 1.18.1, "cum bene completa domus est tempore matutino, cum ad forum stipati gregibus amicorum descendimus . . ." (cf. 4.3.3, "qui erant mecum"); Cic. *Mur.* 70, "a quibus si domus nostra celebratur, si interdum ad forum deducimur, si uno basilicae spatio honestamur, diligenter observari videmur et coli."

13. *Comment. Pet.* 37; Cic. *Mur.* 70, "totos dies . . . ista adsiduitas"; Sen. *Ep.* 22.9, "nudum . . . latus? incomitata lectica?"; Mart. 3.46.5, "in turbam incideris, cunctos umbone repellet" (cf. *Laus Pisonis* 134–36; Pliny *Ep.* 3.14.7, slave). *Anteambulones*: Suet. *Vesp.* 2.2; Mart. 2.18.5, 3.7.2, 10.74.3.

14. Cic. *Mur.* 71, "neque ulla re alia quae a nobis consequuntur nisi opera sua compensari putant posse"; cf. 70, "operam atque adsectationem."

15. S. M. Treggiari, *Roman Freedmen during the Late Republic*, pp. 75–78. Clodius: Cic. *QFr.* 2.3.2 and 4, *Att.* 4.3.3, etc.

16. Cic. *Verr.* 1.130 f., esp. 144 (D. Brutus), 151 (Iunius' status).

17. Hor. *Epist.* 1.7.46–95, esp. 61–70.

18. Cic. *Mur.* 72, "locus et in circo et in foro"; *Att.* 2.1.5, "Siculis locum gladiatoribus dare." We do not hear of places in the theater for *ludi scaenici.* Perhaps there was less demand for comparatively highbrow entertainment.

19. Ulp. *Dig.* 9.3.5.1; cf. Lucian *De merc. cond.* 3 (οἰκεῖν ἐν καλῷ) and 20 (συνοικίας); Horace's Sabine farm is an extreme example.

20. The word *parasitus* is little used except in comedy or with reference to comedy (e.g., Cic. *Amic.* 98, Hor. *Epist.* 2.1.173).

21. E.g., Plaut. *Mil. Glor.* 666–68, *Capt.* 473–75, 482 f., etc.

22. Cic. *Mur.* 70, "tenuiorum amicorum et non occupatorum est ista adsiduitas"; *Comment. Pet.* 37, "ab iis plane hoc munus exigito, qui per aetatem ac negotium poterunt, ipsi tecum ut adsidui sint." For an example (Cicero's client T. Agusius), see *Fam.* 13.71.

23. Tac. *Hist.* 1.4.3; *Comment. Pet.* 35.

24. Hor. *Sat.* 1.6.62.

25. Phaedr. *Fab.* 2.5; Mart. 2.7, 4.78.

26. Manilius 5.61–66, Sen. *Tranq.* 12.4.

27. Juv. 3.41–57; Hor. *Sat.* 1.9, esp. 23–25, 56–60; Cic. *Cael.* 21.

28. Cic. *Fam.* 3.9.2, "quod te adeunt fere omnes, si quid velis."

29. For these terms, see Cic. *Mur.* 70–71, *Comment. Pet.* 35 f., etc.; cf. Cic. *Fam.* 9.20.3 on *salutantes*, "qui me quidem perofficiose et peramanter observant."

30. Cic. *Arch.* 4–5, "cum praetextatus etiam tum Archias esset."

31. Cic. *Arch.* 6; S. M. Treggiari, "Intellectuals, Poets, and their Patrons in the First Century B.C.," *Echos du monde classique: Classical News and Views* 21, no. 1 (1977): 26.

32. Cic. *Arch.* 19. The *nam* exemplifies Archias' devotion "ad populi Romani gloriam laudemque celebrandam."

33. Cic. *Arch.* 7 and 26.

34. G. Williams, *Change and Decline: Roman Literature in the Early Empire*, p. 115. Compare Alcaeus (*Anth. Pal.* 7.247, *Anth. Plan.* 5), Polystratus (*Anth. Pal.* 7.297), Crinagoras (*Anth. Plan.* 61, *Anth. Pal.* 9.283).

35. Contrast Cic. *Arch.* 19 ("attigit," cf. 28) with 21 ("bellum . . . totum . . . expressum est").

36. Cic. *Arch.* 25, "quem nos in contione vidimus, cum ei libellum malus poeta de populo subiecisset, quod epigramma in eum fecisset tantum modo alternis versibus longiusculis, statim ex iis rebus quas tum vendebat iubere ei praemium tribui."

37. Varro ap. Gell. *NA* 1.22.5, Nep. *Att.* 14.1, Pliny *Ep.* 5.19.3; cf. Cic. *Att.* 1.12.4, *Fam.* 5.9.2 (*anagnostes*).

38. Cic. *Att.* 12.6.2. For *acroaseis*, see *Att.* 15.17.2, Varro *Sat. Men.* 517B, Suet. *Gram.* 2.2, etc.

39. Cic. *Att.* 1.15.1, *QFr.* 1.1.28, *Flac.* 9, cf. *Arch.* 12; Plut. *Cic.* 5.2, Dio Cass. 46.18.1.

40. Cic. *Arch.* 18, "quotiens ego hunc *vidi* . . . quotiens revocatum. . . . Quae vero accurate cogitateque scripsisset, ea sic *vidi* probari ut ad veterum scriptorum laudem perveniret." The verb and the participle suggest a public performance. For *revocare*, cf. Cic. *Sest.* 120 and 123, *Tusc.* 4.63; Val. Max. 6.2.9, etc.

41. Cic. *Att.* 4.11.2, "ego mecum praeter Dionysium eduxi neminem." For Dionysius, see Treggiari, *Roman Freedmen*, pp. 119 f.

42. I.e., either the A. Terentius A.f. Varro who was quaestor in Delos about 88 B.C. (see E. Badian, review of *ILLRP: Imagines* (*CIL Auctarium*), ed. A. Degrassi, *JRS* 58.[1968]: 245 f.) and later legate in Asia (*ILS* 8772–73), or else his father. On M. Terentius Varro Lucullus (Cic. *Arch.* 6 for Archias' enfranchisement), see D. R. Shackleton Bailey, *Two Studies in Roman Nomenclature*, p. 132.

43. Ps.-Asc. 193 and 218St, Schol. Gron. 349St, scholiasts on Hor. *Sat.* 2.1.49 (garbled); cf. Cic. *Div. Caec.* 24, *Verr.* act. pr. 17, 40, *Clu.* 130. On the identity of Hortensius' cousin Terentius Varro, scandalously acquitted on this occasion, see D. Magie, *Roman Rule in Asia Minor*, pp. 1125 f. He had been *procos. Asiae*, and may well be identical with A. Varro (see Badian, review of *ILLRP*, p. 245). W. G. Arnott in "The Praenomen of Archias," *Hermes* 99 (1971): 254–55, argues *ex silentio Ciceronis* that Aulus cannot derive from a noble patron, and suggests that it is a pun on αὐλός.

44. Lucian *De merc. cond.* 3 (trans. H. W. and F. G. Fowler, *The Works of Lucian of Samosata*, vol. 2, p. 2). Philodemus: Cic. *Pis.* 68–71.

45. Cic. *Brut.* 132. Cf. *De Or.* 2.154 on the fluency of his Greek; *Acad.* 2.148, *De Or.* 2.152, 3.21 on his mastery of Greek philosophy. See in general H. Bardon, *La littérature latine inconnue*, vol. 1, pp. 115–23.

46. Cic. *Brut.* 132; quoted at second hand by Plut. *Mar.* 25–27.

47. Quoted in Gell. *NA* 19.9.14; cf. Callim. *Anth. Pal.* 12.73; another in Cic. *Nat. D.* 1.79.

48. On the *communis historia* of "Lutatius," see Bardon, *La littérature latine inconnue*, vol. 1, pp. 121–22, for the meaning of the title, and Peter, *HR Rel*, vol. 1, p. cclxviii, for the identity of the author; fragments in Peter, vol. 1, pp. 192–94 and Funaioli, *Gramm. Rom. Frag.*, pp. 122 f.

49. Cic. *Brut.* 132 on Furius, whose *Annales* are attested in Gell. *NA* 18.11 and Macrob. *Sat.* 6.1.31–34. Antipater: Cic. *De Or.* 3.194. On Archias as a poet of the *Garland*, see A. S. F. Gow and D. L. Page, *The Greek Anthology: The Garland of Philip and Some Contemporary Epigrams*, vol. 2, pp. 434 f.

50. Suet. *Gram.* 3.5 (Daphnis), Cic. *Fam.* 16.10.2 (Tiro); cf. Treggiari, "Intellectuals, Poets, and their Patrons," pp. 27 f.

51. Cic. *Att.* 1.19.10, cf. Plut. *Luc.* 1.5 for his Greek history of the Marsic war; Cic. *Acad.* 2.1–4, Plut. *Luc.* 42.3–4, etc. on Lucullus and Antiochus of Ascalon, for whom see J. Glucker, *Antiochus and the Late Academy*, pp. 13–27 and 380–86.

52. Cic. *Arch.* 21, *Att.* 1.16.15, where "Lucullis" suggests it also included M. Lucullus' *res gestae* in Thrace.

53. T. W. Hillard, *The Claudii Pulchri, 76–48 B.C.: Studies in their Political Cohesion*, pp. 174–208, a long and valuable digression on Plutarch's sources in order to place the origin of the episode of Appius and Tigranes at Antioch (Plut. *Luc.* 21). See also T. Reinach, *Mithradate Eupator, roi de Pont*, p. 427, and F. P. Rizzo, *Le fonti per la storia della conquista pompeiana della Siria*, pp. 31–35 and 79.

54. Hillard, *The Claudii Pulchri*, pp. 193–97 on Plut. *Luc.* 12.1–2, 13.4, 16, 24.6–8, etc.; also 19.4, Lucullus' entry into Amisus. One might add that the *Luculleia* (Plut. *Luc.* 23.1) offered scope for a good Homeric ἆθλα episode.

55. Plut. *Luc.* 12.1.

56. E.g., Cic. *Fam.* 13.1.2, 25, 78.1 (Greeks), 69.1 (freedmen), etc. See Cic. *De Or.* 2.276 for the visits of Nasica and Ennius.

57. Cic. *De Or.* 2.365, 3.75, 194.

58. Cic. *De Or.* 2.228; cf. *Brut.* 143, "cum gravitate iunctus facetiarum et urbanitatis . . . lepos."

59. Cic. *Att.* 1.16.15; T. P. Wiseman, *Cinna the Poet and Other Roman Essays*, pp. 138–46, esp. 144 f. Cf. Longinus' epigram on Tiberius' grotto at Sperlonga: F. Coarelli, "Sperlonga e Tiberio, Review of R. Hampe, *Sperlonga und Vergil.*" *Dial. Arch.* 7 (1973): 117.

60. Archias' poem on Roscius and the snake (Cic. *Div.* 1.79—to illustrate Pasiteles' engraving?) was just the sort of thing Philippus might have included.

61. Gow and Page, *The Greek Anthology*: Antipater nos. 3, 16, 30–31, 41–45; Apollonides nos. 21, 25, 26; Crinagoras no. 36, εἰς ἑτάρων μυρίον εὐσο(ίην).

62. On Crinagoras, see G. W. Bowersock, *Augustus and the Greek World*, pp. 36 f. Similar financial hints in Philodemus and Antipater (*Anth. Pal.* 11.44, 9.92, 428). Antipater's poem on Piso's Thracian campaign (9.428) and that of Boethus of Tarsus on Antony at Philippi (Strabo 14.674) are

closely parallel to Archias' Lucullan epic, and perhaps also to the poem he was about to begin for the Metelli in 61 B.C. (Cic. *Att.* 1.16.15).

63. Cic. *Arch.* 27, *Schol. Bob.* 179St; Val. Max. 8.14.2; for the temple cf. Pliny *HN* 36.26, Nepos fr. 26P (ap. Prisc. 8.17 p. 383H).

64. Cic. *Div.* 1.44 f.; Varro *Ling.* 5.80, 6.7, 7.72.

65. Festus, *Gloss. Lat.* 446–48L: temple of Minerva on the Aventine from 207 B.C.

66. *ILLRP* 803.12. Funeral games: *didascalia* to Ter. *Hec.* and *Ad.* Votive games at triumphs: Livy 36.2.3, 39.22.8, cf. Pol. 30.22. Atellan farces played when there was a *pompa*: Fest. (Paulus) 115L, Varro *Ling.* 7.95 (on "Manducus"). Actors needed for funeral procession: Diod. Sic. 31.25.2, Dion. Hal. 7.72.12, Suet. *Iul.* 84.4, *Vesp.* 19.2. Poets needed for *neniae* and *tabulae triumphales*: Festus, *Gloss. Lat.* 154L, Tac. *Ann.* 3.5.6, Livy 40.52.4 f., 41.28.8 f., *ILLRP* 122, 335.

67. Val. Max. 3.7.11. Conversely, the authors were now independent enough to say no to their customers: e.g., Macrob. *Sat.* 2.6.6 on Laberius' refusal of a mime to Clodius. N. Horsfall, in "The Collegium Poetarum," *BICS* 23 (1976): 79–95, denies any continuity between the humble "scribes' and actors'" guild of the third century and the *collegium poetarum* frequented by Accius and C. Caesar Strabo. However, the Augustan "mag[ister] scr[ibarum] poetar[um]" known from a recently found inscription (E. J. Jory, "P. Cornelius P. L. Surus: An Epigraphical Note," *BICS* 15 [1968]: 125 f.) was a freedman, and Horsfall suggests (p. 91) that some of its members may have been humble writers of *elogia* and epitaphs.

68. Wiseman, "The Two Worlds of Titus Lucretius," in *Cinna the Poet*, pp. 11–43, the published version of a lecture delivered in 1971.

69. On whom see Cic. *Brut.* 247. See also G. B. Townend, "The Fading of Memmius," *CQ* 28 (1978): 267–83.

70. Contrast, for instance, Peter Green, "The Penumbra of Power: Review of T. P. Wiseman, *Cinna the Poet and Other Roman Essays*," *TLS*, May 2, 1975, p. 478, and Elizabeth Rawson, Review of T. P. Wiseman, *Cinna the Poet and Other Roman Essays*, *JRS* 66 (1976): 266–67.

71. See now E. J. Kenney, *Lucretius*, p. 17.

72. Walter Allen, "On the Friendship of Lucretius with Memmius," *CP* 33 (1938): 167–81, following Friedrich Marx, "Der Dichter Lucretius," *NJKA* 3 (1899): 534 f.; quotation from Allen, p. 178.

73. Peter White, "*Amicitia* and the Profession of Poetry in Early Imperial Rome," *JRS* 68 (1978): 74–92; quotations from pp. 80 and 81.

74. Kenney, *Lucretius*, pp. 7 f. on Wiseman, *Cinna the Poet*, pp. 25–26; ibid., pp. 5 and 39 on Lucretius' educated audience, "he wrote as a *doctus poeta* for *docti lectores*" (p. 5).

75. Cic. *Off.* 1.147, "etiam poetae suum quisque opus a vulgo considerari vult, ut, si quid reprehensum sit a pluribus, id corrigatur."

76. Hor. *Sat.* 1.4.74–76, "non ubivis coramve quibuslibet. In medio qui / scripta foro recitent, sunt multi, quique lavantes: / suave locus voci resonat conclusus"; *Epist.* 1.19.41 f., "spissis indigna theatris / scripta pudet recitare."

77. Comitium: F. Coarelli, "Il Comizio dalle origini alle fine della Repubblica," *PP* 174 (1977): 166–238, esp. 201–14. Gradus Aurelii: Cic. *Clu.*
93, cf. *Flac.* 66; E. Nash, *Pictorial Dictionary of Ancient Rome*, vol. 2,
pp. 478–81; Coarelli, "Il Comizio," pp. 213 f.

78. Vitr. *De Arch.* 5.11.2, Petron. *Sat.* 90; cf. *ILLRP* 116 (*scholae*,
Nola), 680 (*exedrae*, Tibur).

79. Suet. *Gram.* 2.4, "Q. Vargunteius Annales Ennii quos certis diebus
in magna frequentia pronuntiabat."

80. Hor. *Sat.* 2.3.33 f., 296, cf. Ps.-Acr. on *Epist.* 1.12.20; also Ps.-Acr.
on *Sat.* 1.1.14 (Fabius), *Sat.* 2.7.45, Porph. on *Sat.* 1.1.120, 3.139 (Crispinus).
Cf. Varro *Sat. Men.* 517B, "acroasi bellorum hominum" (in a Cynic context).

81. Cic. *Cael.* 41. Epicureans: *Fin.* 1.13, 25, 2.44, 81, *Tusc.* 2.7, 3.50,
4.6, 5.28.

82. Lucr. 1.922–47, 6.47, 92–95; 1.117–26 on Ennius. Muses' crown:
1.118, 929–30.

83. White, "*Amicitia*," p. 85.

84. Mart. 12.2.15, "ille dabit populo patribusque equitique legen-
dum"; 7.97.11 f., "te convivia, te forum sonabit, / aedes compita porticus
tabernae."

85. Cic. *Att.* 16.2.6 and 3.1, where *dumtaxat* and *arcano* respectively
imply that a more public reading is being deliberately excluded.

86. Pliny *Ep.* 4.7.2, both in Rome and in the towns of Italy and the
provinces.

87. Juv. 7.55, Vir. *Ecl.* 3.26 f.

88. Prop. 2.22.3–6, with the remarks of W. A. Camps, ed., *Propertius:
Elegies, Book II*, pp. 152 f.

89. For discussion of the *ludi compitalici*, see A. K. Michels, *The Calendar of the Roman Republic*, p. 205, n. 28, and A. W. Lintott, *Violence in
Republican Rome*, pp. 80 f.; also L. R. Taylor, *The Voting Districts of the
Roman Republic*, pp. 76 f., and Treggiari, *Roman Freedmen*, pp. 170 f. and
198 f.

90. *Lares* altars: Varro *Ling.* 6.25, Ov. *Fasti* 2.615, 5.129–46. Gossip:
Hor. *Ars P.* 245–47, *Sat.* 2.3.25 f. ("frequentia compita"), Cic. *Mur.* 13,
Prop. 2.20.22, Ov. *Am.* 3.1.18, Livy 34.2.12, Juv. 1.63 f., 9.112, etc.

91. Cic. *Pis.* 8, Asc. 7C (Sex. Cloelius); Livy 34.7.2, *ILLRP* 696–704.

92. On the praetors' tribunals in the Forum, see L. Richardson, "The
Tribunals of the Praetors of Rome," *MDAI(R)* 80 (1973): 219–33 (though I
do not agree with all the details of his argument), and F. Coarelli, "Il Comizio," pp. 212 f.

93. Cic. *Cael.* 61–62, *Rosc. Am.* 18, cf. 132.

94. Petron. *Sat.* 90. The same thing happened when he recited in the
theater.

95. Cic. *Att.* 1.16.11 (whistles at Cicero, unusually absent), Macrob.
Sat. 2.6.1 (stones at Vatinius, who asked the aediles for a restriction to fruit),
Pliny *Ep.* 7.17.8–9.

96. Cat. 95.10, "at populus tumido gaudeat Antimacho"; Callim. *Anth.
Pal.* 12.43.4.

97. *Pugillaria / codicillos*: Cat. 42.4 f. and 11 f. *Tabelli*: 50.2. *Libelli*: 1.1 f. and 8, 14.12. *Volumina*: 22.5–8, 95.6. Books in general: 14.17–19 (booksellers), 14b.2 f., 36.1 and 20, 44.21, 95.7 f. *Scribere*: 22.5 and 16, 36.7, 44.18, 50.4.

98. Callim. *Ait.* 1.24, *Epigr.* 27.3P f. (cf. fr. 465P f. quoted by Athen. 3.72A); T. P. Wiseman, *Clio's Cosmetics: Three Studies in Greco-Roman Literature*, pp. 169 f.

99. Cic. *Fam.* 13.77.3, "bibliothecen multorum nummorum"; A. J. Marshall, "Library Resources and Creative Writing at Rome," *Phoenix* 30 (1976): 254 f.

100. Suet. *Iul.* 73, "hospitioque patris eius, *sicut consuerat*, uti perseveravit."

101. H. Mattingly and E. Sydenham, *The Roman Imperial Coinage*, vol. 1, p. 81, no. 218, dating the *quadrantes* of L. Valerius Catullus to about 4 B.C.; for the moneyership as mark of favor under Augustus, see T. P. Wiseman, *New Men in the Roman Senate 139 B.C.–A.D. 14*, pp. 150 f. Consular: Suet. *Gaius* 36.1, cf. CIL 14.2095, 2466 (Sex. Teidius Valerius Catullus, cos. suff. A.D. 31).

102. Cf. F. Cairns, *Generic Composition in Greek and Roman Poetry*, pp. 243 f.

103. Cic. *Fam.* 5.6.2; M. W. Frederiksen, "Caesar, Cicero and the Problem of Debt," *JRS* 56 (1966): 130 f.

104. Cat. 23.26 f., 41.2, 103. I ignore poem 26 because of the insoluble textual uncertainty in line 1: *whose* villa is mortgaged?

105. Cat. 14.6 f.; cf. Antipater of Thessalonica, *Anth. Pal.* 6.249 (a Saturnalia present to Piso).

106. The situation imagined at Cat. 11.1–14 is that Furius and Aurelius might attend Catullus as an *adsectator* attends his patron. I owe this suggestion to Oswyn Murray.

107. T. Bergk, "Philologische Thesen," *Philologus* 12 (1857): 581. For poets in Nepos' *Chronica*, see Gell. *NA* 17.21.3 (Homer and Hesiod), 21.8 (Archilochus), following Apollodorus (*FGrH* 244 fr. 35, 48, 63, 74 etc.); Nep. *Att.* 12.4 for his high opinion of Catullus.

108. H. A. J. Munro, *Criticisms and Elucidations of Catullus*, pp. 2–5; C. J. Fordyce, *Catullus: A Commentary*, p. 87; G. P. Goold, "O Patrona Virgo," in *Polis and Imperium: Studies in Honor of Edward Togo Salmon*, ed. J. A. S. Evans, pp. 253–64, and *Interpreting Catullus*, pp. 10 f.; G. N. Sandy, "Indebtedness, *Scurrilitas*, and Composition in Catullus (Cat. 44, 1, 68)," *Phoenix* 32 (1978): 76.

109. The paradosis is one syllable short, but "qualecumque quod ⟨est⟩, patrona virgo . . ." gives perfect sense.

110. A. Palmer, "On Ellis's Catullus," *Hermathena* 3 (1879): 298 f.; Wiseman, *Clio's Cosmetics*, pp. 172 f.

111. E.g., Goold, "O Patrona Virgo," p. 262, "the normal relationship of poet and patron."

112. Sparrow: Mart. 1.7, 109.1, 4.14.13, 7.14.3 f., 11.6.16. *Lascivia*: 1. praef.

113. White, "*Amicitia*," p. 79; Treggiari, "Intellectuals, Poets, and Their Patrons," p. 24.

114. Aurelius Opillus ap. Suet. *Gram.* 6.

115. Not Macedonia: see T. P. Wiseman, "Catullus, His Life and Times; Review of F. Stoessl, *C. Valerius Catullus*," *JRS* 69 (1979): 162–63.

116. Q. Veranius pr. before A.D. 18 (Tac. *Ann.* 2.56.4), Q. Veranius Q.f. cos. A.D. 49: R. Syme, "The Origin of the Veranii," *CQ* 7 (1957): 123–25. Cf. note 101 above.

117. For "sinistrae Pisonis," cf. *manus* at Cic. *Verr.* 2.27, Tac. *Agr.* 15.2.

118. Hor. *Sat.* 1.9.58 f., "tempora quaeram, / occuram in triviis, deducam."

119. Cat. 21.9–11 (Aurelius), 23 (Furius).

120. Cic. *Mur.* 13, "adripere maledictum ex trivio aut ex scurrarum aliquo convicio"; Hor. *Ars P.* 245–47, Prop. 2.20.22, etc.

121. Rich: Cic. *Har. Resp.* 42, *Sest.* 39, *Quinct.* 55, 62. Playing ball: Plaut. *Curc.* 296, Lucil. 1134–36M. Malicious wit: Plaut. *Poen.* 1280 f., Cic. *Quinct.* 11, *De Or.* 2.244, 247; cf. *Fam.* 9.21.3, *Verr.* 3.146, *Clu.* 39 (*improbus, petulans*). Urbanitas: Plaut. *Mostell.* 15, cf. *Trin.* 202, *Epid.* 15. See P. B. Corbett, "The *scurra* in Plautus," *Eranos* 66 (1968): 118–25; Munro, *Criticisms and Elucidations*, pp. 57 f.

122. Verrius Flaccus ap. Fest. 378L. The derivation would not apply to the Plautine *scurra* who goes in front (Plaut. *Poen.* 611). Suet. *Gram.* 17 for Verrius' dates (he died *sub Tiberio*).

123. Hor. *Sat.* 1.5.52–55 (Sarmentus), 2.7.15–18 (gambler), *Epist.* 1.15.26–41 (spendthrift, now impoverished); at *Sat.* 1.8.10–11 Pantolabus seems to be part of the *misera plebs*. Cf. Corbett, "The *scurra* in Plautus," p. 125.

124. Hor. *Epist.* 1.17.13–14 and 19 (the philosopher Aristippus). Cf. Ov. *Am.* 3.1.17 f.: the gossip is heard equally at *convivia* and at the *compita*.

125. Hor. *Sat.* 2.8.21–41.

126. *Pace* Sandy, "Indebtedness," pp. 68–72, on Cat. 44.10–12. Lucullus: Plut. *Luc.* 41.4–6.

127. Cic. *Cael.* 73.

Positions for Poets in Early Imperial Rome

PETER WHITE

In this essay I want to discuss the working lives of poets at Rome without raising any consideration that has to do with the quality of their poems. And if this approach should upset the sensibility of the philologist or literary critic, I will confess that the ideal reader I have in mind is Ovid's father, the first Western parent known to have sat down with his artistic son and asked, "Why are you wasting your time on that? There's no money in it."[1]

My argument will be that Ovid's father misjudged the situation. In Roman society poetry was in some ways a practical career which offered opportunities of making money and of getting ahead in the world. But these opportunities were very different from those available to a modern poet; indeed they often had little to do with the actual writing of poetry. What this line of work did entail by way of rewards and burdens I hope gradually to make clear. But let me start with the issue singled out by Ovid's father and ask, What were the sources of a Roman poet's income? In studying the poet's career, that at least will give us something tangible to look for.

In general the resources which support a modern writer were negligible or nonexistent in Rome. Although a lively book trade had grown up by the end of the first century after Christ, the whole empire did not contain book buyers in numbers that would have approached the scale of a modern mass market. Even if such a market had existed, there would have been no means of mass-producing books; nor did an ancient bookseller organize his business so as to reach buyers beyond the confines of his own city. Throughout antiquity the return on sales must have been calculated in modest figures. Moreover we have no reason to think that the limited profit which a bookseller did make was shared with the authors whose works he sold. Although ancient writers sometimes allude to the sale of their books, they never intimate that they gained anything from sales. In *Epigrams* 11.3, Martial says plainly that he did not:

Non urbana mea tantum Pimpleide gaudent
   otia nec vacuis auribus ista damus,
sed meus in Geticis ad Martia signa pruinis
   a rigido teritur centurione liber,
dicitur et nostros cantare Britannia versus.
   quid prodest? nescit sacculus ista meus.

The most that a poet could have hoped would be a lump sum from
the bookseller to whom he gave his manuscript (though such pay-
ments have escaped mention in our sources if they were ever made).
Once a poet released his work he could anticipate no royalties and
no sort of economic protection. Anyone could copy his book and
then sell or give it away. The sale of his books, therefore, would
scarcely have enriched a poet.[2]   *except for fame.*
   One way in which a poet could make money was by writing for
the stage. On an ever-increasing number of days throughout the
year, public festivals were celebrated in the theaters and arenas of
the capital. One of the most popular events was the performance of
pantomimes, for which librettos were purchased either by the magistrates who sponsored the shows or by the stars who performed.
This demand did create a limited opportunity. Juvenal says that, for
all the merit of his serious poetry, Statius would have gone hungry if
he had not sold plays to the actor Paris (*Sat.* 7.82–87). But this sort
of writing did a poet's reputation no good. Juvenal describes Statius'
work for the stage as literary prostitution.[3] And another writer who
devoted himself to turning out pantomimes was condemned by the
elder Seneca for "polluting his talent."[4] Although there was money
to be made here, it was tainted.
   Apart from pantomimes we know virtually nothing about the
demand for theater scripts. Varius is said to have received a million
sesterces for a tragedy of Thyestes produced at the Actian games of
Augustus.[5] It is not clear whether this remarkable sum represents a
gift or a purchase by the emperor. Many other tragedies and comedies as well were written during the empire, but there is not one
which we know was purchased for performance at a festival program
or which was written with any thought of performance. From time
to time an imperial extravaganza would offer some variation in the
standard dramatic fare. Horace composed a choral piece for the secular games of 17 B.C. and he probably received some recompense for
it. But performance at the secular games was literally a once-in-a-
lifetime opportunity—not a very practical solution for the poet who
required a regular source of income.
   Writing for the stage, although it could bring in some money,

cf. Catullus' Diana hymn, & epithalamium

was clearly not an adequate foundation for a career in poetry. And in fact few of the Roman poets of whom we know had anything to do with the theater. — *see Wiseman, Catullus & His World, on Attis poem (63)*

Except for scripts, the chances of direct remuneration for poetry were slim. The emperors loved to proclaim their magnificence in dazzling bursts of largess, and sometimes the lucky recipient was a poet rather than a drinking companion or an athlete or a freak or a talking parrot. Yet poets in Rome never became paid retainers or imperial laureates who could count on sustained assistance. Most who crowded around to catch the emperor's occasional bouquets watched someone else walk home with the prize.

Among private citizens, munificence was more discreet and great handouts were rare. A poet might hope that the timely laudation of birthdays, weddings, and achievements would prompt a wealthy friend to reach for his purse, but it was only a hope. For reasons I will explain in a moment, commissioned poetry, which stipulated recompense in exchange for verse, would have been considered extremely bad manners in Roman society. Even if deployed in this direction, the poet's craft could not guarantee its practitioners a living.

Unless there is a possibility I have overlooked, it appears that Roman poets did not support themselves directly through their literary production. The basis of their livelihood must have lain elsewhere. But where?

Most poets did not have to make a living by their poems because they were already bolstered against the pinch of basic needs. From the time of Cicero on, almost all the poets whose works we read today were either *equites* or senators: certainly Horace, Tibullus, Propertius, Ovid, Persius, Seneca, Lucan, Silius Italicus, Valerius Flaccus, and Martial; probably Catullus, Virgil, Statius, and Juvenal.[6] Senators and knights comprised the upper class of Roman society, and one of the bluntest proofs of their superiority was that they could satisfy a property qualification. The floor at which fortunes began to be counted was four hundred thousand sesterces: no one could claim the title of a Roman knight unless he could prove assets worth at least that much. A capital of this amount invested according to the usual practice in land and loans would have yielded just enough income for a man to live in modest comfort with no further exertion.[7] Even the poorest Roman knights, therefore, must be recognized as men of property who could subsist on rents and interest. For such men the problem was not how to secure their basic income but how to enhance it.

The affiliation of poets with the Roman upper class has two economic consequences. In the first place, it is a good part of the reason why their poems brought in little or no money. And second, it
opened to the poets an altogether different set of opportunities.

Since poetry was primarily an avocation of propertied gentlemen, its direct potential for producing income was bound to be
slight. Many of those who wrote poetry would simply not have
needed to earn money by it. Furthermore, as I said earlier, a strong
prejudice stood between the practice of poetry and any direct form of
recompense for it. A poet could not have taken money for his craft
without lowering himself to the despicable status of those who
worked for hire, mercennarii. Any sort of work done for pay was
thought demeaning, but payment for poetry would have seemed particularly abhorrent, since poetry belonged to the domain of liberal
studies. The prejudice that operated in this area is best seen in the
Roman attitude toward another of the liberal arts. Oratory contributed services that were essential in Roman society, and it was a calling respected in a way that poetry was not. Yet the orators' efforts to
make their work a paid activity repeatedly brought down public cen-
sure. Under Augustus the old republican ban on taking gifts or payment for forensic service was reaffirmed. Sixty years later, when the
issue arose again, Claudius decided that the law had to be accommodated to the facts of life, and so he legalized fee-taking. But the pro-
test was still so bitter that fees were held to a low ceiling, and advocates who exacted more were threatened with harsh penalties.[8]

For poets the barrier between profession and profit remained
nearly insuperable. But if their work yielded little profit, their ac-
ceptability as gentlemen opened other doors. This point will require
a somewhat longer development than the first.

Equestrian and senatorial poets could find the same profitable
appointments as other men of their class. Catullus' poems on Memmius have made one sort of appointment notorious. When a governor swept down upon a Roman province in his official capacity, he
took along a suite of friends who shared in the proceeds according to
the station of each. I have no more to say about ventures of this sort,
except that they seem to have dwindled after the end of the republic
and that they were probably related to a second and perhaps less familiar sideline. Poets sometimes took up temporary commissions in
the army, all of whose officer positions were filled by men of equestrian or senatorial rank. That army service represented a good short-
term financial opportunity is shown especially by the elegists.
These poets repeatedly inveigh against the gain-seeking of their age,

while extolling the loftier ideals of the cup and the couch. It is to the villainous gain seekers that I want to call attention. One of the stock figures of elegy is the soldier who campaigns through distant lands in quest of spoils, *praeda*, and then returns to poach the girl friends of the poets. These men are not uncouth outsiders who have unaccountably elbowed their way into respectable society. They too are often *equites*,[9] who took the opportunity to make their fortunes in the last great round of foreign adventures before the empire settled down under peace and the *princeps*. They were not foot soldiers but officers, with the perquisites of rank. Apart from whatever they might manage to seize for themselves in the territories they overran, they would have shared in the gifts with which a victorious general customarily rewarded his staff at the close of a successful campaign.[10] As the elegists knew, the award of *praeda* was the great lure of campaigning, and for a period of thirty years or so the spoils could be enormous. If the liberators had won at Philippi, they would have shared out the booty they had brought from Asia as well as the wealth to be confiscated from the triumviral army. The tribune Horace would have returned home a rich man.[11]

Influenced by the two civilians Propertius and Ovid, we tend to see these military adventurers as the very antitype of the poet. But in Tibullus soldiering and poetry are not yet irreconcilable activities. He evidently accompanied the legate Messalla on a tour of duty in the East just after Actium,[12] and according to the fragmentary *vita* that is transmitted with his poems he received military decorations after Messalla's campaign in Aquitanian Gaul. Several of Tibullus' contemporaries also varied their poetic lucubrations with stints of campaigning. Cornelius Gallus is the most famous case; Horace may be considered another. Among minor talents whose work has perished we may count the neoteric Ticida, slain by Pompey's men at Thapsus; Cassius of Parma, last of Caesar's assassins to forfeit his life; Cornificius, who fell in battle when he was deserted by his troops; and Tibullus' friend Aemilius Macer. Bavius, the target of Virgil's and Horace's barbs, is reported to have died in Cappadocia, and military service probably accounts for his visit to that turbulent province.[13]

Military service therefore appears to have been one means of fiscal improvement to which a poet might resort. But after the early years of the principate wars of conquest became fewer, the initiative of commanders was reduced, and bookkeeping grew more strict. Even in the good old days not all expeditions showed a profit, and whether they did or not the life of the campaigner was always at risk. One must assume that poets followed the headlines in the *acta diurna*: TICIDA SLAIN AT THAPSUS; BAVIUS DIES IN CAPPADOCIA. It would be unwise to assert when our information is so sparse that this opportunity dried up altogether. We know that Martial was commissioned as a military tribune,[14] which may but need not mean that he once went campaigning. A baffling legend in the Juvenal tradition reports that the satirist was posted to a garrison in Aswan.[15] Nevertheless there are fewer soldier-poets to whom we can point in the period after the death of Augustus than before. Statius never saw in person the Domitianic campaigns which he glorified in his epic on the German war.

After the prospect of lugging home a fortune from the wars receded, one might have expected poets to embrace another opportunity, leaner but still substantial, which opened up under the gray regulations of peacetime. In the palace and throughout the empire, the emperors organized a veritable army of officials to help them manage their financial and administrative affairs. These men belonged to the equestrian order, like so many adventurers of Tibullus' time; they drew a regular salary for work which was respectable and even prestigious, and which was much safer than soldiering. Furthermore, practitioners of the liberal arts enjoyed an advantage in securing appointments within certain areas of this bureaucracy.[16] But although men with other sorts of literary interests did enter the emperor's service—for example, the elder Pliny, Suetonius, and in a sense perhaps Quintilian—there is not much evidence that poets did. The only examples I can think of are Seneca, whose tragedies may or may not have been written after his summons to the palace, and Seneca's friend Lucilius, who dabbled in philosophy and poetry while pursuing his career as an imperial procurator. Faced with a comparable opportunity, Horace had said no, and that appears to reflect the attitude of most poets. Entry into the emperor's service had two disadvantages, as compared with signing on for a campaign abroad. The administrative hierarchy became increasingly stratified, so that advancement to the most desirable positions depended on steadfast performance in a series of lowlier employments. And at every level, work for the emperor demanded a large investment of one's energies. It could not be managed as a casual or temporary sideline.

Either from the spoils of a good campaign or in administrative service under the emperors, poets could acquire riches which the writing of poetry itself did not produce; both possibilities therefore deserve mention among the opportunities which were open to them. But soldiering seems gradually to have lost its appeal, while administrative work did not engage at least most of the poets we know about. In general these were not the sorts of activities that poets took up in order to increase their wealth.

Poets had a readier way to fortune, and they owed it both to the ease with which they could assimilate themselves in good society and to the particular art which they possessed. These qualifications put them in the company of certain other professional men of Rome: the orators, jurisconsults, and philosophers. None were supposed to charge fees for the work they did, but they all shared an advantage which helped to make up for that disability. At least in Rome, these professions involved not simply the independent pursuit of an art or discipline but engagement in the life and interests of well-to-do society. Their practitioners provided services which beguiled the leisure or abetted the business of the leading citizens. By these services they established ties of *amicitia* which yielded far greater rewards than any system of fees or commissions would have done. Testamentary bequests, gifts of cash or property, and large loans on easy terms might fall into the lap of a rich man's friend. A sinecure or a military commission or a richly dowered bride could be fixed up through a timely word from one of the *principes*.[17] Moreover, the friends of the rich had every reason to expect a steady flow of such favors. The exchange of gifts and benefits had an important and well-defined place in the Roman code of friendship; and the wealth which accumulated in the hands of the rich during the early empire gave them rare means of putting in practice the virtue of liberality. Gift-giving on the Roman scale thus created a significant opportunity for individuals with the suppleness and manners which would commend them to the well-to-do.

The benefits which rich men lavished upon their *amici* are a familiar element of Roman custom. It may be less obvious that the *amici* had a role to carry out which was commensurate with the rewards they coveted. The role of friend and companion was virtually a career. It required both time and art: the time an *amicus* was obliged to keep the great man company during at least a part of his daily activities, and the not inconsiderable art of adapting to the humor and occupations of another. Not only does the role of an *amicus* deserve to be considered a career, but I would suggest that it was the career most readily available in Roman society to an educated man of moderate means.

At this point I must leave the poets temporarily in order to develop what I have just said about the vocation of *amicitia*. I will argue that the Romans themselves considered attachment to the rich to be a career, and in some circumstances even a respectable career.

Then I shall come back to the poets and show how their activities compare with the functions of an *amicus*.

Juvenal *Satires* 3 is ostensibly a dialogue between the poet and a friend who is on the point of quitting Rome forever. The friend asks rhetorically what opportunities the city can offer to an honest man like himself, then answers his question as follows:

> quid Romae faciam? mentiri nescio; librum,
> si malus est, nequeo laudare et poscere; motus
> astrorum ignoro; funus promittere patris
> nec uolo nec possum; ranarum uiscera numquam
> inspexi; ferre ad nuptam quae mittit adulter,
> quae mandat, norunt alii; me nemo ministro
> fur erit, atque ideo nulli comes exeo tamquam
> mancus et extinctae corpus non utile dextrae.
>
> [3.41–48]

Every detail in this tirade, which continues for another eight lines, presupposes that attachment to a wealthy *amicus* is the main livelihood a man can find at Rome. Martial indicates in *Epigrams* 3.38 that it is one of the main opportunities. He asks a new arrival in Rome how he plans to make a living, to which the newcomer responds that he will practice law. When Martial derides that proposal, the newcomer says that he will take up poetry. After that fantasy too is dispelled, the immigrant resolves that as a last resort he will frequent the houses of the great: "atria magna colam." A century or so earlier, Horace addresses *Epist.* 1.17 and 1.18 to young men who are about to join the entourage of a greater friend. The tone of his advice in both letters implies that the young men are embarking on a long career. And at *Epist.* 1.18.2 he describes the intended step by the phrase "profiteri amicum," "setting up as an *amicus*," which seems to equate this role with professions properly so called, like law and teaching.[18]

In all these passages attendance on the rich is treated as a long-term occupation, a way of life to be contemplated as carefully as any vocational decision. That is a perfectly ordinary way for a Roman to speak of such activities. We on the other hand sometimes interpret them in ways which are un-Roman. I have in mind two attitudes in particular.

In the first place, the association between the rich man and his regular companions should not be understood as clientage or patronage. The Romans did not use words like *patronus*, *patrocinium*, or *clientela* in speaking of these relationships. They did sometimes re-

fer to the rich man's humbler associates as clients, *clientes*. But for
the most part the vocabulary they used consists overwhelmingly of
words like *amicus* and *amicitia*.[19] To substitute the notion of clientage is misleading for several reasons. It sets between the rich man
and his entourage a great social gulf that did not really exist: when
their social origins can be identified, "clients" often turn out to belong to the equestrian order.[20] Words like clientage and patronage
also tend to suggest a formal arrangement based on reciprocal rights
and obligations, rather than on the more elusive promptings of liberality and personal esteem. And finally these words may create the
impression that nonmaterial forms of assistance, like protection before the law, were more important to the friends of the rich than pe-
cuniary benefits. Yet none of these presuppositions fits the situation
of Juvenal's friend or of the other client characters we encounter in
first-century literature.

Another bias affects the way we perceive the role of the rich
man's friend and companion. It is very difficult for a modern ob-
server not to feel repugnance for activities which appear basically
parasitic—and that is often the light in which we see the companion. But the Romans applied the words "parasite" and "parasitic" far
less often in this context than we do. I believe that a significant difference in social organization accounts for the difference in percep-
tion. In the society with which most of us are familiar, men generally support themselves by salaried work, and there is a large variety
of jobs and careers from which they can choose their work. Men who
find no place in this system are a conspicuous and suspect minority.
But in Roman society, at least in upper-class society, the opposite
was true. Men at this level owed their maintenance to earnings on
capital and not to salaried work, which was felt to be incompatible
with *dignitas*. Not surprisingly, since respectable professions were
in principle not paid occupations, few professions evolved. In a society in which so many men did no work, it would not have been
easy to say who was a parasite and who was not.

Furthermore, Roman tradition strongly encouraged the forma-
tion of *amicitiae* not merely between equals in rank and wealth but
also between unequals. Attachments of this sort had a positive value
in the eyes of the leading citizens: by surrounding themselves with a
large entourage, they advertised their importance, and they also fulfilled their desire for companionship at their dinners, on their daily
rounds, and in their other leisure pursuits. On the other side of the
relationship, respectful attendance on one's superiors won approval
because it expressed the correct hierarchical alignment of orders and
individuals. Especially for a young man, this behavior had a power-

ful sanction behind it. In the late republic and early empire, the sons of good families often completed their education for public life by obtaining an introduction to a leading orator or statesman and joining his retinue. A passage from Cicero's *De officiis* is revealing. Discussing how an *adulescens* is to get himself established in the public eye, Cicero says that it is best if one can capitalize on a famous family name. Precocious distinction in military affairs affords another opening. But for young men to whom these routes are closed, Cicero recommends a third course: "facillime autem et in optimam partem cognoscuntur adulescentes qui se ad claros et sapientes viros bene consulentes rei publicae contulerunt, quibuscum si frequentes sunt, opinionem adferunt populo eorum fore se similes, quos sibi ipsi delegerint ad imitandum."[21] Attachment to prominent citizens, therefore, far from being the recourse of drones was a natural movement which drew the young, the less distinguished, and the less affluent into appropriate participation in Roman social life. It was a role commonly filled by men who to begin with possessed a certain measure of financial independence and respectability. Its functions were determined by the need of a leisured class for display, companionship, and diversion; and its rewards flowed from the liberality which a great gentleman was expected to practice toward the circle of his friends.

Poets had ideal qualifications for this role. Of their actual performance in the role I think there can be no doubt: Horace, Martial, and Statius have left ample testimony about their obligations in high society. Rich men certainly were accustomed to take poets into their entourage. But why should they have taken up poets in particular?

The answer is that poets, those acknowledged masters of *otium*, were able to improve the leisure of the rich. It must be understood that this leisure was not unencumbered by rules of behavior. It had to be managed decorously, like one's style of dress or the planning of a townhouse: Latin writers who touch upon the problem of *otium* are often concerned to disavow a hankering for boorish entertainment. In this area of life the standard to which well-bred persons aspired was *elegantia*, smartness and correct taste, and they welcomed company who could set off the sparkle of *elegantia* in their homes. Polish and accomplishments were therefore in great demand. When Cornelius Nepos in his biography of Atticus tried to account for the extraordinary prestige of a man who resolutely avoided every political commitment, it was to this facet of Atticus that he turned. Despite his equestrian origins, observes the biographer, Atticus eventually became (through the marriage of his daugh-

ter) an in-law of the emperor Augustus, "cum iam ante familiarita-
tem eius consecutus nulla alia re quam elegantia vitae qua ceteros
ceperat principes civitatis dignitate pari, fortuna humiliores" (*Att.*
19.2). There were many accomplishments[22] which could lend the
desired sheen to the prospective socialite, and one was literary talent. The younger Seneca links literary and social distinction at
Epist. 19.3. His friend Lucilius, he says, will find it harder than most
men to retreat into philosophy because society is bent on lionizing
him. "In medium te protulit ingenii vigor, scriptorum elegantia,
clarae et nobiles amicitiae; iam notitia te invasit." But the most
explicit statement about the special entrée of literary men comes
from the young poet who wrote the *Laus Pisonis.* In it he says that
Piso's mansion is always charged with the excitement of artistic
enterprise:

> cuncta domus varia cultorum personat arte,
> cuncta movet studium; nec enim tibi dura clientum
> turba rudisve placet, misero quae freta labore
> nil nisi summoto novit praecedere vulgo;
> sed virtus numerosa iuvat. tu pronus in omne
> pectora ducis opus, seu te graviora vocarunt
> seu leviora iuvant.

[133–39]

The presence of poets added distinction to the great man's entourage. But it would be a mistake to think that their presence represented only his bashful tribute to genius. Poets found welcome for
other reasons too. The leaders of society, like all who trained with
the *grammaticus,* had studied poetry above every other subject.
Many (Silius Italicus and Pliny are typical) developed literary crav-
ings which never left them in later life, and in their years of eminence they sought the company of poets and others who might share
their belletristic avocations. Finally, even those socialites who were
impervious to the Muses' inspiration took a keen interest in attracting publicity. To be celebrated in the dedications and occasional
verse of fashionable authors brought notice which was effective, but
not so extravagant that it would arouse the mistrust of emperors.

Here at the door of the great man's house I end this survey of the
possibilities open to poets. For them, as for many others whose resources consisted more in their wits than in capital, one of the most
practical ways to tap the wealth of Rome was to gain the friendship
of leading citizens. Since poets practiced an art which suited the leisure pursuits of that class, they had a certain advantage over other
aspirants to friendship and favor.

This advantage suggests that one last question should be considered. I have argued that the poets' expertise made them desirable *amici*. But if a talent or even a mere determination for verse could find favor in the eyes of the rich, is it not likely that would-be *amici* sometimes took up poetry for just that reason? My answer will be a cautious yes. Although they fall well short of proof, there are some indications that Romans of the early empire began to realize that there could be a lucrative side to the poetry business.

Let me point out first that this attitude would be entirely consistent with the new money-mindedness observable in other careers during this period. In the middle of the first century, the orators finally won their point that payment for services was a legitimate demand. And Seneca's brother was simultaneously discovering the "brevius iter acquirendae pecuniae" which lay in following the career of an imperial procurator.[23]

That poets too should turn a profit seems widely assumed, by poets at any rate, during the second half of the century. This attitude is expressed in increasingly mercenary ways of talking about poetry and in bitter complaints when expectations are unfulfilled. Let me begin with Persius, who contended that poets of his day were prompted entirely by materialistic aims:

> quis expedivit psittaco suum "chaere"
> picamque docuit nostra verba conari?
> magister artis ingenique largitor
> venter, negatas artifex sequi voces.
> quod si dolosi spes refulserit nummi,
> corvos poetas et poetridas picas
> cantare credas Pegaseium nectar.
> [*Prologus* 8–14]

But expectations about money are most fully exposed in the first hundred lines of Juvenal *Satires* 7, which denounce the rich for their stinginess toward literary friends. The unpleasant tone of a poet on the make comes out most clearly in the following lines, in which Juvenal trundles the old clichés about poetic inspiration into a scene of daily scrounging:

> neque enim cantare sub antro
> Pierio thyrsumque potest contingere maesta
> paupertas atque aeris inops, quo nocte dieque
> corpus eget: satur est cum dicit Horatius "euhoe."
> [7.59–62]

The mercenary note is sounded in subtler tones as well. In the silver age, wistful catalogs rehearse the benefactions done to poets in times past: what is emphasized is not encouragement and praise, as in Horace's catalog at *Sat.* 1.10.81–90, but financial aid.[24] Poets also take up the metaphor of the sterile and the fecund field and apply it to their labors in the field of poetry. In the poems of Ovid, who popularized the figure, the hoped-for "yield" is fame;[25] but for poets after Ovid the yield is money.[26] Finally, the word *imputare* creeps into the poets' discourse with their great friends. *Imputare* comes from the language of bookkeeping, and it denotes the charging of goods or money or services to the person who owes for them. Statius sometimes speaks in this way of "crediting" poems he has written to the account of the persons honored in them.[27] The language is metaphorical. Statius does not mean literally that he charges so and so many sesterces for each poem, but only that the conferment of a poem is a *beneficium* and, like every *beneficium*, it establishes a claim to gratitude from the recipient. Nevertheless, given the realm from which it is drawn, the metaphor does hint broadly at the form which gratitude might suitably take.

These passages and turns of expression show that poets of the first century were increasingly preoccupied about getting money. Since the only substantial chance of making money was for a poet to gain the favor of rich men, it is evident that these poets must also have been intensely interested in forming connections with the rich.

But is that why they took up poetry in the first place? Again, what I can present is far from proof. A ubiquitous character in Roman society, however, ought at least to rouse our suspicions. He is the young man who seeks entry into another's circle of friends and who counts on his poetic activities to commend him. It is significant that he is a young man because that is the age at which it was most acceptable to join another man's entourage.

The most perfect example is the author of the *Laus Pisonis*. He tells us that he is not yet twenty years old (261); that he is aware that Calpurnius Piso has no use for undistinguished clients of the common sort, but prefers to befriend individuals who can demonstrate artistic accomplishment (133–37); and that he himself happens to be a poet—not yet a very skillful poet, but one who will certainly improve if he is granted the advantage of Piso's company (212–19).

It is almost the same with the author of the *Panegyricus Messallae*. He too indicates that he is a young man (205–6). Formerly wealthy but now abruptly humbled in fortune (183–89), he begs to be admitted to Messalla's friendship (193–200). Although he concedes that his powers are frail (2–7, 26, 176–80), he promises repeatedly that in return for recognition as an *amicus* he will devote his entire career in poetry to celebrating Messalla's name (16–17, 24–27, 191, 203, 211).

The *Ciris* differs from these poems in that it is not a poem of introduction by which the poet seeks entry into a great man's circle. The author is already associated with Messalla: he says that they have on occasion passed time in writing verse together (19–20), and that the *Ciris* itself had long ago been promised to Messalla (47; cf. 9). But otherwise the parallels with the encomiasts of Piso and Messalla are noteworthy. The author of the *Ciris* had been thwarted in his hope of a political career: "etsi me, vario iactatum laudis amore / irritaque expertum fallacis praemia vulgi" (1–2). These lines suggest a man who has lost an election, perhaps a political beginner of about twenty-five.[28] He goes on to say that in his hour of discouragement he sought comfort in the study of Epicurean philosophy (3–4), at which, he says, he is still a novice (36–42). Although he does not apologize for the poor craft of his verses, he does in another way confess that the poem for Messalla represents a deviation from his true interests: when the promised work is completed, he will devote himself entirely to philosophy (5–11). A remark he makes in presenting the *Ciris* reveals incidentally how poetry acquired its vocational role for young men in the society of that time. He would have preferred, he says, to compose a grand epic in the Lucretian manner for Messalla, but does not know enough about natural philosophy. So instead he offers an epyllion about a mythical heroine—"haec . . . quae possumus, in quibus aevi / prima rudimenta et iuvenes exegimus annos" (44–45). These lines evidently allude to the training received in school, where students spent so much time on reading and imitation of the poets that they often ended by acquiring the rudiments of a technique themselves.

Although the traits which distinguish the type of poet I am talking about are most clearly united in these three examples, one frequently encounters elements of the type elsewhere. To deal only with the testimony of Horace, his pronouncements on the *ars poetica* are cast in the form of instructions to the sons of Piso, and the sons are identified as *iuvenes* (24, 366). *Epist.* 1.18 contains advice for Lollius, who is entering service as companion to a rich *amicus*. Lollius is both a poet (40–47) and a young man (50–64). Horace gives no clue to the age of the acquaintance who tries to wangle an introduction to Maecenas in *Sat.* 1.9. But the man obviously believes that a reputation as a poet would count heavily as a recommendation, because he reminds Horace of his poetic activities (7, 23–24).

The last text is more famous than all the rest. Its value for my argument is that it seems to presuppose exactly the situation I have been describing. In *Epist.* 2.2, Horace relates how he returned penniless to Italy after fighting on the wrong side at Philippi. It was at that moment, he says, that he felt obliged to take up poetry in order to escape poverty: "paupertas impulit audax / ut versus facerem" (50–51). One can readily believe that this statement is ironical, masking the truer and deeper sources of Horace's vocation. But the irony must contain a grain of truth. If not Horace himself, at least some of his contemporaries (the author of the *Panegyricus Messallae*, for example) must have illustrated the real possibility of getting ahead by trading on a facility for verse.

I have no thought of giving these suspicions about poetic opportunism a universal application. The best Roman poetry can hardly have been the work of men who sidled into their role for the sake of its social opportunities. But beneath the level of the best, poetry can be regarded as a career with a practical orientation: men with literary abilities found openings in Roman society that other men did not, both in private and in public life. Young men in doubt of a career cannot have failed to think about the preference consistently shown to virtuosi in the liberal arts.

NOTES

1. Ov. *Tr.* 4.10.21–22: "saepe pater dixit 'studium quid inutile temptas? / Maeonides nullas ipse reliquit opes.'"
2. The scanty evidence which has to do with the ancient book trade is best discussed by T. Birt, *Kritik und Hermeneutik nebst Abrisse des antiken Buchwesens*, pp. 315–22; K. Dziatzko, "Buchhandel," *RE* 3 (1897): 973–85; and H. Widmann, *Geschichte des Buchhandels vom Altertum bis zur Gegenwart*, vol. 1, which has an up-to-date bibliography on pages 1–3. Opinion differs as to whether book merchants paid authors in order to obtain original manuscripts; see especially K. Dziatzko, "Autor- und Verlagsrecht im Alterthum," *RhM* 49 (1894): 559–76, and T. Birt, "Verlag und Schriftstellereinnahmen im Altertum," *RhM* 72 (1917–18): 311–16.
3. Juvenal's salacious metaphor in the lines on Statius was correctly interpreted by R. Pichon, *De sermone amatorio apud Romanos elegiarum scriptores*, p. 6.
4. *Suas.* 2.19, "[Arbronius Silo] pantomimis fabulas scripsit et ingenium grande non tantum deseruit sed polluit."
5. According to a didascalic notice preserved in two manuscripts from Monte Cassino, the text of which is given in M. Schanz and C. Hosius, *Geschichte der römischen Literatur bis zum Gesetzgebungswerk des Kai-*

sers *Justinian*, vol. 2, p. 162. The didascalic notice is partly corroborated by Ps.-Acr. on Hor. *Epist.* 2.1.246.

6. Equestrian poets of the republic are listed and briefly discussed by C. Nicolet, *L'Ordre équestre à l'époque républicaine*, vol. 1, pp. 447–56. The list is carried down through the early empire by L. R. Taylor, "Republican and Augustan Writers Enrolled in the Equestrian Centuries," *TAPA* 99 (1968): 469–86; and P. White, "*Amicitia* and the Profession of Poetry in Early Imperial Rome," *JRS* 68 (1978): 88.

7. The relationship between the cost of living and the equestrian census is set out in greater detail by White, "*Amicitia*," p. 88. For the amount of income needed to maintain a genteel standard of living, see in addition to the passages cited there Nep. *Att.* 13.6 (Atticus' monthly budget of three thousand sesterces) and Cic. *Att.* 16.1.5 and 12.32 (the annual allowance of eighty thousand given to the young Marcus).

8. Augustus' renewal of the provisions of the *Lex Cincia* is mentioned at Dio Cass. 54.18.2. The debate which took place about advocates' fees in A.D. 47 is recorded by Tacitus at *Ann.* 11.5–7.

9. For examples after Catullus' Mamurra, see Tib. 1.2.65–78, Ov. *Am.* 3.8.9–22, Prop. 2.16 (about a military man of senatorial rather than equestrian rank) and 4.3 (the *hasta pura* mentioned in line 68 implies that "Lycotas" is of equestrian rank). For other soldiers of fortune who appear to have respectable origins, see Prop. 3.4 and 3.12.

10. See P. Cagnat, "Praeda," in *Dictionnaire des antiquités*, ed. C. Daremberg and E. Saglio, vol. 4, pp. 610–11, and K. H. Vogel, "Praeda," *RE* 22 (1953): 1200–13, especially columns 1208–9.

11. For a contemporary illustration of what might have been, see the good story told by Pliny (*HN* 33.82–83) about one of Antony's veterans whose fortune was founded by a solid gold statue which he carried home from the East.

12. Tibullus seems to be saying in 1.7.9–22 that he beheld the wonders of the East at Messalla's side, but this interpretation has sometimes been doubted.

13. For Ticida (or Ticidas), see F. Münzer, "Ticida," *RE* 6A (1936): 844–46; for Cassius of Parma, Schanz and Hosius, *Geschichte der römischen Literatur*, vol. 1, p. 315; for Cornificius, ibid., pp. 308–9; for Macer, Tib. 2.6, and Schanz and Hosius, *Geschichte der römischen Literatur*, vol. 2, pp. 164–65; for Bavius, ibid., p. 98.

14. Cf. Mart. 3.95.9–10 and 5.13.1–2.

15. The story and its variants are discussed by G. Highet, *Juvenal the Satirist*, pp. 20–31.

16. This fact has recently been emphasized by F. Millar, *The Emperor in the Roman World*, pp. 83–101.

17. Some actual examples of these various *beneficia* are collected by White, "*Amicitia*," pp. 90–91.

18. For parallel expressions, cf. "grammaticum se professus," Cic. *Tusc.* 2.12; "me iuris consultum esse profitebor," *Mur.* 28; "profiteri philosophiam," *Pis.* 71; "profiteri medicinam," Celsus *proem.* 13 and Suet. *Iul.*

42.1; "profiteri ducem," Ov. *Ars Am.* 1.181; and "professus obscenum," lines 1–2 of the Oxford fragment of Juv. 6.

19. This assertion is defended at some length by White, *"Amicitia,"* pp. 78–82.

20. For example, Naevolus, the unscrupulous companion of Juv. 9.10, and the Egyptian *scurra* Crispinus, Juv. 4.32.

21. Cic. *Off.* 2.46. In Horace's survey of the ages of man, notice the character assigned to the young man who has just emerged from the wildness of adolescence: "conversis studiis aetas animusque virilis / quaerit opes et *amicitias*" (*Ars P.* 166–67).

22. It is at precisely this point that society made room for that other specialist, the *scurra.* Or perhaps it would be more correct to describe the *scurra* as a failed *elegans*: the performer whose routine kept straying beyond the borderline of refined wit.

23. Tac. *Ann.* 16.17.3.

24. Cf. *Laus Pisonis* 230–45; Mart. 12.36; Juv. 5.109, 7.94–95.

25. E.g., *Tr.* 2.327, 5.4.48; *Pont.* 1.5.25–26 and 33–34, 4.2.16.

26. *Laus Pisonis* 234; Mart. 1.107; Juv. 7.48–49 and 103; cf. Calp. *Ecl.* 4.23 ff.

27. Stat. *Silv.* 2 *praef.* 31, 4 *praef.* 21 (Klotz, 2d ed.); cf. the accountant's phrase *laturus accepto* just before the first example.

28. That the reference here is to politics or oratory is the most common interpretation of the passage, but see the commentary of R. O. A. M. Lyne (*Ciris: A Poem Attributed to Vergil*, p. 95), who thinks the *Ciris* poet is referring to earlier endeavors in literature.

Literature and Society in the Later Roman Empire

BARRY BALDWIN

Although I reserve the right to look backward and forward for purposes of illustration and comparison, my termini are essentially Hadrian and Diocletian, the period covered by the *Historia Augusta*. This period subsumes the Gibbonian age of gold or Antonine Indian summer, the grim Severan dynasty and grimmer fifty years of anarchy, the totalitarianism of the tetrarchy, and the eve of the triumph of Christianity.

As we shall see Hadrian affords a convenient starting point, not least because he may be the Caesar of Juvenal *Satires* 7, the great hope of men of letters. Before coming to that, however, it might be as well to anticipate and answer an unspoken question. When someone announces the intention of discussing literature of the second and third centuries A.D., especially poetry, the natural response is, What literature? A good deal was being written and this essay will disclose some of it; anyone wishing the full story can pursue it at leisure in the second volume of Bardon's *La littérature latine inconnue*.

To a large extent we know what we have lost. The question is how much that loss is to be regretted. A three-pipe problem, as Sherlock Holmes used to say, but one that may turn out more alimentary than elementary. It is generally assumed that the later losses are of second- or third-raters only. That is the recurring theme from Teuffel-Schwabe's vast register of names to recent treatments by such distinguished scholars as Timothy Barnes[1] and Gordon Williams.[2] They may of course be right. But we should never forget that it is essentially a Queen of Hearts verdict, reached without evidence.

Fronto, it is true, lost his reputation by being discovered. That does not mean that the same would be bound to happen to all the other literary *pulvis et umbra*. After all we do know that we have lost one great Roman classic from earlier times in Lucilius. Some would make a similar claim for Gallus. The loss of so much early

Roman poetry and drama, despite the interest of Hadrian, Aulus Gellius, and the late grammarians, further attests to the unreliability of survival statistics.

Furthermore, unless one is willing to assert that Roman taste was bad in practically every period, we must assume that at least some of what is lost was good. Of the fifteen or so literary figures accumulated by Horace at the end of *Sat.* 1.10, only one (Virgil) survives. True, some discount must be made for the mutual admiration society in which Horace moved. Obviously when Tibullus says of Valgius (one of Horace's gallery) "aeterno propior non alter Homero," we are not obliged to believe him (*Panegyricus Messallae* 180). But when Ovid looks back over thirty years to the Augustan apogee, he includes along with Horace and Virgil the names of Ponticus, Bassus, and Macer—all lost to us.[3] The same is true of the poets listed by Quintilian in his tenth book.

Voltaire made this point ("Ovide nomme une foule d'écrivains illustres de son temps, inconnus aujourd'hui");[4] one is happy to be in such good company! It is a recurring situation. We happen to know the names of some of the Latin poetry winners in the Capitoline *Agones*.[5] Most intriguing of these is a boy wonder, the thirteen-year-old L. Valerius Pudens.[6] Did he go on? Or burn himself out like that better attested teen-age prodigy of the Antonine age, Hermogenes?[7] None of these winners' works survive. Personally I think we can trust Roman taste at least once: in its refusal to give the prize in A.D. 90 (or 94) to Statius. Here of course we do have examples of the work of a loser,[8] verses not so much aesthetic as anaesthetic, whereas nothing survives by his father, who was a winner.

One of Aulus Gellius' acquaintances was a poet called Annianus. A few lines of his *Carmina Falisca* are preserved.[9] They are unmemorable snippets ("uva uva sum et uva Falerna" is a typical example). Yet Annianus was well enough known in the fourth century A.D. to be adduced as a model and vindication for indecent centos by Ausonius. The Flavian satirist Turnus evokes praise as late as the sixth-century A.D. from Byzantine bureaucrat John Lydus.[10] And, along with Juvenal, it was a now lost writer who topped the literary hit parade of the late fourth century's Roman aristocracy, according to the disgusted observation of Ammianus Marcellinus[11]—namely, the imperial biographer Marius Maximus, currently battling it out with Syme's *Ignotus* for the dubious honor of being the prime source of the *Historia Augusta*.

This is not to go to the other extreme of *omne ignotum pro magnifico*. The situation may still lend itself to the words of the caustic Aper in Tac. *Dial.* 10: "mediocres poetas nemo novit, bonos pauci." I certainly do not claim that the period in question abounded in great writers. The point is, there is a chance that it was less of a desert than is commonly claimed.

My essay explores four themes: the literary interests of emperors; literary activity in general (especially poetry); reasons for the state of literature (Greek as well as Roman); and the position of the writer in society. All are interconnected and all coalesce with Hadrian.

His reign was a pivotal one, albeit we could be a little misled by his being the starting point of the *Historia Augusta* and by the absence of any *vitae* of Nerva and Trajan. By and large, we reckon Hadrian among the good emperors and I have no special desire to exclude him, but his position is due more to Gibbon than the sources. Both Dio and the *Historia Augusta* are equivocal, though when the latter says he was buried "invisus omnibus" we cannot be sure whether that means "hated" or "unseen" by all.[12] A good deal of the hostile tradition was inspired by his treatment of men of letters. Captious and aggressive, he would assail them both verbally and in pamphlets. This was remembered as late as Ammianus, who adduces Hadrian's behavior to support his own criticisms of Valentinian (30.8.10).

It was obviously better to be attacked in that way by this Roman version of Housman than to be up on a *maiestas* charge and be sent into exile or to death. This reminds us of the Julio-Claudians. There is the evocative case of Cremutius Cordus,[13] and the fact that the first two victims of *maiestas* trials under Nero in A.D. 62 were both satirists.[14] I suggest, however, that there is mitigation if not justification in all such cases. Fergus Millar's recent formulation "The emperor was what the emperor did" should be extended to read "and what was done to him." Given the large number of assassinations and genuine plots, and given that opposition to the throne was not of her majesty's loyal variety, emperors were hardly paranoid when they tried to stay alive and worried over what their enemies might do. Domitian said it best—"condicionem principum miserrimam quibus de coniuratione comperta non crederetur nisi occisis"—and by his own fate proved his point.[15]

In saying this I am partly influenced by my inability to accept Lord Acton on power and corruption as universally binding. Lack of power can very often be just as corrosive. Whatever one thinks of that, it is Hadrian rather than a Julio-Claudian who best typifies the tensions some find inherent between *princeps* and artist. One of the most exotic characters in the pages of Gellius, Philostratus, and others was a philosopher-rhetorician, the eunuch or hermaphrodite

Favorinus of Arelate. One day he was rebuked by friends for throwing a debate with Hadrian over some philological matter. But their reproaches turned to wry laughter when he replied, "non recte suadetis, familiares, qui non patimini me illum doctiorem omnibus credere qui habet triginta legiones."[16]

That nicely anticipates the famous question posed by Joseph Stalin when asked if he did not fear papal reaction to something he was planning to do: "The Pope? How many divisions has he got?" It also had a Roman pedigree. Macrobius has a story in which Asinius Pollio declined to reply to some Fescennine verses written against him by Augustus, commenting, "at ego taceo, non enim est facile in eum scribere, qui potest proscribere."[17]

In neither story is the emperor in question a bad one. Nor is the dilemma just that of the writer. An emperor who was not a fool (and very few of them were) appreciated that it was hard for him to hear the truth. Hence perhaps their use of *scurrae*, licensed jesters employed by good rulers and bad.[18] I often think that this is what lies behind the motif, frequent in the *Historia Augusta*, of bad emperors roaming through the city in disguise. The biographer inevitably maintains that they were in search of low life. In reality they were (like Peisistratus) looking for something much more elusive: the truth.

A Greek versifier, Pancrates, produced a poem in which Hadrian is encouraged to name a lotus for his boy friend Antinoos, claiming that it had sprung from the blood of a lion killed by the pair.[19] Gordon Williams uses this incident to prove that, in his words, poetry had dried up in both cultures.[20] But this is to make far too much of a small piece of poetic nonsense. It no more destroyed poetry than did Tiberius when he gave two hundred thousand sesterces to Asellius Sabinus for a dialogue between a mushroom, a figpecker, a thrush, and an oyster.[21]

Far more worrying might be the seeming ease with which poets who were imperial encomiasts flourished. A recently discovered case is that of Aelius Paion of Side, whose efforts earned him the title, not unique to himself, of Philokaisar.[22] Or take the Caesarian games held at Corinth in A.D. 127: every prize-winning poet named in the commemorative inscription had written a eulogy of the emperor.[23]

Still, one may be cautiously optimistic. Modern scholars tend to take this sort of production too seriously. Stilted and derivative pieces in honor of a ruler do not imply that they were the beginning and the end of the literature of their time. Coexistence with different and better literature is quite feasible; posterity after all would be very wrong to judge twentieth-century British poetry on the basis of the dutiful verses of Masefield or Betjeman.

Hadrian had many hobbies. He was devoted to painting and music, keen on geometry, and a good fencer. Other emperors were similarly versatile. Commodus, who rarely gets into literary discussions, molded goblets as one of his more innocuous hobbies.[24] He also sang and danced, the reward for which was to be told that such pastimes did not befit an emperor.[25] Given this, his notorious mania for the arena could be viewed with some sympathy as a case of overcompensation.

There is a point to be made here. Students of literature sometimes forget that there are other arts. When a Roman emperor is not conspicuously rewarding poets or rhetoricians, it need not mean that he is a philistine. No one could call Hadrian that with any truth. Yet in the biographer's register of the arty types loved by him, the only genre not present is poetry. Nor is there a single poet among the deipnosophists of Athenaeus. There are two musicians, and their presence has evoked surprise from that most expert of quarters, Glen Bowersock.[26] In point of fact, they were culturally quite respectable. Lines of demarcation must not be too sharply drawn; elsewhere Athenaeus describes Agrippus Memphius, an Antonine mime, as a philosopher-dancer.[27]

Versatility is also an important issue. An inscription probably dating from the second century discloses the septuagenarian Hermogenes.[28] Chiefly famous as a doctor, his bibliography is immense: local histories of his native Smyrna and of many cities in both Europe and Asia; biographies of Romans and Smyrniots; a work on military strategy; mileage charts of Europe and Asia, and more. Galen is a more familiar example of this type of polymath. We have his bibliography, drawn up by himself—it is overwhelming.[29]

On the Latin side, consider Apuleius. His many lost works include love poems, miscellaneous *ludicra* (some verses on the merits of tooth powder survive, of which the line "complanatorem tumidulae gingivulae" is certainly designed to set one's own teeth on edge),[30] and what may or may not have been a money-spinning panegyric, *De virtutibus Orfiti*. There is a case for believing that too many writers of this sort spread themselves too thin, and so achieved little that was great in any genre.

With regard to Hadrian's own poetry, most people will be familiar with the "animula vagula blandula" piece (if really by him)[31] and the "nolo esse Florus" exchange. One or two of his Greek efforts are included in the *Anthology*: 6.332 is a tactful epigram extolling Trajan's conquests; 9.402 (*pace* the Loeb editor's error in calling it *ade-*

spoton) is a one-liner on the fate of Pompey;[32] 7.674 praises Archilochus, a salutary reminder that Hadrian was not restricted to archaic Latin.[33]

For all that, it is for archaism and eccentricity that Hadrian is best known. This side of him, and his age, is often misrepresented and misunderstood. For instance, when the emperor proclaimed the superiority of Antimachus over Homer, did he set the world of letters by its ears? George III's animadversions upon Shakespeare may come to mind. The *Historia Augusta* gives the impression that Hadrian was being typically perverse; in fact he was merely extending a commonplace judgment. We have Quintilian's word for the popularity of Antimachus in his day: "ei secundas fere grammaticorum consensus deferat" (10.1.53).

Hadrian was not doing anything very revolutionary in knocking Homer and Virgil from their pedestals. It was a popular sport; the *-mastix* type of pamphlet was the ancient version of the hatchet job. In the case of Ennius, it is not clear to what extent Hadrian was making or following the fashion. As Cicero, Horace, Tacitus, and many other sources make clear, there was almost always an archaizing movement at Rome. Rather than accumulate the usual texts, I shall simply adduce the strikingly cynical and rarely quoted prologue to book 5 of the *Fables* of Phaedrus: "Aesopi nomen sicubi interposuero / cui reddidi iam pridem quicquid debui / auctoritatis esse scito gratia [a comparison with fraudulent paintings and statues follows] / adeo fucatae plus vetustati favet / invidia mordax quam bonis praesentibus."

Ennius was a cult figure. Marcus Aurelius read him, if only to please Fronto.[34] Gellius went along with friends to hear an *Ennianista* give readings from the *Annales* in the theater at Puteoli.[35] This was not just provincial taste; Gellius once encountered and overwhelmed an illustrious expert in Ennian studies in Rome.[36]

The enthusiasms of Gellius and his contemporaries are still too often ridiculed or deplored as a sign of intellectual sterility. On the contrary, I see them as a sign of cultural health.[37] Gellius was roughly as remote from Ennius as we are from Shakespeare. Why should Romans not study and reassess what had become their classics? It is quite explicable that the generations after Seneca should have turned back to early Latin literature for change and relief, much as our own cultural nostalgia, at least for the moment, skips the sixties for the fifties.

Again, this is not new. The academic atmosphere of Gellius' circle is often strikingly similar to that of the coteries described in the

De viris illustribus of Suetonius. The main difference is a suggestive social one: Gellius and his friends have no freedman scholars in their midst.[38]

Whatever one thinks of Gellius and Fronto, it must not be forgotten that there was a parallel development in Greek literature. The Second Sophistic bypassed the Hellenistic tradition and lived in a make-believe literary world of themes drawn from the fifth and fourth centuries B.C. Along with this went the lexicography of a Phrynichus, seeking in a prescriptive and often ill-informed way to establish what it fondly thought to be Attic Greek as a sort of BBC standard English.

So if Latin literature is held to have collapsed in the second century A.D., then the same must be said of Greek. How and why did this happen in an age of relative prosperity and imperial virtue? On the reckoning of those who do not esteem Gellian tastes, one can understand the very different third century taking refuge in literary reaction and nostalgia—but why the second?

Hadrian had intended that Aelius Ceionius Commodus should succeed him. From the point of view of literature, his premature decease was a blessing. That is, if (and this conditional should be assumed for the balance of my essay) we can believe the *Historia Augusta*. For Aelius, said to be *versu facilis*, regarded Martial as his Virgil. Such a lapse of taste is only partially redeemed by his other bedside books: Ovid's *Amores* and the recipes of Apicius, an arresting combination of food for thought and thought for food.[39]

At first glance, the reigns of Antoninus Pius and Marcus Aurelius do not look very propitious for poets, at least in terms of patronage and support. Pius is not credited with any literary interests or activities apart from some speeches, the authorship of which was questioned.[40] His involvement in poetry is restricted to cutting the stipend of the lyric poet Mesomedes.[41] To judge from the latter's surviving productions[42] this seems a sound decision, but there may have been more in it than meets the eye. It is not safe to assume, as does Bowersock, that poets such as Mesomedes and Strato were political nullities.[43] That is an inference based on too narrow a reliance upon the *Lives of the Sophists* of Philostratus. But this is a highly selective gallery of rhetoricians and philosophers; had we only it to go by, we should know nothing of the existence of Lucian or Galen.

Thanks to the correspondence of Fronto and his own *Meditations*, we can trace the evolution of Marcus Aurelius' interests from student to prince. At first absorbed by history, he came to find it monotonous and depressing,[44] and he thanks the gods for restraining him from rhetoric and poetry.[45] In such an atmosphere, one can see why the kept man of letters in Lucian's *De mercede conductis* furnishes the radical chic with philosophy, not poetry.

Yet although you will not find the word "poetry" in Haines' index of the topics discussed by Fronto, and although Gellius never had a thing to say about the productions of his two poet friends Annianus and Julius Paulus,[46] poetry was being written. And it was not all the old hat Juvenal used to complain about. For whatever reasons, and novelty was certainly one, there was an eruption into iambic dimeters. One effort in this vein is the Latin version of Plato's epigram on the soul in the kiss contributed by an anonymous friend of Gellius.[47] More fascinating is the attempt by a certain Alphius Avitus to treat Roman history in this meter.[48] Up to a point that prefigures a development in early Byzantine literature—the epics of George of Pisidia in the early seventh century, written in iambics rather than hexameters. The metrical arguments to Terence and Virgil from the pen of Gellius' teacher Sulpicius Apollinaris offer a similar precedent. They can hardly be called poetry but anticipate the full-blown versified commentaries on Homer by John Tzetzes.

Nor does it seem impossible that some poets attracted the favor even of Antoninus Pius. His favorite pastime was celebrating the vintage.[49] Now Gellius did this on the Faliscan estate of the poet Annianus. The latter, as we have seen, wrote *Carmina Falisca* about the *vindemia* and cognate themes. It is tempting to draw the connection that Gellius does not draw.

I have more than once seen the Antonine age compared to the Victorian. That is right but for the wrong reasons. When one reflects on some of the disparate phenomena of nineteenth-century England (the theological ferment aroused by Darwin, the growth of socialist thought, the decadents in painting and literature, Gilbert and Sullivan, and some choice pornography), one realizes how foolish the usual talk about stuffiness and conformity is. So too with the Antonines. The period produced Apuleius, Lucian, Galen, some great legal brains, and the first flowerings of Christian literature. Supporters of Marmorale would insist on adding Petronius. Nor should we forget the many examples of amateur poetry in both languages disclosed by epigraphy. Had the walls of Pompeii still been in use, I have no doubt that *puellae defututae* would have been immortalized on them.

As always, the *Historia Augusta* clouds the issue. There is no sign in it, for instance, of the drug addiction of Marcus Aurelius. The perfect Stoic prince as a junkie is a piquant picture, if a trifle crude.[50] The biographer portrays Antoninus Pius as a kindly old uncle, almost a plaster saint, whose only exotic achievement was to die from a surfeit of Alpine cheese. It comes as a shock therefore to find him depicted in the *Caesars* of Julian as sexually unbridled and as a "cumin splitter."[51] No doubt the reason the earnest Julian did not find Pius congenial was the latter's witty reason, preserved in the *Digest*, for removing immunity from taxation and liturgy from philosophers: "If they quibble about the size of their estates, they will make it clear that they are not really philosophers."[52] It is a line worthy of Lucian, and one repeated more than once in the future.[53]

Compared to the second century A.D., the third looks much more of a literary wilderness. Careful digging unearths a *Medea* in the perennial form of a Virgilian cento.[54] The wearisome acrostics of the Christian Commodian may belong to this period.[55] Rather more rewarding is the *Iudicium coci et pistoris* of Vespa,[56] a squib in a tradition extending from the aforementioned dialogue by Asellius Sabinus past Lucian's *Iudicium vocalium* down to the fourth-century *Testamentum porcelli*.

This dearth is no doubt what gave the *Historia Augusta* the need or temptation to people the period with the greater bulk of its fictions. Nevertheless it is reasonable to assume that they were plausible ones. Thus even if untrue what the biographer offers by way of imperial literary interests deserves a glance. It is credible that Pertinax, himself a failed teacher, should go at least once to the Athenaeum to hear a poet—credible too, given the tastes of the times, that when someone wanted to insult him they should do it by quoting Lucilius.[57]

The literary interests of Septimius Severus are emphasized, partly to point a contrast with his defeated rivals Niger and Albinus, Black and White, both of whom are separately dubbed as *eruditus mediocriter litteris*, though this does not prevent Albinus from producing an arresting combination of georgics and Milesian tales.[58]

Young Geta is said to have been an archaist; like Tiberius he enjoyed confounding professors with obscure points.[59] With Alexander Severus we have to be especially careful, since the *vita* of him is notoriously full of fabrications. As portrayed therein, the paragon prince seems to react against archaism by parading Virgil as the Plato of poets. But this is not quite consonant with a passage in which he lists Horace and Serenus Sammonicus as his favorite poets, much less with the one in which he is indifferent both in and to Latin literature! He himself produced some versified *vitae principum bonorum*.[60] A cognate claim is made for Gordian I, who is said to have wished to outdo Cicero's verses and to have composed an *Antoniniad* in thirty books on Pius and Marcus Aurelius.[61]

Towards the end of the century there is one interesting replica-
tion, which may be false, of Hadrian. In a textually corrupt passage,
the emperor Numerian is said to have competed with Nemesianus
in poetry, as a result of which "in omnibus coloniis [or *colonis*]
inlustratus emicuit" (*Carus* 11.9). This makes no obvious sense,
although the Loeb editor retains it without comment, and Pet-
schenig's *coloribus* (adopted in Hohl's Teubner) seems forced. I am
attracted to Casaubon's *coronis*, which makes emperor and poet
meet in formal competition.

Of course, it is not only the *Historia Augusta* that pads out the
literary history of the third century. Modern scholars have been
equally tempted—hence those fashionable phantoms, Syme's *Ignotus* and Ennmann's *Kaisergeschichte*. One such effort, however, is
rather different and of more interest. Edward Champlin has recently
proposed shifting the *Eclogues* of Calpurnius Siculus from the reign
of Nero to that of Alexander Severus.[62] His case is not implausible,
though naturally far from invulnerable.[63] A prime attraction of the
idea is, as he says, that it would give us a recurring tradition of Roman pastoral poetry: Virgil, the *Einsiedeln Eclogues*, Calpurnius
himself, and Nemesianus.

We can certainly appreciate the attractions of pastoral for the
third century, especially when it is laced with political comment.
One other detail may be suggestive. There is a discernible note of
brutality, especially sexual brutality, in post-Virgilian Roman pastoral. Calpurnius includes a homosexual rape (*Ecl.* 6.84–87), while
Nemesianus has a young girl ravished by two fifteen-year-old shep-
herds (*Ecl.* 2.1–9). Could this element reflect the horrors of the third
century?

In one respect the apparent dearth of poetry is to the credit of
the times. Until the Roman recovery under Claudius II, Aurelian,
and Probus, there are few great victories and no triumphs to celebrate. We notice, incidentally, that these three good emperors are
about the only ones to whom the *Historia Augusta* imputes no literary interests at all. Is that a curious truth or one of the biographer's
willful paradoxes? There was little scope for epic or triumphal odes.
Reality, not repression, is the cardinal factor. Also strikingly absent
from the *Historia Augusta*'s account of the period is the treason
trial. No emperor, apart from the ephemeral Didius Julianus in A.D.
193, is attacked for misuse of *maiestas* proceedings, not even Gallienus, the biographer's *bête noire* of the third century.

In the preface to his *Cynegetica*, Nemesianus contrasts the
practical virtues of his didactic poem with the *crambe repetita* of
other poets still churning out epics on mythological themes. In its

derisive style and choice of examples, this diatribe is a clear reminder of Juvenal *Satires* 1. However, unless it is entirely a derivative exercise the sequence does imply the existence of traditional es-
capist poetry in the third century.

But things have improved by the late third century. The sons of
Carus have won great victories which the poet undertakes to celebrate. One notices, as he wished us to, how precisely the poetic record of Nemesianus reproduces that of Virgil: pastoral, didactic, epic.
The point is, as things improve for Rome so poetry makes something of a comeback. The same is true on the Greek side: the exploits of Diocletian and his colleagues provoke the epic utterances
of Soterichus.

It is in social and material considerations that the most feasible
explanation for the vicissitudes of later Roman and Greek poetry
can be found. "Et spes et ratio studiorum in Caesare tantum" is how
Juvenal opens *Satires* 7 on the troubles of men of letters.[64] With this
we may conveniently juxtapose an extract from Fergus Millar's recent and healthily controversial *Emperor in the Roman World*. Having shown with an abundance of documentation just how lavishly
men of letters could be rewarded, Millar concludes, "In this respect,
as in so many others, the pattern of the *beneficia* which the emperors distributed accurately reflects the values of the society over
which they ruled."[65]

Juvenal predictably devotes about five times as much space to
the plight of poets as to any other type of writer. Needless to say, the
satirist exaggerates. His famous jeremiad on the woes of Statius,
compelled to keep alive by writing a hack libretto, is fine poetry but
historical nonsense on a par with the ending of *Satires* 4. Statius, on
his own showing, won some favor from Domitian and enjoyed at
least two wealthy patrons, Pollius Felix and Julius Menecrates, and
their Neapolitan villa.[66] One should not overlook this, as it were, Roman California of affluent culture; and, thanks to John D'Arms' *Romans on the Bay of Naples*, there is no excuse for so doing. Nor did
one always have to be to the manner (or manor) born. Seneca's
friend, the younger Lucilius, demonstrates the upward mobility that
was possible. He rose from poverty and low birth to a Neapolitan
villa, thanks to poetry and philosophy.[67]

But Juvenal has put his finger on something vital. Poetry was
never so solidly respectable at Rome as in Greece. Aper makes the
point in his usual blunt fashion in the *Dialogus* ("ut si in Graecia
natus esses, ubi ludicras quoque artes exercere honestum est"); it is
significant that Maternus does not argue against this, or against
much of the central charge of the uselessness of poetry.

Indeed it is a point that is forever coming up, explicitly or by implication. When Ovid announced that he wanted to be a poet, his father replied, admittedly with some paternal exaggeration: "studium quid inutile temptas? / Maeonides nullas ipse reliquit opes."[68] The *centonarius* Echion at Trimalchio's banquet is equally practical about his son's career.[69] Not quite "Get into plastics" as in *The Graduate*, but get into law; "habet haec res panem, nam litteris satis inquinatus est" (note the verb).

Hence, *inter alia*, a class of reluctant littérateurs. Probus, for instance, only became a *grammaticus* after a long and vain wait for a military commission,[70] an experience that perhaps does something to corroborate the truth of Juvenal *Satires* 16. The younger Pliny laments the fate of the senator Valerius Licinianus, whose unfortunate affair with a vestal had reduced him (*eo decidit ut*) to exile and the position of professor.[71]

Poetry did not have a solid base. One of the innumerable points of value made in Gordon Williams' *Change and Decline* is that by long tradition senators did not write poetry, at least not seriously.[72] It was an attitude that persisted, one that is well exemplified by the younger Pliny's justifiable modesty about his own squibs. It is just as manifest in the case of the emperors; the exception is Nero, and the Tacitean reaction to his poetry underlines the point. For all his private encouragement of some poets, Augustus did not think it a matter for inclusion in the *Res Gestae*.

And Maecenas is excluded from that tendentious document. Indeed after him it is very hard to find anyone who could be called a second Maecenas, with the possible exception of Titinius Capito in Trajan's time.[73] At no period, it might be added, do many literary men turn up as *amici principis* in the imperial councils.[74]

Hadrian was a watershed. And even this emperor, with all his liberality, was capable of saying no to mendicant poets, as the sharp exchanges that make up *Anth. Pal.* 9.137 demonstrate. A writer appeals: "Half of me is dead; hunger is crushing the other half. Save, your majesty, a musical semitone of me." To which Hadrian rejoins: "You wrong both Pluto and the sun by still looking at the latter and not going to the former."

After Hadrian the combination of hard-headed emperors and harder times brought many pressures to bear on literature, especially poetry. After the heyday of Papinian, Ulpian, and Julius Paulus in the Severan period, soldiers take over the praetorian prefecture from lawyers. Alexander Severus is said to have convoked historians to his military councils, but only for their practical wisdom in matters of strategy.[75] What the world of the third century A.D. required was rhetoric with which to persuade emperors and soldiers, and philosophy for an argument against the growing voice of Christianity or as a spiritual refuge from the terrible realities. It is little wonder that the instant wisdom of the *Dicta Catonis* belongs to this period.

A man of letters had to prove himself useful and, in the debased modern sense, relevant. Philostratus provides two cogent examples. When Heracleides lost a debate to his fellow sophist Apollonius, Septimius Severus rubbed salt in the wound by depriving the loser of his immunity. Caracalla refused immunity to Philiscus, professor at Athens, bawling, "Not for miserable little speeches would I deprive cities of men who can perform liturgies."[76]

Poets did not have much of a chance in that atmosphere. The emperor Philip, in whose reign Rome celebrated her millennium, summed their situation up in a laconic refusal to a certain Ulpian: "poetae nulla immunitatis praerogativa iuvantur."[77] Nor would poets have found much favor in Platonopolis in Campania, where Gallienus and his wife Salonina intended, until dissuaded by civil servants stressing the cost, to set up Plotinus and comrades in a philosopher's dreamland.[78]

The other major blow to poetry was the sharp decline in literacy. As early as Commodus we find the telling paradox of an illiterate village scribe! By Diocletian's time a law had to be passed sanctioning illiterate decurions.[79] This prefigures the situation in Byzantium, where it has been calculated that only three hundred or so people were receiving higher education at any given time, thus ensuring a very small audience for anything topical.[80] And Byzantium produced notoriously little poetry after the sixth century.

One area of the later Roman world presents a brighter view. It is Egypt, untypical here as in so many things. A late third-century papyrus from Oxyrhynchus lists over the period A.D. 261–62 to 288–89 the names of prizewinners in competitions entitled to tax exemptions.[81] There are three categories: heralds, trumpeters, poets. Some have inferred that Upper Egypt was relatively prosperous. Given the state of the Roman world and the normal state of Egypt, that does not seem too likely. Remembering Eunapius' comment "The Egyptians are mad about poetry,"[82] it may be permissible to see this policy as a quixotic one, comparable to the tax exemptions granted nowadays to bona fide artists by that not notably rich country, the Irish Republic.

Whatever the motive, the policy had good consequences for the future of poetry, for it is in Egypt that we get a spectacular renaissance of poetry between the late fourth and sixth centuries,[83] which produced not only an unexpected Greek interest in such difficult

Latin poets as Juvenal, but also the last great poet of pagan Rome, Claudian.[84]

Not every man could or would go to Egypt any more than to Corinth. True, things would get better. The temporary stabilization of the fourth century is concomitant with the Latin poetry of Ausonius, the *Epigrammata Bobiensia*, Prudentius, Paulinus of Nola, and so on—not to mention Ammianus Marcellinus or the growth industry of Christian literature of apologetics and doctrine. Not a few men of letters of this period, both Greek and Roman, feature in the first volume of the *Prosopography of the Later Roman Empire*. Subsequent correlations between material and literary rise and fall in both the Latin West and the Greek East confirm the general argument.

For poets and others the third century remained bleak. How many, it is only partly frivolous to ask, followed the example of the hero of this tombstone inscription in Rome?

> I was once a man versed in music,
> A poet and lyre player,
> But most of all a traveler.
> After many perils on the sea,
> Exhausted by my wanderings,
> I became, my friends, a dealer in beautiful women.[85]

NOTES

1. T. D. Barnes, *Tertullian: A Historical and Literary Study*, pp. 188 f.; cf. his "The Lost *Kaisergeschichte* and the Latin Historical Tradition," *Bonner Historia Augusta-Colloquium 1968–69* (1970): 13.

2. G. Williams, *Change and Decline: Roman Literature in the Early Empire*, pp. 310 f.

3. *Tr.* 4.10.41 f.; cf. Williams, *Change and Decline*, p. 54.

4. F. M. A. de Voltaire, *Carnet Piccini*, ed. T. Besterman, vol. 2, p. 384.

5. Cf. L. Friedländer, *Roman Life and Manners under the Early Empire*, trans. A. B. Gough, vol. 4, pp. 264–65.

6. *CIL* 9.2860.

7. Philostr. *VS* 577–78.

8. This is not to overlook his prize-winning *declamationes* and victory in the *Sebasta*, both at Naples (Stat. *Silv.* 5.3.215–19; 225–27).

9. Text in Morel, *FPL* 138–39.

10. Lydus *Mag.* 1.41. Adduced also by Sid. Apoll. 9.266–67 and Rut. Namat. 1.603; cf. my "Turnus the Satirist," *Eranos* 77 (1979): 57–60.

11. 28.4.14: "quidam detestantes ut venena doctrinas Juvenalem et

Marium Maximum curatiore studio legunt, nulla volumina praeter haec in profundo otio contrectantes, quam ob causam non iudicioli est nostri."

12. *Hist. Aug., Hadr.* 25.7. D. Magie (in the Loeb) translated as "hated"; cf. A. R. Birley, *Marcus Aurelius,* p. 61, for the other view.

13. His tragedy is so much to modern taste that we sometimes forget that he anticipated a verdict by suicide, and that his work was later back in circulation, although with the offending passages removed; cf. Quint. 10.1.104.

14. Both were unsavory characters (Antistius Sosianus and the notorious Fabricius Veiento), on the evidence of Tac. *Ann.* 14.48−50; see my "Executions, Trials, and Punishment in the Reign of Nero," *PP* 117 (1967): 425.

15. Suet. *Dom.* 21.

16. *Hist. Aug., Hadr.* 15.13.

17. Macrob. *Sat.* 2.4.21.

18. The tensions between various types of courtier are no doubt exemplified in the famous and to us enigmatic claim of Maternus (Tac. *Dial.* 11) to have broken the power of Vatinius at Nero's court. It is significant that Vatinius was *studiorum sacra profanantem.*

19. Text in E. Heitsch, ed., *Die griechischen Dichterfragmente der römischen Kaiserzeit,* pp. 52 ff.

20. Williams, *Change and Decline,* p. 310.

21. Suet. *Tib.* 42.2.

22. See L. Robert, "Deux poètes grecs à l'époque impériale," *Stele: In Memory of N. Kontoleon,* pp. 10−20.

23. Text in W. R. Biers and D. J. Geagan, "A New List of Victors in the Caesarea at Isthmia," *Hesperia* 39 (1970): 79.

24. *Hist. Aug., Comm.* 1.8.

25. The sentiment is plausible enough, although one is reminded of the similar attitudes towards philosophy evinced by that disparate pair, the mothers of Nero (Suet. *Nero* 52) and Agricola (Tac. *Agr.* 4.3).

26. G. W. Bowersock, *Greek Sophists in the Roman Empire,* p. 14 (noticing only one of the two).

27. *Deip.* 1.20c; cf. my "The Minor Characters of Athenaeus," *Acta Classica* 20 (1977): 39.

28. *IG. Rom.* 4.1445.

29. Ranging, apart from his medical writings, from work on the diction of Old Comedy to a polemic against the spotters of solecisms. Complete details are furnished by Gal. *Libr. Propr.*

30. Text in Morel, *FPL* 140.

31. Hadrian's authorship was doubted by T. D. Barnes, "Hadrian's Farewell to Life," *CQ* 18 (1968): 384; upheld by myself in "Hadrian's Farewell to Life: Some Arguments for Authenticity," *CQ* 20 (1970): 372. Now that I know more about the *Historia Augusta,* I would be less confident.

32. We owe the line to Dio Cass. 69.11.

33. Notice in this connection Ath. 3.115b for Hadrian's advancement of the Old Comedy actor Aristomenes.

34. Fronto, *Ad M. Caes.* 3.16 (= van den Hout 17).

35. Gell. *NA* 18.5.2.

36. Gell. *NA* 20.10.3.

37. Argued at length in my *Studies in Aulus Gellius*.

38. For freedmen in scholarship. Cf. S. M. Treggiari, *Roman Freedmen during the Late Republic*, pp. 110–28.

39. *Hist. Aug., Aelius* 5.3, 5.9.

40. *Hist. Aug., Pius* 11.3.

41. *Hist. Aug., Pius* 7.8.

42. Text in Heitsch, *Die griechischen Dichterfragmente*.

43. Bowersock, *Greek Sophists*, p. 116.

44. Marc. Aur. *Med.* 3.14; cf. A. S. L. Farquharson, ed., trans., *The Meditations of the Emperor Marcus Antoninus*, vol. 1, pp. 401, 856–57.

45. Marc. Aur. *Med.* 1.1.17.4.

46. Gell. *NA* 6.7.1; 9.10.1; 20.8.1 (Annianus); 1.22.9; 5.4.1; 16.10.9; 19.7.1 (Paulus).

47. Gell. *NA* 19.11; cf. my "An Anonymous Latin Poem in Gellius," *Arctos* 13 (1979): 5–13.

48. Text in Morel, *FPL* 143; the work was apparently entitled *Libri excellentium*.

49. *Hist. Aug., Pius* 11.2.

50. Cf. T. W. Africa, "The Opium Addiction of Marcus Aurelius," *Journal of the History of Ideas* 22 (1961): 97–102. Sources for Marcus' condition are listed by A. R. Birley, *Marcus Aurelius*, p. 114, n. 1.

51. Julian, *Caes.* 312a; cf. my "The *Caesares* of Julian," *Klio* 60 (1978): 462.

52. *Dig.* 27.1.6.7.

53. See Papinian (*Dig.* 50.5.8.4), and the emperors Diocletian and Maximianus (*CJ* 10.42.6).

54. Referred to by Tert. *De praescr. haeret.* 39.

55. Cf. B. Altaner and A. Stuiber, *Patrologie*, pp. 181 f.

56. *Anth. Lat.* 199.

57. *Hist. Aug., Pert.* 11.3; 9.6.

58. *Hist. Aug., Alb.* 11.7–8.

59. *Hist. Aug., Geta* 5.1 f.

60. *Hist. Aug., AS* 3.4; 27.5–8; 30.3; 31.4.

61. *Hist. Aug., Gord.* 3.1.

62. E. Champlin, "The Life and Times of Calpurnius Siculus," *JRS* 68 (1978): 95–110.

63. Far too much is made of the words "facundo comitatus Apolline" (4.87) as implying the notion of an emperor's association with a divine *comes*, a third-century concept.

64. Much has been written on the question of which emperor is meant. See in particular, apart from Highet and commentators on Juvenal, G. B. Townend, "The Literary Substrata to Juvenal's Satires," *JRS* 63 (1973): 148; N. Rudd, *Lines of Enquiry: Studies in Latin Poetry*, pp. 84–118. Hadrian seems to me the most likely candidate.

65. F. Millar, *The Emperor in the Roman World*, p. 493.

66. The literary and archeological evidences are assembled by J. H. D'Arms, *Romans on the Bay of Naples*, pp. 220–21.

67. Sen. *Ep.* 49.1; 53.1; 70.1.

68. *Tr.* 4.10.21–22.

69. Petron. *Sat.* 46.7.

70. Suet. *De vir. illustr.* 24.

71. Pliny *Ep.* 4.11.

72. Williams, *Change and Decline*, p. 53.

73. For Titinius in the role of a Maecenas, see R. Syme, *Tacitus*, pp. 92–93.

74. To judge by the prosopographical index to J. A. Crook, *Consilium Principis*, pp. 148–90.

75. *Hist. Aug., AS* 17.3.

76. Philostr. *VS* 601 (Heracleides), 623 (Philiscus).

77. *CJ* 10.53.3.

78. Porph. *Plot.* 12; cf. J. M. Rist, *Plotinus: The Road to Reality*, pp. 12–14. It will be observed that the *Hist. Aug.* has no mention of Plotinus.

79. *CJ* 10.32.6; for the illiterate scribe, cf. H. C. Youtie, *Chron. d'Egypte* 41 (1966): 132–35. See the valuable discussion by R. MacMullen, *Roman Government's Response to Crisis: A.D. 235–337*, pp. 58–60.

80. By P. Lemerle, *Le Premier humanisme byzantin*, pp. 255–57; cf. R. Browning, "Literacy in the Byzantine World," *BMGS* 4 (1978): 39.

81. *POxy.* 2338.

82. Eunapius *VS* 493.

83. Documented in the admirable article of A. Cameron, "Wandering Poets: A Literary Movement in Byzantine Egypt," *Historia* 14 (1965): 470.

84. The Antinoë papyrus text of Juv. 7.149–98 was published by C. H. Roberts ("The Antinoë Fragment of Juvenal," in *JEA* 21 [1935]: 199–209) (= 37 in R. Cavenaile, *CPL*).

85. *Epigr. Gr.* 613.

LITERARY AND ARTISTIC APPROACH

The Poetics of Patronage
in the Late First Century B.C.

JAMES E. G. ZETZEL

Determining the nature of literary patronage ought to be crucial to our understanding of Roman poetry, for the existence of a developed system of patronage would imply that the poems mirror the wishes and attitudes of the addressees rather than of the poets, that the texts are to be read as social documents as much as, or even more than, literary works.[1] The issues are not of course quite so stark as that; most critics if pressed would probably say that the wishes of a patron—be it Fulvius Nobilior, Memmius, or Maecenas—act as boundaries for the poet, limits within which he writes what and how he wishes. But the idea that the Roman poets of the classical period (for the purposes of this essay defined as that from Catullus to the death of Horace) were at the mercy of such unpoetic pressures is not a comforting one to a literary critic, although it might be suggested that it is only my residual romantic sensibility that is unwilling to admit social constraints on the poetic spirit. The question of patronage, however, deserves to be looked at from a literary as well as a historical point of view, and in that context I will propose that a good case can be made for denying utterly the importance of patronage to Latin poetry. Not necessarily to the poets, I hasten to add, but to their literary productions. That the literature even of praise has two sides was well known in antiquity, and a story found in Plutarch's *Apophthegmata Laconica* (217 DE) formulates the issue neatly: when a sophist was about to deliver an encomium of Heracles, Antalcidas said τίς γὰρ αὐτὸν ψέγει;—"Who is criticizing him?"[2] And it is with that cynical outlook that I will approach the issue of patronage here.

Peter White has recently analyzed much of the evidence for patronage in great detail, so that it is not necessary to repeat it. I can begin by citing from the conclusion of his article:

Poets attached themselves to wealthy households for reasons which had little to do with their poetic interests. . . . They were drawn almost inevitably into some attachment by the forces which aligned all men in a hierarchy of orders and individuals.[3]

The truth and common sense of this conclusion are apparent, and have the great merit of placing Roman poets as Romans of the first century B.C. or A.D. in their proper social context. On the other hand, it says little about Roman poets as poets. The identity of the two facets should not lightly be assumed: every Roman poet was aware that he adopted a persona or a series of personae in his verse. If we accept without question the identity of either poet with persona or of real *patronus* with poetic addressee, then we are in danger of draining the poetic texts of much of their meaning in order to gain mere historical information.

I want here to try to expand on White's argument in two directions at once, to suggest that there is both more and less patronage than he suggests. In the first place, even if the relationship of poet to patron is merely a specific case of the normal Roman bond of *clientela* or *amicitia*, that is not the only form of patronage affecting Roman poets. There is some—admittedly not much—evidence that in some cases *patroni* did act in the manner of Renaissance patrons, supporting their authors financially as well as socially and expecting that support to have a direct effect on the subject and even the style of the literary product. In some cases, too, even if financial support was not involved it seems that some poems were written in order to attract the interest and support (financial or moral) of a prospective patron. This background of artistic patronage as opposed to *clientela* (I use the term "artistic patronage" to refer to the Renaissance type) must be kept in mind when considering those major poets, particularly Catullus, Horace, Virgil, and Propertius, for whom artistic patronage was in fact unimportant.

If the historical context—the existence of artistic patronage—represents one side of this argument, the literary texts themselves are the sole material for the other. Given the fact that almost all the evidence for patronage is derived from poetic texts, it is worth taking the trouble to examine it as part of the poetry rather than as historical fact. In particular I will look at the poetic function and context of direct address in Latin poetry, and within that most closely at some poems addressed to Maecenas. In the first place, I will suggest that the choice of addressee is not necessarily a function of the relationship between the poet and the person whose name is in the vocative, but can be seen as a correlate of both the subject and the style of the poem. I will not go so far as to suggest that the poet need not know the person addressed (although I think that is a defensible position), but I would certainly say that in the case of organized poetic books there is no reason to assume that the individual poems ever had an independent existence prior to the creation of the whole.[4] A corollary is that there is no reason to believe that the individual poem, for example *Odes* 1.6 to Agrippa, was ever sent to the addressee as a separate work. And if that is the case, then we must assume that the poet intended such direct addresses to affect not the addressee but the reader; in other words, their function is poetic not political.

Two other points arise from this. If the dedication is seen as a part of the poem, then its tone and meaning should be judged in relation to the rest of the poem. A high poetic form, such as epic or didactic, is bound to have a dedication more serious and solemn than that of neoteric *nugae* or elegy, where the wit and irony of the form, together with the deliberate pose of reversing social conventions, inevitably affect our reading of the dedication itself. Thus I would suggest Virgil's attitude to Maecenas and Augustus is more straightforward and respectful than that of Horace, and Horace's dedications are in turn more serious than those of Propertius or Catullus. My final point, which is related to this, will be that there is one addressee who stands at the top of what might (not without some oversimplification) be called the two opposing scales of poetic value—that in which social value is paramount, where epic is the highest form, and that in which the importance of poetry itself is paramount, which might also be called the scale of Callimacheanism. That addressee, of course, is the Muse, and I will suggest that the substitution of the Muse for the human patron, which is necessary in epic, is in other genres to be taken as an indication of the poet's attitude both to his society and to his craft.

We should begin from the question of true artistic patronage. It may seem that to demonstrate the existence of artistic patronage is not really relevant to and indeed contradicts the second part of the argument, which is intended to demonstrate the unimportance of patronage as objective fact in poetry. But the existence of artistic patronage must be understood as the social reality against which the major poets were working, the convention that they transformed in their verse. In the first place, there now seems little doubt that none of the major poets was in need of financial support.[5] Horace makes the clearest allusion to his own poverty—"Paupertas impulit audax / ut versus facerem" (*Epist.* 2.2.51 f.)—but this retrospective explanation of his poetic career is certainly not to be taken seriously. Horace's father, and Horace himself at least before the civil wars, had the financial if not the social qualification for equestrian status, and even after the war Horace seems to have been able to obtain the post of *scriba quaestorius* before encountering Maecenas.[6] The assertion of poverty is as little true for Horace as it is for Tibullus or Propertius.

But if the poets were financially self-sufficient, then how are we to interpret the second-person addresses to real and often important people? They cannot all be people in whose *clientela* the poet was, and if they are all to be seen as *amici* of some sort it seems curious that so many poems to important people are couched in the form of *recusatio*, either refusal to write an epic or refusal to do something with or for the addressee (as for example in Prop. 1.6). In the last poem to be discussed here, Catullus' dedication of his *libellus* to Nepos, the relationship between these two men seems extremely odd given the literary beliefs and associations that emerge elsewhere in the Catullan corpus. If we recall, however, that poetry was not the profession of any of these poets in the sense of an income-producing occupation, that it was the product of *otium* not *negotium*, we may find some explanation. Poetry may have been the business of some people, particularly writers for the stage, and at an earlier period, and for some Greeks, but it was not the business of Catullus. It was the leisure pastime of men who had the education and wealth to indulge in it.[7] My own solution to the puzzle of the dedication of poems is that these wealthy gentlemen, the poets, employed as a literary conceit what was, for less fortunate contemporaries as for earlier generations, a reality. There were or at least there had been poets who needed patronage, either social or financial, and whose poetry reflected that need. But it may be significant that little if any of the production of such poets survives, and I can think of only one clear example from the late republic, a poet whose works survive in some twenty-two fragments.

The poet in question is scarcely one of the leading lights of Roman literature. It is P. Terentius Varro of Atax, "interpres operis alieni" as Quintilian calls him (10.1.87), best known for his translation of the *Argonautica* of Apollonius of Rhodes. He also translated two other Hellenistic poems, Aratus' *Diosemeia* and the lost geographical poem of Alexander of Ephesus, the *Chorographia* or *Cosmographia*. It is one of his other works, however, that is most significant as far as patronage is concerned, an epic poem called the *Bellum Sequanicum*. If we can trust Jerome's *Chronicle*,[8] Varro was born in the village of Atax in Gallia Narbonensis in 82 B.C. and did not even learn Greek until 47 B.C. We may safely assume that the epic, presumably on Caesar's Gallic wars, was his first work and that it was written in his native Gaul in order to attract the attention of, or in gratitude for having attracted the attention of, Julius Caesar. It was thus a work whose creation is directly related to the desires of a patron; it was a piece of propaganda not only on Caesar's behalf but on his own.

Some further guesses, no more than that, can be made about the rest of Varro's poetic career. There is only one other person in this period who translated the *Diosemeia*, and that of course was Cicero. But there is also only one other person who is known even to have read the *Chorographia* of Alexander of Ephesus, and that too was Cicero, who refers to it in two letters of 59 B.C.[9] And there is an easy link to be made between Varro Atacinus the Caesarian and Varro Atacinus the Ciceronian: the other person writing poetry in Gaul during Caesar's campaigns was Quintus Cicero, who composed tragedies at great speed during his enforced leisure at Alesia.[10] There is thus a plausible connection between Varro in Gaul and Cicero in Rome, and we may well conclude that the choice of subject for his works was not totally unrelated to the powerful men whose attention he wished to attract. Indeed, in the case of Varro of Atax the few fragments make it possible to detect the influence of patronage on style as well as subject: the fragments of the *Bellum Sequanicum* provide an imitation of Ennius, while the moderate neotericism of the fragments of the *Argonautae* offers at least one quite learned imitation of Catullus 64.[11] Perhaps it is only a matter of fitting style to genre, but it may also be that Varro attained more independence in style after his first, highly traditional poem got him attention in Rome.

There is not enough left of Varro Atacinus for us to be able to know exactly what his relationship to Caesar or to Cicero was. It may have been *amicitia* rather than artistic patronage. On the other hand, if Jerome's report that he did not learn Greek until he was thirty-five is true, then financial support may have been necessary; the obvious explanation of his Greekless youth is that he simply could not afford the expensive education that Catullus and the others so clearly had. And that simple fact, the affluence of the neoteric and postneoteric poets, must always be kept in mind.

The wealth of Catullus and the others is not something that was shared by all literary men; neither earlier Roman poets nor contemporary Greeks, groups that should be used as controls for understanding neoteric and Augustan poets, were known for their wealth. Ennius certainly needed financial support, as did Livius Andronicus the schoolteacher and the various early playwrights. But more important are the Greeks. In the first place, it had been acceptable since the time of Simonides for Greek poets to live off their poetry.

And what is true of the early Greeks was also true of those who were the literary hangers-on at Rome, that is, that financial support by Roman patrons was obviously necessary and had considerable influence on what and how they wrote. One need only mention Archias' epics or the long string of Crinagoras' epigrams for significant occasions in Augustus' household. In the late republic, at least to judge from the extant evidence, house philosophers were at least as numerous as house poets. Philodemus, Staseas, Diodotus, and many others dedicated works to the patrons with whom, and on whom, they lived.

I emphasize the fact of artistic patronage because it provides the necessary background for any interpretation of its metamorphosis in neoteric and postneoteric poetry. Indeed, it is important to remember that with Catullus there is an extraordinary change not only in the style of Roman poetry but in its social significance as well, and that not only was an acquaintance with Hellenistic poetry a prerequisite for these poets, but so was a sufficiency of cash. Catullus and his contemporaries display a total alteration—one might even say a reversal—of social values. Where earlier poets if they were well-to-do, Lutatius Catulus for example, could not have regarded their literary endeavors as anything more than a relaxation from public life, the neoterics seem to regard poetry as a way of life itself, a social code with its own exclusively literary hierarchy of values and relationships. This inversion of values affects the attitude to the social conventions of patronage as well.

This description is, I think, borne out in the attitude of Catullus and others to political figures. Even if it might be argued that a Catullus or a Virgil needed support or publicity from a leading public figure, which may indeed be true, there is remarkably little in their poetry to show it. Varro of Atax may have got his start from a poem praising Caesar's deeds, but it was necessary for an industrious and witty poetaster in the reign of Tiberius to supply an equivalent, the *Culex*, in Virgil's career. And Catullus, whose family did have Caesarian connections, far from writing an epic on Caesar's deeds wrote insults. If we judge by normal social patterns of advancement, it is clear that Memmius, who took Catullus to Bithynia as a *contubernalis*, must be regarded as one of Catullus' patrons, but he too receives invective rather than flattery.

Horace's poetic career too is puzzling in the light of social expectations. If patronage in any sense of the word was important to a poet, it should have been at the beginning of his career when the poet was young and unknown, struggling for success and recognition. But the only time that any major Augustan poet seems seri-

ously to be influenced in his choice of subject by the wishes of a patron is at the end of Horace's life: *Odes* 4, *Epistles* 2, and in a
different way the *Carmen saeculare.* To judge by all these cases, in
fact, it would seem that Catullus and the Augustans were well aware
of the social expectations of patronage but deliberately flouted them.
Whatever poems Virgil or Horace wrote in their youth to attract the
attention of Maecenas, if they ever deliberately wrote such occasional verses, do not survive and for a very good reason: they would
be totally inconsistent with the social attitude of poetry, which was
one that ranged from inversion of to at best indifference to accepted
social norms. In the realm of poetry—perhaps I should say the republic of letters—it is the poet who stands at the top. When Horace
in *Odes* 3.30 (on which see further below) calls himself *princeps*, he
is not joking.

A more detailed demonstration of some of these suggestions
about second-person address is in order. That dedications are more
intimately a part of ancient poems than of modern ones is obvious;
far from being on a separate page they are embedded in the text of
the poem. And in a number of poems it is immediately clear that the
choice of addressee is closely connected to the subject. Propertius
addresses Ponticus in 1.7 and 1.9 because he is an epic poet; Sallustius Crispus is a suitable recipient for Hor. *Odes* 2.2, a poem on
greed. One may wonder, moreover, whether these gentlemen would
have been particularly grateful for the advice offered them. Indeed it
is extremely doubtful that the addressee was the primary recipient
of many poems, even those not included in a larger poetic form. One
famous example is Cat. 50, "Hesterno, Licini, die otiosi." As has
been noted, Calvus did not need to be told what he had done the day
before; he was there.[12] The point of the address is to give a context to
the poem for other readers. Although the choice of Calvus may reflect a real event, it is far more important to recognize the appropriateness of a fellow poet as the recipient of a poem about the plea-
sures of poetry and about the equivalence of the writing of poetry
and the act of love.

A story told by the younger Pliny ought to be cautionary for interpreters of dedications (*Ep.* 6.15). When the elegist Passennus
Paullus, a descendant of Propertius, began a recitation with "Prisce
iubes," Iauolenus Priscus, a friend of the poet and presumably the
Priscus addressed, said, "Ego uero non iubeo." Pliny goes on to say
that Priscus was more than a little unstable, but the point is still
clear: the alleged order to write is fictional and the address need not
be either expected or welcome. The most famous "order" to write
poetry of course is in the *Georgics,* Virgil's reference to Maecenas'

"haud mollia iussa" (3.41). Here too the dedication is, as befits the seriousness of the poem, rather solemn, but it is *haud mollia* that is important, not *iussa*, and the presence of Maecenas' name indicates to the reader that the concerns of the poem are not disparate from those of Maecenas and Augustus.

Of all second-person addresses in Augustan poetry, it is those to Maecenas that deserve to be, and are, taken most seriously, and of all the addresses to Maecenas it is those by Horace that are most numerous and significant. I will not examine them all, but I would suggest that in several of them, as in the two in Propertius, it is poetry not patronage that is paramount. Four of Horace's books are addressed to Maecenas: the first epode, the first satire, the first ode, and the first epistle all bear his name. What is more, in at least three of those poems the subject matter, the priamel on the choice of careers, is markedly similar. One might indeed go so far as to suggest that this combination is, for Horace, a *sphragis* much as the name of Cyrnus is for Theognis. But there is more to it than that. In at least the *Satires* and the *Odes*, the name of Maecenas has a poetic function: he is part of the subject as well as the addressee.

The clearest example of the fusion of subject and dedication is in the *Liber Sermonum*, Horace's first completed work.[13] The book names Maecenas in the opening line, but it is not a perfunctory address made and then ignored in the rest of the poem. The first satire is written in the persona of a street philosopher; in form it is a diatribe in the manner of a latter-day Bion the Borysthenite. What is more, the speaker is not a profound or even a competent philosopher, and he is tactless to boot. He addresses Maecenas on the subject of human discontent and greed and includes him in the category of those who are perpetually seeking more. The picture that the poem gives—and as it is the first public poem of Horace one should not approach it with preconceptions derived from his later works—is of an importunate cynic buttonholing the great man in the street. As the book progresses, however, the portraits of the speaker and of Maecenas, and of the relationship between them, become clearer. We learn of the basis of their acquaintance and of its development. We also acquire a sense of the "circle" of Maecenas and its meaning for the poet in the last two poems, and the book ends with a list of the whole coterie. The whole is done with great skill and irony: the counterpart of Horace's encounter with Maecenas in the street in 1.1 is the meeting of the *molestus* with Horace in 1.9; the book shows a clearly delineated progress from outside the circle to inside, as it does from philosophy to literary criticism.

The *Liber Sermonum* is not a collection of unrelated poems but

the deliberate creation of a poetic *vita*, one which may or may not
reflect the true state of affairs in Horace's real life. Maecenas is not   *yes*
merely the addressee or patron, he is an element in a work of art. As
that is the case, it becomes impossible to tell what the truth underlying the stories told in the book really is. What is more, and this is
confirmed by the appearance of Maecenas in *Sat.* 2.6, it is not impossible to believe that the relationship of patron to client, of elect circle to importunate outsider, is itself only a vehicle for discussing the
role of the poet in society, and for giving concrete expression to the
Callimachean scorn for the *demosia*. In the *Satires*, as in most poetry of the Augustan age, art not life is both the subject and the object of poetic creation.   *art is life / life is art*

My description of the *Satires* here is both more serious and
more dogmatic than it ought to be. There is much humor in the
book, and a great deal of deliberate self-contradiction. No one moreover should doubt that the portrait of Maecenas, Virgil, and Horace
himself in 1.5 is meant to be funny and not primarily, as is sometimes claimed, a portrait of the Epicurean ideal of friendship. When
we turn from the *Satires* to the *Odes*, we find less humor, as one
would expect in a more elevated genre, and the dedication to Maecenas clearly means much more. Even so, it is possible to pick out
some elements that suggest that his presence in *Odes* 1.1 has at
least as much to do with poetics as with patronage. But humor is not
totally missing even from the addresses of the *Odes*; indeed there is
conscious irony in the arrangement of the first poems of book 1.
Starting from Maecenas we have addresses to all the appropriate men of standing: after Maecenas comes Augustus, then Virgil,
then Sestius, consul in 23 B.C., the year of publication, then Agrippa,
and finally Plancus, the consul of 27 B.C. But between Sestius and
Agrippa there is Pyrrha, the charming and fictional addressee of
"Quis multa gracilis." I cannot help thinking that, even if the *recusatio* to Agrippa demanded that Horace have already demon-
strated his capacities as a love poet, there is a certain self-mockery
in the arrangement.

In 1.1 alone, however, such a light touch is not apparent. It reads
as a perfectly straightforward plea for support from Maecenas:

quodsi me lyricis uatibus inseres
sublimi feriam sidera uertice.
[1.1.35–36]

Even though the second person here may also be an address to the
reader, it is primarily a statement that this is a new poetic form and
that Horace hopes for the approval of his friend and patron Maece-

nas. Although that may be the significance of the poem taken alone, it is not the only possible reading. In Horace poems are almost invariably parts of larger structures which reflect on or modify the meaning of the poems themselves. The first ode of book 1 is not an exception to this; it is, I think, part of a phenomenon which might be called the paradigm of the displaced patron, which I will discuss later in Catullus.

Odes 1.1 clearly corresponds in structure to the last ode of book 3; they are the only two poems in the collection that are written in stichic Asclepiadean meter, they open and close the book. One element of 1.1 not present in 3.30, however, is the address to Maecenas. And while 1.1 concerns both the choice of careers and Horace's poetic aspirations, these two elements are severed at the end of book 3. *Odes* 3.29 deals with the opposition of public and private (in it Horace summons Maecenas from the cares of city and empire to relax at Tibur), while 3.30 deals with the poetic achievement of the *Odes*, Horace's status as a monumental poet. *Odes* 3.30 is scarcely a modest poem. Where Horace had been content with Bacchic ivy in 1.1, he demands from Melpomene Delphic laurel in 3.30; where in the first poem he merely hoped to become one of the *lyrici uates*, in the last he has become poetic *princeps*; most important, where in 1.1 he asked for Maecenas to acknowledge him, in 3.30 he has passed beyond the need for any mortal patron. His monument is higher than the royal pyramids; so much for Maecenas the descendant of kings. From the company of nymphs and satyrs he has moved to that of the *pontifex* on the Capitol, from mortal delights to immortal glory. "Princeps Aeolium carmen ad Italos / deduxisse modos" is indeed, as David Ross has shown, a proud statement of the combination of Callimachean poetics and Roman subject;[14] but it is also an image of the poet as conqueror and *princeps*. Horace has by becoming a leader transcended the need for Maecenas or even for Augustus, and by addressing the Muse—indeed, commanding her—his poetry has become the virtual equivalent of epic. Far from rounding off his collection with a graceful adieu to Maecenas, as he does in the lesser 2.20, he has displaced Maecenas entirely, because the mortal patron no longer has any function. It is no longer the patron who supports or creates the significance of the poet, it is the poet's own craft.[15]

One other element of *Odes* 1.1 needs to be considered, because it is important in the sequel. The poem is a priamel, and as such it must be considered an implicit *recusatio*; the connection of the *recusatio* to Maecenas is not surprising. The implicit argument is that different people have different desires and abilities; writing lyric is my desire and therefore I hope that you, Maecenas, will approve. The obvious reason for directing such a poem to Maecenas is not only that he is a friend or patron of Horace but that, as someone identified with Augustus, he is a proper addressee. It would make no sense to offer a *recusatio* to someone for whom the implied epic would be inappropriate.

There is another reason for the appropriateness of Maecenas, however, as the poem presents the argument: even though Maecenas was of royal descent, he had not aspired to the senatorial career, and by remaining an *eques* he never held *imperium*. When presented in this way, the portrait of Maecenas is at best peculiar, although it is normally not questioned. Granted Maecenas remained an *eques*, but that is the only way in which he did not attain the pinnacles of power and influence. He did not avoid public responsibilities; all that he avoided was the *cursus honorum*. The reason for this presentation of Maecenas is not that it is true, but that it offers an attractive parallel between the retiring nature of Maecenas and the modesty of the poet who is unwilling to write epic.

It is Propertius who makes the clearest use of this homology, in 3.9, and he clearly got it from Horace:

Maecenas eques Etrusco de sanguine regum
    intra fortunam qui cupis esse tuam,
quid me scribendi tam uastum mittis in aequor?
    non sunt apta meae grandia uela rati.

                    [3.9.1−4]

Both the imitation of Horace and the logic of the argument are clear: Maecenas although of royal descent has remained an *eques*; why should not Propertius, whose talents are slender, also limit himself to what he can do? The parallel is drawn explicitly:

at tua, Maecenas, uitae praecepta recepi,
    cogor et exemplis te superare tuis.

                   [3.9.21−22]

After grouping his books with those of Callimachus and Philetas, he continues:

te duce uel Iouis arma canam caeloque minantem
    Coeum et Phlegraeis Oromedonta iugis. . . .

                  [3.9.47−48]

As Commager observes, the point of *te duce* is clear: it does not mean "at your request" but "when you become *dux*."[16] That this is an *adunaton*, moreover, is shown by the example, the wars of the gods and giants; as Propertius had said in 2.1.39 ff., Callimachus does not sing of the Phlegraean battles of Jupiter and Enceladus, and as Callimachus himself had said (fr. 1.20 Pf.), βροντᾶν οὐκ ἐμόν, ἀλλὰ Διός. The battle of the gods and giants was the subject that a true Callimachean could never attempt.

It would not be relevant here to offer a full interpretation of the other poem to Maecenas, 2.1, but once again a case can be made for taking the presence of Maecenas there as less the function of personal relationship than as a part of the *recusatio*; the clear allusion to the Callimachean *adunaton* makes that quite apparent. Starting from the statement that Cynthia, rather than the Muses and Apollo, is the source of his *ingenium*, Propertius proceeds to subsume various subjects within love poetry, ending with *Iliad*s in bed and

> seu quidquid fecit siue est quodcumque locuta,
>   maxima de nihilo nascitur historia.
>
> [2.1.15–16]

From *historia* to Maecenas, in the next couplet, the link is clear: the subjects for Propertius' major endeavors will be Cynthia, but if he could write real epic he would speak of Maecenas and Augustus (18). The poem is a statement, as we should expect in the first poem of a book, about the nature of Propertius' poetry, and is certainly not to be taken as a reply to any literal request from Maecenas for an epic.

In short, while Maecenas was obviously an important person to the Augustan poets, one should not try to draw precise historical facts from the relationships suggested by the poetry. Whatever the real Maecenas did for the real people Horace, Virgil, and Propertius need not be connected in any very clear way to what they wrote about him. He is an element in poetry, and as such is subject to the same creative transformations that anything else in poetry is. While poems are themselves historical facts, they do not convey and normally do not even wish to convey precise historical information.

Maecenas is not the only recipient of poetry at Rome, and other addressees may be subjected to the same type of interpretation that I have tried to give of him. In poem 6 of the *Monobiblos*, Propertius addresses Tullus, the recipient also of the first, fourteenth, and last poems in the book, as well as of 3.22. The background implied by 1.6 is fairly simple: Tullus has allegedly invited Propertius to go with him to Asia as a *contubernalis*, and Propertius declines because of Cynthia's opposition. Francis Cairns finds it odd that Propertius places his allegiance to Tullus second to his fear of, or love for, Cynthia; he thinks it demeaning to Tullus and "in ancient literature it is impossible that a poem addressed to a patron-cum-dedicatee should be uncomplimentary." He produces an elaborate explanation in terms of the propempticon form.[17]

But to worry about complimentary and uncomplimentary in a poem like this is misleading. Like most poems in the first half of the *Monobiblos*, 1.6 is to be read as a definition of love and love poetry, which are of course identical in Propertius, by opposites. The poem is an exposition of the "militat omnis amans" theme, and from the contrast of Tullus the man of patriotic action and duty and Propertius the frivolous lover it develops a deeper opposition: Tullus is going to the decadent East, "mollis Ionia," while Propertius lives "duro sidere" at Rome. Tullus' invitation is not the true occasion of the poem, it is merely the vehicle for the literary conceit.

Comparison of 1.6 with 3.22, the last poem addressed to Tullus, confirms the unimportance of historical fact here. In the later poem he writes to Tullus after a long interval, and it becomes clear that the Tullus of that poem has been in Cyzicus sampling the delights of the East for some years, perhaps since the dramatic date of 1.6.[18] In terms of fact, it is impossible to tell what has happened to Tullus. Did he in fact abandon his career and stay in the East? Or is Propertius merely using his name as an echo of the poem in the *Monobiblos*, redoubling the irony of 1.6? If the poems are read as a pair, it is clear that the Propertius who in 1.6 represents both the rigors and the decadence of staying in Rome with Cynthia is in 3.22 urging the former soldier, now decadent expatriate, to return home to take up his career. And while in 1.6 Propertius' mistress keeps him in Rome, in 3.22 it is in order to marry and raise a family that he urges Tullus to return. Once again the dedication is revealed as part of the fiction of the poem: Tullus in 3.22 is not chosen for social reasons, but in order to echo and alter the effects of 1.6. Tullus does not meet with the humble respect that Cairns thinks suitable for "patron-cum-dedicatee" because the real addressee is not Tullus but the reader.

Finally, I would like to look briefly at one other author. All the major elements of the use of patronage that I have tried to identify in the Augustan poets are to be found in the poetry of Catullus: the use of second-person address for connotation rather than denotation, the emphasis on the primacy and internal cohesion of poetry itself, the use of social relationships, including that of patronage, as a foil or even a metaphor for the assertion of literary values. When we read the epigrams, particularly the reference to the "aeternum sanctae foedus amicitiae," it is evident that Catullus is transferring the language of masculine social relations to the erotic relationship between himself and Lesbia; he is implicitly rejecting the traditional values of Roman society in favor of a new hierarchy of values.[19] That this is a precursor of the explicit inversions of value inherent in Roman elegy is clear too from poem 11, where Catullus substitutes for the dangerous voyage to the ends of the earth and the visit to "Caesaris monumenta magni" the short and unpleasant visit to Lesbia, "pauca nuntiate meae puellae / non bona dicta."[20] Far from being a praise of Caesar, this poem is an oblique assertion that the *militia amoris* is more serious than military expeditions.

Intimately connected with the social model proposed by Catullus is the poetic model; along with the rejection of contemporary social values is the rejection of history. Some aspects of this are obvious—one need only think of Catullus' use of Romulus and Remus or the rejection of the *Annales Volusi* in poems 36 and 95—but it is nowhere more emphatically stated than in the first poem, to Cornelius Nepos. Much of the interpretation of this poem was elegantly set out by J. P. Elder: "Catullus . . . is amiably telling Nepos that he, Catullus, is not going to do in poetry what Nepos has done in prose, i.e. that he is not going to follow the Ennian model of lengthy historical narrative. Nor the style of writing that goes along with that kind of narrative."[21] Elder does not explicitly state the logical conclusion of his argument: the contrast between Catullus' book and Nepos' *Chronica* is an implicit *recusatio*, in which the *Chronica* are the functional equivalent of the "reges et proelia" of *Eclogue* 6. I would prefer to read the poem not as a plea for support from Nepos the person but as a contrast of Catullus' literary values with those represented by Nepos' works.[22]

In the last footnote of his article, Elder also points the way to the solution of the largest problem in the poem—why Nepos is replaced at the end by the *patrona uirgo*.[23] He cites the report of Suetonius (*Gram.* 6) on the grammarian Aurelius Opillus, who considered writers and poets to be "sub clientela Musarum." Elder accordingly suggests that, while Nepos is the patron of past and present, "for the future the patron must be divine." What I find in this poem, however, is precisely the same paradigm of the displaced patron that was found in Horace's *Odes*. Along with the rejection of history, *annales*, and the social code of Rome is the rejection of the human patron: the switch to the Muse is an assertion of poetic pride and of the eternal value of Catullus' work. It is this replacement that demonstrates most clearly the irony of Catullus' self-disparagement; the presence of the Muse signifies the enduring worth of Catullus' slight poetic forms.

Since the approach to the question of patronage in this paper has been so resolutely antihistorical, it is worth while in concluding to try to put the argument in a slightly more historical perspective. In the middle of the first century B.C. a group of educated and well-to-do men discovered, through their reading of Callimachus and the other Alexandrian poets, a system of poetic values that elevated poetry, that emphasized the importance of the poet not as the reporter of reality but as its creator. Catullus and presumably his contemporaries as well adapted this system to their own social situation. What was apparently in Alexandria an emphasis on the proper style of poetry was extended to include subject as well, and the dismal situation of Roman politics in the mid first century easily lent itself to such inclusion. Because they had neither the financial need nor the poetic belief nor the moral desire to write of kings (or consuls) and battles, their poetry developed into that set of countercredos which we refer to under the general rubric of neotericism.

Neither poetry nor society of course remained static. The Rome of Augustus, whatever drawbacks it may have had, was not a subject automatically to be scorned, although different poets reacted to it in different ways. One feature did remain constant: the recognition that poetry was a society in itself, and that literary values, not social ones, were paramount. The fact that poetry is immortal and can share that immortality with its subject is itself a reversal of the traditional Roman roles of patron and client. That Augustus, directly and through Maecenas, provided subjects that poets thought worthy of song, I would suggest, is a far more important conclusion to be drawn from their presence in the works of Horace and Virgil than any inferences about the workings of patronage in Rome. The Roman poets had their sights set not on contemporary social approbation but on eternity, and it is *sub specie aeternitatis* ultimately that we should read their dedications. In the long run it is only because of Catullus, Virgil, and Horace that we care at all about Nepos or Maecenas. It is not the poets who are the clients, but the patrons.

NOTES

1. In keeping with the origins of this essay as a lecture, I have not altered the style and have kept the notes to a minimum, referring only to ancient texts and to modern scholarship which I actually used in writing this. In oral presentation, I offered a dedication to Wendell Clausen, J. P. Elder, and Michael Putnam, friends and teachers to whose writings and conversation my debt is obvious. This particular essay, however, owes much to two generous and perceptive critics: my colleague J. A. Hanson and my wife Susanna Stambler of Cornell University.

2. I am indebted to my colleague A. T. Grafton for bringing this passage to my attention.

3. P. White, *"Amicitia* and the Profession of Poetry in Early Imperial Rome," *JRS* 68 (1978): 92.

4. Whether or not the Catullan corpus was organized by the poet (as suggested most cogently by T. P. Wiseman, *Catullan Questions*, pp. 1–31) is irrelevant: the most that can be said is that the organizer of the book, whether Catullus or another, arranged preexisting poems in a rough pattern; that the Catullan corpus differs completely from Augustan poetic books is obvious.

5. See White, *"Amicitia,"* pp. 88 f., with references to earlier studies.

6. See E. Fraenkel, *Horace*, pp. 13 f.

7. Note particularly the use of *otiosi* in Catullus 50.1 and of *otium* (clearly referring to the leisure for the composition of poetry) in 51.13–16.

8. Jerome, *Chron.* A. Abr. 1935.

9. *Att.* 2.20.6 and 2.22.7. The judgment expressed in the latter passage is worth citing: "libros Alexandri, neglegentis hominis et non boni poetae sed tamen non inutilis, tibi remisi."

10. Four plays, including an *Electra*, in sixteen days (*QFr.* 3.5.7).

11. Morel, *FPL* 11 was, as Servius (*Aen.* 10.396) reports, taken verbatim from Ennius. The verse belongs not to the *Argonautae* but to the *Bellum Sequanicum*; see F. Skutsch, "Q. Ennius, der Dichter," *RE* 5 (1905): 2616. Fr. 7 is an imitation of Catullus 64.119; see W. Clausen, "Ariadne's Leavetaking: Catullus 64.116–120," *Illinois Classical Studies* 2 (1977): 219–23.

12. See E. Fraenkel, "Catulls Trostgedicht für Calvus," *WS* 69 (1956): 281 f.

13. This summarizes part of the argument of my "Horace's *Liber Sermonum:* The Structure of Ambiguity," *Arethusa* 13 (1980): 59–77.

14. D. O. Ross, Jr., *Backgrounds to Augustan Poetry*, pp. 133–37.

15. On the role of Maecenas in *Odes* 3.30 (as well as in *Epistles* 1), see M. C. J. Putnam, "Horace *c.* 3.30: The Lyricist as Hero," *Ramus* 2 (1973): 1–19.

16. S. Commager, *A Prolegomenon to Propertius*, pp. 55 f. with n. 42.

17. F. Cairns, *Generic Composition in Greek and Roman Poetry*, pp. 3–16.

18. On 3.22 and its relationship to the *Monobiblos*, see M. C. J. Putnam, "Propertius' Third Book: Patterns of Cohesion," *Arethusa* 13 (1980): 97–113.

19. See Ross, *Backgrounds*, pp. 8–15.

20. See M. C. J. Putnam, "Catullus 11: The Ironies of Integrity," *Ramus* 3 (1974): 70–86.

21. J. P. Elder, "Catullus 1, His Poetic Creed, and Nepos," *HSCP* 71 (1966): 146.

22. For another view, see T. P. Wiseman's essay in this volume and his *Clio's Cosmetics: Three Studies in Greco-Roman Literature.*

23. Elder, "Catullus 1," p. 149 n. 22.

Propertius 3.9:
Maecenas as *Eques, Dux, Fautor*

BARBARA K. GOLD

Propertius 3.9 is the second of the two Propertian poems addressed to Maecenas, but unlike 2.1 it is not the first poem of its book.[1] Hence it is regarded as an anomaly, a program poem which does not start off the book and which, in addition, announces a program that Propertius has no intention of fulfilling, as is evidenced by the very next poem. Like 2.10, 3.9 flirts briefly with the idea of turning to new and more serious themes and pursuits but then renounces these themes. Both 2.1 and 3.9 are immediately followed by an amatory poem which contrasts strongly with the proposed new program and which reaffirms Propertius' intention to continue writing elegy.

Editors and commentators have been bothered by 3.9 because of its anomalous nature. Ross and Hubbard interpret 3.9 as a prelude to book 4.[2] Ross declares that lines 43–56 form a palinode to 2.1.39–40, and that Propertius in 3.9.43–44 is saying he will follow the Callimachean style even while he sings Augustan themes. Hubbard calls 3.9 a difficult and ambiguous poem, and claims that in it Propertius is professing readiness to accept Maecenas' urging to a higher task—Roman and Callimachean *aitia*. Richardson explains the odd placement of 3.9 by saying that either Propertius wrote it as a genuine programmatic poem, intending to take up more serious themes but later changing his mind, or he wrote it as an introduction to book 3 but, finding it unsuitable for that purpose, positioned it as an advertisement for book 4.[3] It is neither necessary nor, I believe, correct to view 3.9 as a prelude to book 4. Rather, 3.9 is similar to other passages in Roman poetry, which mark new beginnings. Virgil in *Eclogues* 4 anticipates singing "maiora" (1) and "silvae consule dignae" (3), and in *Aeneid* 7 at the beginning of the second half of the work he claims "maior rerum mihi nascitur ordo / maius opus moveo" (44–45). Propertius like Virgil states that he is setting out on a new path and will attempt to write a new kind of poetry if certain conditions obtain.

If we look closely at Propertius books 2 and 3 we find that there has been a slow shift of focus. Propertius seems in the first five elegies of book 3 to have gained a new awareness of his position as a literary figure in the Callimachean style, and to have dropped any claim to subjective elegy.[4] His programmatic poems become more formal; he becomes more concerned with his own fame and literary achievements. In 3.1–3 we find new themes introduced: Propertius as a *sacerdos* who will win *mollia serta* (3.1.1–20); Propertius' fame and immortality as a poet (3.1.21–38); a flirtation with the idea of writing epic and a commandment from Apollo to gain fame from *mollia prata* not *heroum carmen* (3.3.15–18).

These ideas are continued in 3.9, but the poet addresses them to Maecenas and provides some bold twists on the standard *recusatio* theme. The gist of the poem is as follows: Propertius praises Maecenas' moderation and humility (1–2, 21–30), then states that different people find different rewards in different fields (7–18), that each person must follow his own nature (19–20), and that he will take his cue from Maecenas' moderate behavior by refusing to step outside of the appropriate bounds himself (21–22, 35–37). He recites the subjects he will not talk about (Thebes, Troy) and claims that his fame lies in writing love poetry (37–46). But then quite suddenly he changes and says that if he is given Maecenas' guidance he will write about the Titans and the giants, Roman history, and Augustus' wars (47–56). He ends by asking for Maecenas' support in this endeavor (57–60). Without the volte-face in the middle of the poem the argument would be quite clear. As it stands, there is considerable room for disagreement over the interpretation of its meaning. Let us examine it in closer detail.

Propertius' opening address to Maecenas in line 1

> Maecenas, eques Etrusco de sanguine regum

is very similar to the first line of Hor. *Odes* 1.1

> Maecenas atavis edite regibus[5]

but two elements distinguish these opening addresses. First, Propertius specifically calls Maecenas an *eques*, a point central to the poem. Horace does not refer to this, perhaps because the fact that Maecenas was only an *eques* would have diminished his position as a descendant of royalty. There are further implications of *eques*. Propertius too was probably an *eques*.[6] This is Propertius' way both of establishing a common bond between himself and Maecenas and of pointing up the discrepancy between Maecenas' noble ancestry and his social position. A third possible reason for the prominence of *eques* is that it may foreshadow the use of the horse metaphor at the end of the poem (57–58) and serve as an example of the associative language which Propertius uses throughout to refer both to Maecenas and politics and to himself and poetry.[7] This will be examined later in the essay. A second element lacking in Horace is the adjective *Etruscus*. It is used here for the fifth and final time in Propertius' poetry.[8] The other four uses all refer to the Perusine war in which Propertius suffered the loss of a kinsman, and it appears in the only other poem addressed to Maecenas, 2.1. Propertius makes much of the proximity of Perusia, an Etruscanized city in Umbria near Maecenas' place of birth, to the town in Umbria where he himself was born. The word *Etruscus* strengthens the bond between Maecenas and Propertius, already suggested by the word *eques*, by associating Maecenas' birthplace with that of Propertius.

The position of Maecenas is described in line 2: "intra fortunam qui cupis esse tuam"—"you who desire to remain within your bounds."[9] The word *fortuna* is deliberately vague: it is unclear whether the *fortuna* of Maecenas is the lot of a knight or of an Etruscan king. Why then, Propertius asks, do you want to send me into so vast a sea, when I am far more content to stay near shore? Line 3 implies that Propertius' firm rejection of Maecenas' purported request for epic and his strong statement of his intended subject of discourse in 2.1 had not convinced Maecenas, and that Maecenas had made another attempt to persuade Propertius. After continuing the sailing imagery in line 4 with *grandia vela*, he defends his position in lines 5–6 with a different metaphor:

> turpe est, quod nequeas, capiti committere pondus
>   et pressum inflexo mox dare terga genu.

The rest of the first part of the poem is devoted to developing the maxim "omnia non pariter rerum sunt omnibus apta" (7). *Aptus* in lines 4 and 7 is a key word in the poem; Propertius justifies his refusal to write epic on grounds that diverse talents are suitable to diverse activities. He argues that when one exceeds what is suitable (*apta*, 7) and what one is capable of (5), the consequence is *turpe*. This would be the result of any attempt by Propertius to stray from elegy into the field of epic. He enlarges on this point by a catalog of Greek artists, each of whom has won fame in his particular limited field of excellence.[10]

The first section is rounded off in line 20 by another maxim:

> naturae sequitur semina quisque suae.[11]

Thus with a series of maxims, some universally applicable and some individualized, and a catalog of *exempla* to support the cumulative force of the maxims (9–16), Propertius sets the scene for his second *recusatio.*[12]

In lines 21–22, Propertius turns again to Maecenas, applying the principles which he has propounded to Maecenas and to himself:

> at tua, Maecenas, vitae praecepta recepi,
>   cogor et exemplis te superare tuis.

Line 21 and line 2, which it recalls, both portray Maecenas as a role model for Propertius and an example of the precepts of Epicureanism. Maecenas chooses to live according to his personal limitations and capabilities and to limit his involvement in political affairs. Propertius claims that he has adopted these teachings from Maecenas, which will compel him to apply earnestly the same principles to his own literary endeavors. Propertius then illustrates Maecenas' *vitae praecepta* in lines 23–34 and his own attempt to follow them in lines 35–46.

In lines 23–34, in a series of three couplets each beginning with *tibi* (23, 25, 27) picking up the *at tua* in line 21, Propertius lists the magistracies and powers which would be available to Maecenas if he were to exceed his *vitae praecepta*: the consulship (23), praetorship (24), generalship (25–26). Propertius lists here magistracies and commands which could not be held by an *eques* but only by a senator. These would therefore have been impossible for Maecenas, just as are the choices which Propertius lists for himself. The adjective *dominus* (23) is used to provide another link—this time linguistic—between Maecenas, who might obtain the *dominas secures* if he so desired, and Propertius, who in an equally unlikely situation might become *dominus* of his mistress or of epic poetry. *Dominus* is used as an adjective only here in Propertius. The noun *domina* is used frequently but always in amatory contexts (1.7.6, 2.9.45, 3.6.2, etc.). In lines 27–28 Propertius again expresses Maecenas' alternative in a way calculated to remind Maecenas and the reader that an *eques* is the subject:

> et tibi ad effectum vires det Caesar, et omni
>   tempore tam faciles insinuentur opes.

The subject under discussion in this couplet is property and wealth. Although Roman senators were supposed to hold a larger amount of property than knights to qualify for their rank, knights traditionally had more cash. Propertius implies this with the phrase *faciles opes* and further underlines the idea with the use of the word *in-*

sinuo, which literally means "to make its way into the *sinus* of." The word is repeated in part (*sinus*) in line 30. *Vires* in line 27 is another ambiguous term. What powers exactly does Augustus grant to Maecenas? Propertius is not describing constitutional powers, such as the *imperium* given to a senator, but the positions or *curae* held by knights and especially by Maecenas which were probably more alarming to many people than legally conferred powers. Maecenas may have declined the highest magistracies and legal commands but he received instead something far greater and less controlled. It appears then that neither Maecenas nor Propertius is particularly modest in the honors which he refuses, and that the description of Maecenas' humility and restraint in lines 29–30 is tongue in cheek.

In lines 29–30 Propertius reintroduces the sailing metaphor used in the beginning (3–4) and rounds off the first section of the poem. He applies to Maecenas' chosen way of life here vocabulary and imagery which he most often applies to love poetry—*parcis, tenuis, humilem* (29), *velorum plenos . . . sinus* (30).[13] *Tenuis* corresponds to the Callimachean use of λεπτός, lean or highly polished poetry. Propertius, as with the word *eques* in line 1 and *dominus* in line 23, uses associative language here to describe Maecenas' political career and Epicurean precepts on the one hand and his own literary endeavors on the other. By doing this he creates a common denominator between these two apparently disparate pursuits.

This section on Maecenas is completed by two couplets in which Propertius once again plays with accustomed meanings and ways of thinking (31–34). He opens with an emphatic asseverative, *crede mihi* (31), followed by a resounding Ennian echo (32) in "venies tu quoque in ora virum."[14] In this epic-sounding verse there is perhaps a reference to Virgil's *Georgics* and certainly one to an earlier poem of his own, 2.1. The third book of the *Georgics* contains in lines 8–9 Virgil's assertion in Ennian language that he will attempt a loftier theme one day:

> temptanda via est, qua me quoque possim
> tollere humo victorque *virum volitare per ora.*

Propertius' first two lines in his other poem to Maecenas, 2.1, are the following:

> Quaeritis, unde mihi totiens scribantur amores,
> unde meus veniat mollis in ore liber.

Thus the Ennian echo in 3.9.32 serves to connect the world of epic to which Propertius says he aspires with the world of elegy through the mediation of Virgil, and also to connect Maecenas' alleged aspi-

rations with Propertius' own.[15] In lines 31–32 Propertius claims that
Maecenas' true greatness lies not in his own position but in his trust
in and loyalty to Caesar. These are his *vera tropaea*.[16] *Fides* here
may also refer to Maecenas' *fides* to his own principles and nature.
Maecenas and Caesar exemplify the maxim in lines 7–8: different
fame is gained from different pursuits. Maecenas' fame will come
from his restraint in accepting powers and offices and from his loyalty to Caesar, despite their differences, and to his own way of life.
This section appears to be a genuine compliment but may also con-
ceal an allusion to Maecenas' fame, which comes from refraining
from most of the positions and goods offered to him. Propertius then
will be like Maecenas in his judicious use of restraint in matters
which do not interest him or are beyond him—such as writing epic.

Lines 35–46 constitute the answer to lines 23–34, an explanation of Propertius' way of life. The anaphora *tibi . . . tibi . . . tibi* in
lines 23–27 is answered by the resounding *non . . . non . . . nec* in
lines 35–39. Returning to the sea imagery of lines 3–4 and 30, Propertius claims that he will not cleave the *tumidum mare* (35) because his place is *sub exiguo flumine* (36). *Exiguus* love poetry will
be his fare, not *tumidus* epic.[17] Propertius' explanation is given in
negative terms: he tells us what he does not propose to do. In three
couplets Propertius outlines subjects he will not undertake; these
balance the three couplets above describing the offices and powers
which Maecenas rejects (23–28). In line 43 the words *sat erit* strike
the same note of moderation, or contentment with less, which he
praises in Maecenas. Propertius implies that it is here in the "lesser"
field of love poetry that his natural abilities lie, and here where he
can achieve the greatest fame.

Suddenly in lines 47–48 Propertius seems to alter his position
completely:

> te duce vel Iovis arma canam caeloque minantem
> Coeum et Phlegraeis Oromedonta iugis.

The Titans, early Roman history, and the triumphs of Augustus
are the very topics which he has already rejected as unsuitable in
2.1.19 ff. In line 52 Propertius says that when he sings of these subjects "crescet et ingenium sub tua iussa meum." The *tua iussa* picks
up the *te duce* and continues the idea expressed there: "If you will
give me inspiration by leading the way and doing it yourself, my talent will grow in proportion to the biddings which you as *dux* give."
In the phrases *te duce* and *sub tua iussa*, Propertius is again using
words with both literal and literary meaning. *Dux* is a military word
first and means a general, but can also mean more loosely a leader of

men in any field.[18] Propertius uses it here partly to say that he will alter his writing habits if Maecenas alters his political aspirations. But there is more. There is, I believe, a subtle reference in this phrase to Hor. *Odes* 2.12, where Horace tells Maecenas much the same thing: if he wants a poem in honor of the *proelia Caesaris* (10) he must write it himself, *pedestribus historiis*. It was well known that Augustus viewed Maecenas' peculiar writing style with a jaundiced eye, and that Maecenas was a far better judge of other writers than of his own work.[19] Thus the suggestion from either Horace or Propertius that Maecenas might want to take up epic or panegyric poetry would have been highly amusing.

The phrase *tua iussa* can also be understood in a more literal sense in the context of the poem and within the broader literary tradition. If Propertius calls Maecenas a *dux*, a general, then the obvious meaning of *iussa* is the general's orders. A good general such as Hannibal or Caesar never gave any orders which he himself could not carry out. Thus Propertius is simply emphasizing here that Maecenas must be prepared to do first what he bids others do. What that is Propertius leaves uncertain. But *tua iussa* also recalls a famous phrase in *Georgics* 3—*haud mollia iussa* (41)—which is used in a similar context to refer to Maecenas. Later Ovid uses *iubeo* in *Tristia* 2—"at si me iubeas" (333)—in announcing his intention to attempt a gigantomachia and his unfulfilled intention to write a praise of Augustus, as Propertius does in 3.9.[20] The word *iubeo* had clearly become a literary convention by Ovid's time and was used of promises not meant to be kept. I would maintain that in Propertius it is already used this way in reference to Virgil.

Thus in the phrases *te duce* and *sub tua iussa* we have a subtle *recusatio*. The catalog of proposed epic topics in lines 47–52 provides another kind of *recusatio*. There are certain peculiarities and disturbing mistakes in detail in the poet's catalog of epic subjects. In line 48 Propertius claims that he will sing of "Phlegraeis Oromedonta iugis." Huschke was the earliest editor to change *Oromedonta* to *Eurymedonta*; he observed that Oromedon is known only as a mountain in Cos and not as a legendary monster. Shackleton Bailey, however, defends *Oromedonta*, partly because the corruption from *Eurymedonta* cannot easily be explained.[21] In lines 49–51 Propertius describes the early history of Rome—the twins and the wolf (51), the laying out of the walls and the slaying of Remus (50), the Roman cattle grazing on the Palatine (49). These are perfectly legitimate subjects but Propertius seems to have them in reverse chronological order. The transposition of lines 49 and 51 proposed by Peiper and the comments of other baffled editors show at least that this section is puzzling.[22] In any case, Propertius rejected the possibility of writing about these subjects earlier, in 2.1.19–34. In line 55 Propertius refers to the *castra Pelusi*. Several editors (Palmer, Lipsius, Camps) change *castra* to *claustra* because Pelusium was not a camp but a fortified town. *Claustra* also suits the verb *subruta* better than *castra*. Furthermore, as Camps points out, Pelusium surrendered; it was not taken by force.[23] While it is true that Propertius is not a historian and cannot be pressed too hard for correct facts, there are enough worrisome errors here to give us pause.[24] Yet Propertius uses a similar technique and makes such errors in other poems. In 2.34.67–77 Propertius describes the *Eclogues* of Virgil by weaving together details which are imperfectly remembered from the individual poems.[25] His pastoral catalog is close enough to what Virgil actually wrote to make it clear that Propertius has the *Eclogues* in mind, but it is less a careful rendering than a dreamlike fusion of Virgil, Theocritus, and Propertius. In 3.3 Propertius gives an example of the epic topics he intends to treat before Apollo rushes in demanding that he cease his epic attempts and return to the elegiac fold. In this catalog he makes five errors of detail and chronological sequence.[26] In every case it can plausibly be argued that Propertius makes these "mistakes" in order to prove his point: he cannot write the genre in question—in 2.34, pastoral and in 3.3 and 3.9, epic. This is not simply an example of Propertius the blundering poet who is unable to keep straight his historical facts, as some critics think, but part of a clever *recusatio*.

Lines 47–56 operate as a *recusatio* on another level as well. Each topic which Propertius proposes is already the property of one of his predecessors or contemporaries. Horace in *Odes* 3.4.42–80 dealt with the gigantomachy that Propertius mentions in lines 47–48.[27] The legendary history of Rome formed the most famous part of Ennius' *Annales*. And Augustus' triumphs over the Parthians, Eastern peoples and Egyptians had been celebrated by Horace and by Virgil in *Aen.* 8.675 ff.[28]

Thus we have a *recusatio* combined with a promise to write on epic themes if Maecenas will be the *dux*. Propertius says that if Maecenas changes his mode of living he will change his in response and commence writing an epic; Propertius will do what Maecenas does, not what he says. Propertius, however, knows full well that Maecenas will not change and thus makes a safe promise which he never intends to fulfill.[29]

The final two couplets, in which he asks Maecenas to be his *fautor* and to guide his course, refer not to epic but to his earlier theme of love poetry.[30] Lines 57–60, then, do not continue directly from *te duce* but return to the development of thought in lines 1–46 before the parentheses in lines 47–56. In lines 59–60 Propertius asks Maecenas to guide his continued composition of elegiac poetry and tells Maecenas that all of his glory will be due to him who like Propertius has limited himself to the path most suited to his natural abilities. The language itself in lines 57–60 indicates that Propertius is referring to love poetry and not epic. *Mollia* in line 57 is a word which Propertius uses repeatedly to describe his elegiac verse,[31] and it turns our minds back to elegy.[32] The *mollia lora* must refer to the "pliant reins" of elegy. *Coeptae iuventae* (57) refers to elegiac writing which he began at a younger age.[33] In line 57 then Propertius asks Maecenas to take the reins of his chariot of elegy.[34] The chariot and horse motifs have already appeared in various forms throughout the poem. We have mentioned that *eques* in line 1 may foreshadow the horse and chariot metaphor at the end. Likewise Calamis sculpts horses in line 10, the Olympic chariot race is mentioned in line 17, and the Trojan horse in line 42. Propertius uses the image of the chariot race for his poetry also in 3.1.9–14, where he imagines himself as a *triumphator*. Thus the horse and chariot metaphor and related images and phrases have a wide range and are used to describe Propertius' and Maecenas' social rank and various pursuits, artistic and poetic. The metaphor embraces both Maecenas and Propertius and serves to bind them together into a common sphere.

Fautor and *dextera da signa* (58) continue the prayer for guidance in *te duce*.[35] *Dextera signa* and *immissis rotis* could refer to the epic which Propertius jokingly says he may write or to the elegy which he intends to continue to write. In lines 59–60 the final couplet continues this ambiguity:

> hoc mihi, Maecenas, laudis concedis, et a te est
> quod ferar in partis ipse fuisse tuas.

The *laus*, which is left unclear here, must be in Propertius' mind at least the *laus* of Maecenas' approval of the *mollia lora* of elegy. Propertius says in the last couplet that if Maecenas realizes that Propertius' fame will come from elegy and not from epic and gives his favor accordingly, then it will be due to this realization that Propertius will have joined his ranks. *In partes tuas* is a phrase adopted from the political sphere.[36] *Partes* was widely used by historians to refer to an amorphous group with a common basis of political thought.[37] Propertius takes the word *partes* here from the political sphere and sets it in a literary context, saying that if Maecenas gives him favorable signals he, Propertius, will come over to Maecenas' *vitae praecepta* and be like Maecenas in doing only what he does best.[38] Lines

57–60 should read: "Patron of my early youth, take the gentle reins of my youthful course and give me favorable signals now that my wheels have sped forth. Should you, Maecenas, grant me this honor, it will be due to you that I will be said to have joined your ranks."

Propertius' *recusatio* does not stop at the end of the poem. At the beginning of the next poem, 3.10, Propertius picks up the language from the end of 3.9: *signum* (3) echoes *signa* in 3.9.58 and *faustos* (4) echoes *fautor* in 3.9.57. This provides a link between the two poems and underlines his reluctance to write epic verse by using the very language of his refusal in an entirely elegiac poem. Thus 3.9 is an elaborate and complex *recusatio*. Propertius uses language here in an ingenious way. He confounds normally arranged categories of words by stretching their imagistic possibilities; literary terms become political, social terms become literary, and so forth. By doing this he creates a verbal world in which both he and Maecenas can function in their own separate areas of interest, yet in which there can be a common denominator of understanding. In addition he uses the same language both to reject a request by giving a poor sample of it and to create a new poem in the genre within which he is able to operate. The language itself is the same; it is the use of it which differentiates one poet from another and one poem from another.

It is obvious to the reader from the opening line of the poem, the maxims in lines 7–8 and line 20, the catalog of artists in lines 9–16, and the references to the chariot and foot races in lines 17–18 that Propertius is echoing Horatian themes. The whole of the first section up to line 20 is modeled on Hor. *Odes* 1.1, and lines 17–18 resemble *Odes* 1.1.3–6, particularly the *est quibus* (3.9.17), which corresponds to *sunt quos* in *Odes* 1.1.3.[39] These echoes come from Horace's most famous poem to Maecenas. Why does Propertius follow so closely this well-known Horatian ode? Through an actual example he shows Maecenas that two poets, and two poets known well to Maecenas, can use similar themes and language to produce very different poems. Propertius, as I have mentioned, begins with a reference to Maecenas as *eques* and emphasizes throughout his humility and restraint. Horace omits this side of Maecenas entirely. The theme of both poems is "Different people win fame from different pursuits," and Propertius uses this theme as a framework within which he can prove just this to Maecenas. Horace's fame is as a *lyricus vates* (*Odes* 1.1.35); Propertius feels that he can only win fame from the "mollia coeptae lora iuventae" (3.9.57), that is, as a poet of elegy. The language is the same, the theme is the same, but the outcome is different. Propertius proves the thesis that two people using the same tools, in this case two poets using the same theme and language, can produce different but equally praiseworthy results. He both states this thesis in the poem and uses Horatian language to further illustrate his point by means of an *exemplum*.

NOTES

1. A version of this essay was delivered at a meeting of the Southern Section of the Classical Association of the Middle West and South in Sarasota, Florida in October of 1978. I would like to thank J. Griffin, M. Gwyn Morgan, J. E. G. Zetzel, G. Karl Galinsky, and L. Richardson, jr., for their comments and suggestions.

2. D. O. Ross, Jr., *Backgrounds to Augustan Poetry*, pp. 126–27; M. Hubbard, *Propertius*, pp. 109–15.

3. L. Richardson, jr., *Propertius Elegies I–IV*, pp. 348–49.

4. Ross, *Backgrounds*, pp. 122–23.

5. Cf. also Horace *Odes* 3.29 to Maecenas: "Tyrrhena regum progenies" (1).

6. Cf. 4.1.121 ff.; from the evidence of this passage and from his connections, it is assumed that Propertius, like Ovid and Tibullus, was an *eques*. Cf. Hubbard, *Propertius*, pp. 96–97; H. E. Butler and E. A. Barber, eds., *The Elegies of Propertius*, p. xix.

7. Propertius often uses the same language in an associative and metaphorical manner to refer to things literal and literary (Commager, see below, p. 9). The most frequently used words are those which can apply metaphorically to his poetry and literally to an object, or both to poetry and his life. Poem 2.1 is full of these words: e.g., 2.1.2: *mollis . . . liber*; 2.1.41: *duro . . . versu*; 2.1.45: *angusto . . . lecto*; 2.1.72: *exiguo marmore*. All of the adjectives here are used often to describe his poetry (2.1.2, 41) but sometimes to describe objects associated with Propertius which then take on the characteristics of his poetry (2.1.45, 72). Cf. the excellent discussion of the conflation of different kinds of terminology in S. Commager, *A Prolegomenon to Propertius*, pp. 5 ff., esp. p. 8 n. 12; G. Williams' remarks on Propertius' use of associative metaphors in *Tradition and Originality in Roman Poetry*, pp. 781–82.

8. The other references are 1.21.2, 10; 1.22.6; 2.1.29; possibly 2.13.1. For different interpretations of the implications of *Etruscus* see R. Lucot, "Mécène et Properce," *REL* 35 (1957): 195–204; W. R. Nethercut, "The σφραγίς of the Monobiblos," *AJP* 92 (1971): 464–72. The alternate form *Tuscus* appears four times in 4.2 (3 [twice], 49, 50), but all of these instances are in specific reference to Vertumnus, the Etruscan god.

9. The word *fortuna* in line 2 has been much discussed. Bennett makes it roughly equivalent to *natura* or *ingenium*, the talent or native ability which a person has (A. W. Bennett, "*Sententia* and Catalogue in Propertius (3.9.1–20)," *Hermes* 95 [1967]: 228–29 n. 1). J. S. Phillimore (*Propertius*,

p. 107) and D. R. Shackleton Bailey (*Propertiana*, p. 158) take the line to mean "within the bounds of your estate in life." Butler and Barber (*The Elegies of Propertius*, p. 281) give a parallel passage from Ov. *Tr.* 3.4.25–26: "intra fortunam debet quisque manere suam." Propertius uses *fortuna* in different ways: as the equivalent of *fatum* or τύχη (1.6.25; 3.7.32), as a stroke of good luck (1.17.7; 2.28.57), as misfortune (1.15.3; 1.20.3), and as the equivalent of money or wealth (2.34.55; 3.2.21). In 2.22.18 we find *fortuna* used as a synonym for *natura* where both words appear to refer to his lot:

> uni cuique dedit vitium natura creato:
> mi fortuna aliquid semper amare dedit.

This closely parallels the use of *fortuna* in 3.9.2.

10. Line 8, which provides the introduction to the catalogue in lines 9–18, is a textual crux: "palma nec ex aequo ducitur una iugo." The major manuscripts (NFL) give *flamma* as the first word, which most editors have emended to *palma* or *fama*, the reading of the *codices deteriores*. In addition, some take *iugum* as "yoke," others as "height." For other interpretations of the line, see Butler and Barber ("his point is that artists and others may rise to *equal* fame in different branches," *The Elegies of Propertius*, p. 282); Postgate ("the general sense is 'in order to be famous, you must have a province of your own and keep it. You must be *solus* and have no one running alongside you,'" *Select Elegies of Propertius*, p. 170); W. A. Camps ("in art there are varieties of eminence, each offering its several prize," *Propertius: Elegies, Book III*, p. 94); Shackleton Bailey ("from heights unequal men bring down different palms," *Propertiana*, p. 159). The point of the line is not, *pace* Butler and Barber, the opposition of *grandis* to *humilis*, but the diversity of men and their unity in achieving fame. Cf. Bennett, "*Sententia* and Catalogue," pp. 223 ff., 232.

11. Cf. 2.1.46: "qua pote quisque, in ea conterat arte diem." These two very similar statements are both addressed to Maecenas.

12. Cf. Bennett, "*Sententia* and Catalogue," p. 232, for the structure of 3.9.1–20.

13. Cf. Prop. 3.1, 3.3; Callim. *Ait. prol.* fr. 1, 17–28; *Ap.* 105–12. H. Tränkle, *Die Sprachkunst des Properz und die Tradition der lateinischen Dichtersprache*, pp. 77–78, has a note on the uses of *dominus* and other substantives which become adjectives in poetic usage. He gives as a less bold parallel to *dominas secures* the phrase *dominas manus* in Ov. *Am.* 2.5.30.

14. Cf. Ennius *Epigr.* 1.4 ap. Cic. *Tusc.* 1.15.34: "Volito vivus per ora virum."

15. Although the idea in the *Georgics* passage is quite different, the words are the same. The Ennian echo here might also serve as an echo of the Callimachean statement against epic in *Aitia* 1, fr. 1.1–5P f. Cf. H. E. Pillinger, "Some Callimachean Influences on Propertius, Book 4," *HSCP* 73 (1969): 171 ff.

16. With the *fides* of Maecenas we might compare the description of Maecenas in Prop. 2.1.36: *fidele caput*; also *Eleg. in Maec.* 11–12: "foedus

erat vobis nam propter Caesaris arma / Caesaris et similem propter in arma fidem." Shackleton Bailey, *Propertiana*, p. 75, compares the meaning of *vera* here to *vera* in 2.7.15: "quod si vera meae comitarent castra puellae." He says that *vera* denotes the metaphorical meaning as distinct from the literal.

17. Cf. Catullus' only use of *tumidus* (95.10) in reference to the voluminous writings of Antimachus of Colophon; here too it is a pejorative epithet.

18. *Dux* was applied to Caesar, as it was to all of the leading generals of the republic, both as military leader and, in the phrase *dux partium*, as a political leader. Octavian preferred the name *princeps civitatis* to *dux partium* because *dux* had a strong military flavor. The poets of the republic, however, used *dux* of Augustus more frequently than *princeps*. Cf. R. Syme, *The Roman Revolution*, pp. 288, 311–12.

19. Cf. Suet. *Aug.* 86, where Suetonius tells us that Augustus avoided *concinnitas* and that he tried to express himself *quam apertissime*. This certainly was not the aim of Maecenas. Augustus did not like *cacozeloi* and *antiquarii* like Maecenas, we are told, and mocked his *myrobrechis concinnos*.

20. Cf. D. C. Innes, "Gigantomachy and Natural Philosophy," *CQ* 29 (1979): 165–71, esp. 167–68.

21. Shackleton Bailey, *Propertiana*, p. 163. He cites a passage in Herodotus (7.98) where Oromedon is used as a Cilician personal name.

22. Cf. Camps, *Propertius: Elegies, Book III*, p. 100 ad line 51: "This illustrates the fact that Propertius is not fussy about chronological sequence in his enumerations"; p. 101 ad line 55, a reference to "Propertius' vagueness over historical details." It is possible to take *Romanis* in line 49 as proleptic (cf. *Tarpeia arce* in 4.4.29). Whether or not the Roman reader would have been disturbed by this lack of order is not clear; one must remember the order in the catalog of great Romans in *Aen.* 6.756 ff.

23. Camps, *Propertius: Elegies, Book III*, p. 101. Cf. Shackleton Bailey, *Propertiana*, p. 164, who defends the reading *claustra*.

24. Cf. Butler and Barber's pronouncement: "Propertius is a poet and not a historian, and such a point must not be pressed" (*The Elegies of Propertius*, p. 285).

25. Cf. 2.34.67–68, a reference to *Eclogues* 7, which is set not in the *pineta Galaesi* (never mentioned in the *Eclogues*) but on the bank of the river Mincius; line 69, which mentions ten apples sent as gifts to girls; in *Ecl.* 3.70–71, ten apples are sent to a boy, Amyntas. Propertius has throughout this passage conflated Virgilian and Theocritean pastoral. Cf. Richardson, *Propertius Elegies I–IV*, pp. 315–16.

26. Cf. Camps, *Propertius: Elegies, Book III*, pp. 64–65 for a list of the mistakes made in 3.3.7–12. He excuses them there on much the same grounds: that Propertius was concerned with poetical or rhetorical effect and not attentive to accuracy of detail or logical sequence.

27. Propertius himself has already rejected the theme of the gigantomachy as unsuitable for him in 2.1.18–20 and in 39–40, where he con-

trasts the *Phlegraeos tumultus* with the *angusto pectore Callimachi*. Innes
("Gigantomachy," pp. 166 ff.) points out that the gigantomachy was regarded by the ancients as a theme for high epic, and that only Horace and
Ovid of the Roman poets treated this theme (*Odes* 3.4; *Tr.* 2.61 ff., 331 ff.).
Propertius' insistence on the gigantomachy in his two poems to Maecenas
may be a sly joke at Maecenas' expense; the assault of the Titans and giants
on the Olympic gods might have some bearing on Maecenas' "assault" on
the honors and powers of Augustan Rome.

28. Richardson, *Propertius Elegies I–IV*, p. 355, proposes the transposition of 4.1.87–88 to 3.9.48. In this couplet Propertius says that he will
sing of Troy and the wandering Trojans. This would also be a Virgilian theme
which Maecenas has proposed to Propertius.

29. Cf. Camps, *Propertius: Elegies, Book III*, p. 99; Butler and Barber,
The Elegies of Propertius, pp. 285–86; J. P. Boucher, *Etudes sur Properce*,
p. 39. Boucher maintains that Propertius found in Maecenas' nonchalant attitude and rejection of traditional political conventions a good excuse for his
own inaction and a symbol of his personal tastes. Cf. also W. Wimmel, *Kallimachos in Rom*, pp. 260 ff., who translates *te duce* as "if you insist."

30. There is another view. Shackleton Bailey, *Propertiana*, p. 165, feels
that lines 57–60 follow directly on line 56, and that lines 59–60 have no
force if they refer to the continued composition of love poetry.

31. E.g., 2.1.2; 3.1.19 (Propertius' poetry as *mollis*); 1.7.19; 2.34.42 (love
poetry as opposed to epic poetry).

32. Most editors emend *mollis*, the manuscript reading, to *mollia* to
agree with *lora*. Richardson, *Propertius Elegies I–IV*, p. 356, emends it on
the grounds that *mollis* when "applied to a man is always insulting"; similarly Butler and Barber, *The Elegies of Propertius*, p. 286. *Mollia* is also
preferable for metrical reasons; cf. M. Platnauer, *Latin Elegiac Verse: A
Study of the Metrical Usages of Tibullus, Propertius and Ovid*, pp. 37–38.

33. I take *coeptae iuventae* with both *fautor* and *cape lora* as the sen-
tence order suggests. G. Luck (*The Latin Love Elegy*, p. 138) takes *coeptae
iuventae* as referring to his time of life, youth or manhood, in which he is
now contemplating epic.

34. It is interesting to note that both poems to Maecenas end with an
image of Maecenas as a charioteer: in 2.1.75–76 he is a rider, here he is a
driver.

35. Cf. Virg. *G.* 1.40, also a prayer in bipartite form, first for guidance
and then for a favoring sign.

36. For the accusative of *partes* after *fuisse*, cf. Cic. *Div. Caec.* 56, Petron. *Sat.* 42, and other examples in Kühner-Stegmann II (i), pp. 593–94.
The verb *fuisse* here must have the force of *venio*.

37. Cf. J. Hellegouarc'h, *Le vocabulaire latin des relations et des partis
politiques sous la république*, pp. 110–15. *Partes* designates a group of people bound together by political interests, a *parti d'opinion*, but can also have
a more abstract value like *causa*. The phrase *suscipere causam* is analogous
to *suscipere partes*; this is exactly the sense of *partes* in 3.9.60.

38. Butler and Barber, *The Elegies of Propertius*, p. 286, and Camps, *Propertius: Elegies, Book III*, pp. 101–2, take *in partes tuas* to mean "on your side."

39. There may also be an echo of Hor. *Odes* 1.1.6: *terrarum dominos* in 3.9.23: *dominas secures*.

The Creation of Characters in the *Aeneid*

JASPER GRIFFIN

Recent writers on the *Aeneid* have made us more than ever aware of the complexity of the poem. Virgil's sources are numerous and belong to more than one category. Homeric epic, Attic tragedy, Hellenistic poetry, Roman myths, Naevius and Ennius and Catullus, learned etiologies and contemporary politics—all are blended into that great unity which attempts to sum up and to include the whole of the mythical and historical past and to show it as forming a pattern which will forever shape and dominate the future. In this essay I shall examine one aspect of that complexity, attempting to convey not only what the poet is doing in his creation and combination of characters, but what his purpose is and the importance of this side of the poem for the understanding of the whole.

Already in antiquity there were scholars who sought to explain actions of Aeneas by reference to Augustus and events of the poet's own time. The boys who take part in the Troy game at the funeral games of Anchises wear helmets and carry two spears; we read in Servius that "it is agreed that Virgil is here alluding to the presents which Augustus gave to the boys who took part in his games"—that is, the *lusus Troiae* on which he was so enthusiastic (*Aen.* 5.556). When Aeneas celebrates games and offers sacrifices at Actium, Servius observes that Augustus founded the *ludi Actiaci* and that Virgil "in honor of Augustus ascribes his actions to his ancestor" (*Aen.* 3.274). It is right to point out at once that the ancient commentators sometimes give examples of this method which startle us by their crudity; few modern scholars for example would want to accept the view that when at *Aen.* 1.292 Virgil speaks of "Remo cum fratre Quirinus," "the true explanation is that Quirinus is Augustus, while Remus is put for Agrippa, who married Augustus' daughter and waged his wars together with him" (Serv. ad loc.). We remember that this same method was applied to the *Eclogues* with unfortunate results, tending to turn them into a disguised autobiography of the poet. Thus Servius says of *Ecl.* 1.1 with a desperate note: "In this passage we should accept Virgil under the mask of Tityrus; but not everywhere, only where reason demands it." This sort of interpretation is no less subjective than others, and tact and common sense will be as vital here as anywhere else. I give a couple of modern examples.

You will remember the touching complaint of Dido, that Aeneas is sailing away and leaving her without even the comfort of a child by him:

> si quis mihi parvulus aula
> luderet Aeneas, qui te tamen ore referret,
> non equidem omnino capta ac deserta viderer
> [4.328–30]

In 1927, D. L. Drew thought that Sidonia Dido stood for Scribonia, the tiresome wife whom Octavian divorced after she had borne him a daughter; if only she had had a son she might not have been left, as Dido was left. This was, said Drew, a decidedly daring move on Virgil's part.[1] In 1973 A. A. Barrett said the passage was contemporary in reference but in a very different way: it was aimed at those who believed that Julius Caesar had fathered a child by Cleopatra.[2] The intrigue of Aeneas with Dido stands for that of Caesar with Cleopatra; Octavian's line was to deny that his adoptive father had offspring by her, and Virgil obliges by making Dido also explicitly childless.

A second and last example. In book 5 Aeneas opens the funeral games with a boat race. Drew believed that this stands for the boat race in Augustus' Actian games,[3] although unfortunately the sources describe this in a way which makes clear that it was not a race at all but a mock sea battle, a ναυμαχία; Kraggerud on the other hand maintains that it "will have reminded the reader of the triumphs of Roman fleets in Sicilian waters."[4] At least one reader is reminded that of the four craft which enter for the race one runs on the rocks, while the helmsman of a second is thrown overboard by his enraged skipper; the triumphs of Roman fleets seem but hollowly recalled by all this. These examples suggest that we have not left the Middle Ages; they contradict each other and cannot all be true—and yet they cannot be refuted.

The method of finding modern parallels to events and figures in the *Aeneid* has recently been revived, and with a particular twist, that of typology. It is at this that I want to look particularly in view of its vogue; it has been accepted for instance in the last fifteen years by Binder, Buchheit, Gransden, Knauer, Perret, von Albrecht, and Zinn.[5]

It is I think clear enough that Virgil is not simply telling a story about Aeneas interesting for its own sake, but that at least some of the episodes of the poem are to be understood as referring forward through time to contemporary affairs. I shall not enlarge upon this obvious point beyond one clear example: the otherwise unmotivated detail that Aeneas' son Ascanius was particularly fond of a boy called Atys, "from whom the Latin Atii derive their descent" (5.568). Ever since antiquity it has been seen that this is a compliment to the family of the Atii, to which Augustus' mother Atia belonged; the patrician Julii were already linked by affection with that not very distinguished clan in the mythical period. What we need to do is to inquire what is meant by applying the theological idea of typology to the relationships in the *Aeneid* and whether it is illuminating.

Typology is the process of "seeking correspondences between persons and events not (as allegory does) in meanings hidden in language, but actually in the course of history, and looking not to the fulfillment of a prediction, but to the recurrence of a pattern."[6] Before the birth of Christ this method was used by some rabbis in interpreting Old Testament utterances about the Messiah,[7] and it was given a decisive impetus by Saint Paul, above all in 1 Corinthians 10: the wanderings of the Israelites in the desert "happened to them by way of figure (or example: τυπικῶς), and they are written for our admonition, upon whom the ends of the world are come." Thus the rock which produced water to feed them in the desert was Christ, the spiritual rock. It is only the same road which is being followed when Gregory of Nyssa, for example, tells us that the manna on which the Israelites fed in the desert was the word of God, and that the rod with which Moses smote the bitter water and sweetened it was the cross, which makes spiritually palatable what before was bitter with sin.[8] Eusebius actually goes so far as to deny that Moses and the prophets were really concerned with their own contemporary history at all, "for they were not concerned with predicting matters which were transient and of interest only for the immediate future," but with Christology and the destiny of the whole human race,[9] while it is common to find such characters as Jacob, Isaac, Aaron, and Joshua interpreted as types of Christ.[10]

It is now being argued that the *Aeneid* is to be interpreted in this way. Thus Troy becomes a sort of Old Testament type of Rome and so also do the scenes which Virgil adapts from Greek epic, for new Rome transcends and replaces old Troy and also prevails over and replaces Greece, just as the career and significance of Christ transcend, exceed, and replace the typological models in the Old Testament. This is for instance the argument of G. N. Knauer,[11] who goes on to explain that this is also the reason why Virgil makes his Aeneas resemble both Odysseus and Achilles: he is to sum up and outdo the whole of the heroism of Greece. It is even being suggested that Virgil actually derived this conception from contemporary Jewish writers.[12] I shall argue that while Virgil does intend the reader to see the characters of one time in the light of those of another, yet in important respects the typological analogy is misleading; that there is no need or plausibility in invoking Jewish sources; and above all that in the creation of characters, as with other features of the *Aeneid*, complexity serves a deeper and more poetically interesting purpose than this sort of analysis suggests.

I begin by making the obvious point that Virgil was no stranger to suggestive and multilayered writing even before the *Aeneid*. The *Eclogues* are among the hardest poems to pin down ever written; nobody can read them without being aware that at times there is a second and more contemporary reference behind the surface meaning. We no longer fancy that we can pinpoint Virgil's farm on a map by careful study of *Eclogues* 1 and 9, but it remains unavoidable that in a disguised way the poet is glancing at recent political events. As if aware in advance that we should try to turn his poems into history, he has been careful to make his Tityrus both old and a slave and not therefore Virgil himself, just as he gives the farm lost by Menalcas topographical features incompatible with the realities of Mantua.[13] In *Eclogues* 5 his Daphnis both does and does not recall Caesar the murdered dictator; Gallus in *Eclogues* 10 is presented as a cross between a character out of Theocritus and the personification of the unhappy lover in his own poetry. As a pastoral figure he is set in Arcadia carving on the trees the name of his cruel mistress; in reality C. Cornelius Gallus was doubtless far away, and it was not a happy idea of the great Friedrich Leo to suppose that he was visiting Arcadia on leave from the army.[14] In *Eclogues* 4 Virgil has made his meaning so complex and suggestive that we shall never be able to unravel it all.

In all this I think we can be sure of one thing: he took a crucial hint from Theocritus' *Idyll* 7. That poem baffles the interpreters because it presents a real experience—the poet walks across the island of Cos with two perfectly real friends to a harvest festival given by another perfectly real person—in a disguised form: not Theocritus but Simichidas is the name of the narrator, and the encounter with the goatherd Lycidas is described in a way which recalls meetings with gods, and which obviously meant to its original audience some-thing which it cannot convey to us who are not in the know. This is coterie poetry; reality is represented in a disguised and ironic form. Virgil, who has no equal in literature for deftness in seizing and ex-ploiting the hints offered by his literary models, saw in this fascinat-ing poem an indication of the way in which he could maintain the perfection of Hellenistic literary form and polish, with the remote-ness from contemporary Rome which that seemed to entail, but at the same time introduce real life into his poetry. He could thus bring together the two sides that figured in the two different types of po-etry written by Catullus and his friends: the contemporary political poetry and the longer, more polished Hellenistic pieces in the style of Euphorion. This amalgamation of contemporary life and Hellenis-tic artistry and transformation of contemporary figures into poetic form had already been hinted at by Theocritus.

Hellenistic poetry then was a source for Virgil's allusive style of narration, and in particular for his creation of characters. Tityrus and Menalcas cannot be resolved into separate historical constitu-ents: Menalcas is and is not Virgil, as Daphnis is and is not Caesar and Dido is and is not Cleopatra. Other Hellenistic models offered themselves for the presentation of present reality in a mythological form. Callimachus in his *Hymn to Zeus* assimilates King Ptolemy to the god, and explains with curious fullness that Zeus' elder broth-ers were happy to let him be supreme although he was the youngest; we see here an allusion to the circumstances in which Ptolemy II Philadelphus succeeded his father in preference to his older half-brothers.[15] Theocritus at 17.128–34 assimilates the marriage of that Ptolemy with his own sister, repugnant to Greek sentiment, to the union of Zeus with his sister Hera. Virgil could find some partial models in Hellenistic poetry, where another myth was used so as to make us interpret the main myth in a certain complex way. Thus Apollonius of Rhodes makes his Jason, inducing Medea to help him against her own father, tell her about Ariadne, who helped Theseus against her father (3.998 ff., 1074 ff., 1096 ff.); he does not tell her what the poet tells us in case we do not know, that Theseus deserted Ariadne when she had served his turn (4.433 ff.). We see events in the light of that ironic parallel: in the same way Jason will abandon Medea when she has made the sacrifice for him, and although that does not actually happen by the end of the poem it casts its shadow over the union of the pair from its beginning.

But there were many other kinds of parallelism and identifica-tion which were available to influence the inquiring mind of Virgil within the Graeco-Roman tradition. I shall list in a necessarily summary way a number of forms which he could have found suggestive. First, because with *Eclogues* 4 we have touched on it already, oracular utterances. The world was full of oracles in Virgil's time—Augustus collected and burned great numbers of them. Characteristically the oracles preserved as Sibylline pretend to have been composed in the remote past; they "predict" in a cryptic style events which have in fact already happened. They also have a certain vagueness and suggestiveness: they abound in such designations as "a king of Egypt" or "a man wearing a purple cloak upon his shoulders, fierce and unrighteous and fiery" (3.389). The audience had to try to work out a particular application for such terms by looking at history, past and present, and seeing an appropriate person whom they were meant to fit. *Eclogues* 4 is explicitly oracular, and Anchises strikes the same note at the end of book 6 (the address *Romane* translates the 'Ρωμαῖε of the oracles). The oracular technique of hinting at more than is said and of referring to people in a way which is ambiguous among several possibilities was evidently of interest to Virgil.

Another set of ideas is closely related—that of time returning, with the corollary that events and even persons repeat themselves. This conception, which appears both in Pythagorean and in Stoic forms, was so generally familiar that we find, for instance, Virgil's contemporary Dionysius of Halicarnassus opening his work *On the Ancient Orators* by speculating whether the revival of taste for classical Attic oratory should be ascribed to "the natural cycle bringing the old order round again."[16] In *Eclogues* 4 Virgil imagined a second Trojan War and "another Tiphys" to steer the Argonauts again; here we have found another way in which great figures of the past could be seen in the actions of the present. "Redeunt Saturnia regna," said the oracular *Eclogue*: "Augustus shall establish the golden age again in the land where Saturn ruled," says Anchises (6.792 f.).

Such conceptions lead us to the interpretation of history in the light of models from the past. This is a fascinating subject which I can do no more than glance at. We know for instance that Alexander of Macedon compared himself to Achilles, and many historians regard this as central to him. Victor Ehrenberg speaks of "the sensation of mythical analogy so characteristic of Alexander." His tutor Lysimachus gave him the nickname Achilles in youth and called himself Phoenix after Achilles' tutor; he once even endangered the king's life by insisting upon going on a dangerous mission with him, claiming that he was no older than Phoenix when he went to Troy. Alexander also compared himself with Heracles and wore a lion's-head helmet, a symbol of that hero. There is some evidence that he even emulated Dionysus.[17] Alexander himself had an enormous impact upon the imagination of those who came after him. Many of the successor kings claimed descent from him, modeled their portraits on him, and tried to get for themselves as much as they could of the aura which came to surround him, of being the quintessence of royal splendor, glamor, and power.[18] Romans too felt the power of his spell, starting with Scipio Africanus and going on to Pompey and Antony; Cicero, writing a memorandum on government for Caesar, was "intentionally following the example of similar works written by Aristotle and Theopompus for Alexander."[19] Augustus in turn was anxious to assimilate himself to the great Macedonian. He used his portrait as his signet, he made a great show of touching his body at Alexandria,[20] and he seems to have encouraged the story that like Alexander he was conceived by his mother after a visit from a divine snake.[21] Augustan poets took hints from the panegyrics upon Alexander for their praise of Augustus.[22] He was also compared or identified with Romulus; the poets, not least Horace, associated him with Hercules, as G. K. Galinsky has so elegantly reminded us.[23] All this is different from rabbinical or Christian typology because it does not imply that the later figure of each pair outstrips and replaces the former, as the Messiah or the Christ fulfilled and replaced the Biblical models, nor that the whole of history is one story with a single pattern and meaning.

Closely related are the themes of propaganda and of family history. Great Roman families encouraged their young members to emulate the virtues of their ancestors, whose images were kept in the atrium and paraded through the streets at funerals. Augustus' funeral went beyond the normal practice and featured the images not only of his kinsmen but "of other Romans who had been prominent in any way, beginning with Romulus"; all were in a symbolic sense his ancestors.[24] Laudatory speeches also marked these occasions. And we observe that the more eminent *gentes* came to possess a definite character, so that a Gnaeus Piso was expected to be hard and proud, a Lucius Piso to be cultured and civilized, a Domitius Ahenobarbus to be ferocious—and Marcus Brutus was in great part forced to kill Caesar by the success of his own family's propaganda about Lucius Brutus the scourge of the kings. The Latin verb *patrissare*, to act like one's father, suggests by its form a Greek origin, but πατρίζειν is never found in extant Greek. This is an area especially Roman.[25]

Propaganda had long used the device of assimilating or identifying contemporary figures with those of myth, and the visual arts had cooperated. Already in Attic art of the sixth century B.C. the tyrant

Pisistratus had sought to identify himself with Heracles, while the democracy immediately after the overthrow of the Pisistratid dynasty encouraged a great boom in representations of Theseus. The Parthenon frieze offered a vision of recent history transposed into myth: Greeks fought against Trojans, Amazons, and centaurs while the gods fought the giants, a reflection of the struggle of Greece against Persia which made it symbolic, as part of a universal victory of civilization and order over barbarism and chaos.[26] The same sort of conception could be powerful in literature too—Isocrates urged Philip of Macedon to the conquest of Persia by urging on him the example of King Agamemnon, leader of all Greece against the barbarian (e.g., *Panathenaicus* 76 ff.). We have seen that his son Alexander preferred when the conquest came the less statesmanlike but more glamorous role of Achilles. For Romans, we find that the imagination of the educated class thought naturally of contemporary events in Homeric terms already in the second century B.C., when Cato told Polybius that if he ventured to face the Senate again he would be like Odysseus going back into the Cyclops' cave to fetch his cap and belt, and when Scipio Aemilianus, walking on the ruined site of Carthage, quoted the Homeric lines "There will be a day when Troy will fall," seeing in the doom of Carthage a warning of the fate of Rome.[27]

Romans thought of history as a whole, not merely of their own family trees, as full of *exempla*,[28] and the parade of heroes in the sixth book of the *Aeneid* finds its three-dimensional counterpart in the statues of Roman worthies with which Augustus adorned his Forum, declaring in a public edict that they were to be an exemplar by which he himself and later *principes* could be judged.[29] Cicero repeatedly places himself in a sequence of noble defenders of Rome against the demagogues and the assassins: Scipio Nasica, L. Opimius, Metellus Numidicus. At moments he goes so far as to compare himself with the Decii (*Dom.* 64) or even with Romulus (*Cat.* 3.2). Against him he saw his antagonist of the moment as in another succession, that of the villains: the Gracchi, Saturninus, Sulpicius, Catiline, Clodius, Antony.[30] It is natural to him to call Clodius "a lucky Catiline," Apronius "another Verres," L. Piso "that Semiramis" and "a barbarian Epicurus"; Calpurnius Bestia is "another Caesar Vopiscus," while Antony is called "you new Hannibal" and Verres "another Cyclops." Cicero himself by contrast will be "an immortal example of *fides publica*."[31] No wonder he emphasizes that the orator must have in his mind "the whole force of old times and of historical examples," so that, for instance, he can discredit an opponent by saying something like "When I looked at Considius, I thought I was seeing the Blossii and the Vibellii of old,"[32] the proud leaders of a Campania hostile to Rome. All this shows how natural Romans found it to "see through history"[33] and to recognize one event or person in another. We see it again in the quickness of theater audiences in the late republic at picking up and exploiting any allusion in a play which could be made to apply to an unpopular figure of the time. Cicero gives us many examples, and in the speech in defence of Sestius he says that the audience never failed to catch a possible allusion (118).

It is not even a long step from here to the "canons" in which it was natural for Roman poets to arrange themselves. Ovid clearly puts himself in a succession of elegiac poets, number four after Gallus, Tibullus, and Propertius, while Propertius was proud to present himself as a Roman version of a Greek poet, *Romanus Callimachus*.[34] These poets find a form for their own aesthetic ideas and experiences by putting themselves in the position of a predecessor. Thus Virgil, Propertius, and the rest borrow a scene (the poet instructed by Apollo) from the opening of the *Aitia* of Callimachus, who in his turn was producing a variant on a celebrated experience of Hesiod. This blends easily with such things as Mark Antony, after his defeat at Actium, sulking on Pharos and saying that he would "live the life of Timon the Misanthrope, since his experiences had been the same" (Plut. *Ant.* 69.4).

In religion, identifying women and men with goddesses and gods had by this date a long history. Again a few examples must suffice. Pericles was called "Zeus"; Ptolemy II liked to be identified with Zeus by his poets; Ptolemy III had himself depicted on his coins with the attributes of Zeus, Poseidon, and Helios; Mithradates Eupator was greeted by the Greeks of Asia as Dionysus; Antony called himself "New Dionysus." Lunatics claimed to be gods, and sometimes succeeded in attracting a following. Characters in Plautus freely call themselves and others by such names as Jupiter, Juno, Mars, Venus, Achilles, and so on: "O my Juno, you shouldn't be so cross with your Jupiter" (Plaut. *Cas.* 2.3.14). Proverbial expressions abounded, such as "This is another Heracles," "Another Phrynondas" (of scoundrels), "The man is a Theramenes," "Agamemnon's feast," "Ajax' laughter." At a deeper level some religious activities were conceived as reenactments of mythical events. That is clearly true, for instance, of maenadism, where the worshipper acts out afresh the events of the mythical past.[35] Akin to this but more poetical is the practice of Propertius, making the myths "symboles sensibles d'une réalité secrète, une vérité dissimulée dont sa propre expérience lui a donné l'intuition."[36] The amorous and enchanting heroines of his myths present for Propertius a world not only more attractive but also in a way more real than the unsatisfactory and matter-of-fact world of Augustan Rome; he sees himself in the role of Paris or Odysseus to the Helen or Calypso of his beloved. In the novel, both Greek and Latin, characters similarly "see" their own experiences in the light of mythical models. For instance, Chariton 5.10.1: "What Protesilaus is this who has come back to life in my time?"; Achill. Tat. 2.23.3: "There is your Cyclops asleep—be a bold Odysseus"; Petron. 9: "If you are a Lucretia, you have found your Tarquin"; and so on.

The last of this kaleidoscopic series shall be the self-conscious classicism of Augustus and Augustan Rome. The emperor, who claimed to have turned a city of brick into a city of marble, aimed both in architecture and in other arts at the classic style of the fifth century B.C., and in such a work as the Ara Pacis his artists succeeded in creating something distinctively Augustan by combining in one masterpiece the imperial family with Mars and Aeneas and with the symbolic female figures of Rome and Italy.[37] Augustus boasted that he never made innovations, and he liked to present anything new as a revival of the past and himself as an old-fashioned Roman. We can see in this a reflection of the nostalgia for the past which pervades the *Eclogues* and *Georgics*, and which Livy expresses so memorably in the *praefatio* to his history. Messages for the present and feelings about it are in such a time naturally expressed in terms of the past.

The purpose of my long catalog has been to suggest that there is no need to look outside perfectly familiar features of Graeco-Roman thought and invoke the practice of Jewish rabbis in order to find the background to Virgil's practice. What he does is not in reality closer to the typological exegesis of the Old Testament than it is to these other practices. For Virgil there is not simply one present story in the light of which the past is reinterpreted: past history is itself multilayered. The voyage of Aeneas to Italy has echoes of the voyage of Odysseus, but it also recalls in a more distant past the exile of Dardanus, an Italian before he went to Troy, and it places the hero in relation to the wanderings of Hercules, which are themselves outdone by the labors and journeys of Augustus (*Aen.* 6.801). Nor is it only the case that we see different times and various events, all of which mutually illuminate and explain each other. Virgil also uses the device to bring out and to do justice to the complexity of our attitude to his story and to Rome itself.

In the first half of the *Aeneid* the main model for the experiences of Aeneas is of course the Odysseus of the *Odyssey*; in the second half he bears a general resemblance to the Achilles of the *Iliad*, culminating in his slaying of Turnus in a scene evocative of the slaying of Hector. But the picture is far more complex. His relationship to Dido and Lavinia cause his enemies to see him as Paris, the foreigner who seduces or abducts local queens (4.215, cf. 9.592 ff.). From another point of view he plays the role of Menelaus, demanding his wife who is kept from him in a foreign city. Indeed, the scene in book 12 where he is wounded in a breach of the truce puts him in the role of the Menelaus of *Iliad* 4. With Dido, Aeneas is not only Odysseus (telling his adventures to the Phaeacians and having to disentangle himself from Calypso), but he also plays the role of Apollonius' Jason. Jason both abandons Hypsipyle (book 1) and beds with Medea in a cave (book 4), so that we have echoes of two relationships of Apollonius' hero, not one. When he comes to visit Evander, we see him take on some of the coloring of Telemachus visiting Nestor and Menelaus; when he celebrates games at Actium, as we have seen, he foreshadows Augustus, while as for Heracles, in the words of G. K. Galinsky "Virgil assimilates Aeneas to Heracles from the very beginning."[38] He is a Trojan patriot, an Italian (descended from the Italian Dardanus), a Roman, an Augustan.

The other important characters are no less complex. Turnus, who dies the death of Hector, was predicted by the Sibyl to become an Achilles, and was born of a goddess as Achilles was (6.89 f.). The champion of Italy against the invader, he traces his descent back to Agamemnon's city of Mycenae (7.372). Dido at her first appearance is seen in the light of Nausicaa; then she entertains Aeneas just as Arete and Alcinous, queen and king of the Phaeacians, entertained Odysseus. She attempts to hold on to him, like Calypso; she is united with him in a cave, like Medea; when she is abandoned she echoes the abandoned Ariadne of Catullus 64 (4.316). But she also incarnates the national enemy in Carthage, she is a founder of a city like Aeneas himself, and when she comes to review her own career before her suicide she speaks in the style of the Roman general in his *elogium*, his epitaph for himself (4.655 f.).[39] Through the figure of the foreign queen who tries to seduce the Roman from his destiny and his home we feel a certain vibration of the unforgettable Cleopatra.

All this is perhaps obvious enough, but the important thing is what Virgil does with all this learning and all these parallels. As we saw, those who believe in typological explanations see this matter as essentially simple: according to Knauer, for example, Virgil shows how greater Rome exceeds and eclipses lesser Troy,[40] and, according to Perret, Virgil presents in Aeneas a hero who assumes the qualities of earlier heroes such as Odysseus and Achilles, but who supersedes them.[41] The reality is more complex and more interesting. When Dido appears in the light of the young Nausicaa or the touching Ariadne, part of our response to her derives from our response to those models and to the emotional resonance which they bring with them. When she turns to magic like Medea or Circe, we experience a different emotion: the pity appropriate to a young girl is overlaid by the horror and revulsion we feel for a witch. When she struggles to retain her dignity while at the same time asking him to stay, memories of our attitude towards Calypso in *Odyssey* 5 are aroused; when she curses the hero and Rome and invokes the idea of Hannibal as her avenger, we are meant to feel the chill of fear which that terrible memory always had for a Roman.

Even more, the hero of the poem himself, as he appears in different roles and different lights, calls forth different responses. It is wrong to say, as scholars are prone to do, that Aeneas "is" or "is not" Achilles.[42] We respond to him in many different ways in the course of his adventures and experiences, and all of those ways contribute to the total sum of our attitude and judgment on him. In his affair with Dido he puts himself in the line of the seducers of mythology who sail away and leave the weeping heroine behind; our response to him in that role, colored as it is by our response to Jason and to Theseus, must be at least in part negative. In this pattern the heroine is the one who must win our sympathy. When Aeneas in the footsteps of Achilles slays Turnus, our response is colored by our emotions when we see Achilles kill Hector; although Achilles is the great hero, Hector is humanly an attractive figure, and his death is tragic. So too we feel that the death of Turnus is tragic. On the one side Virgil has given full justification for his slaying and he must die; on the other he has used our emotional memory of Hector to cause us a certain reluctance to see his death. In the same way we feel a certain unease when Aeneas, urged on by heaven and the bidding of manifest destiny, sails away from a deserted heroine who has recalled some attractive and glamorous literary models.

All this might of course be a mere chaos of contradictory directives and muddled purposes on Virgil's part. It is in reality more than that, because this complexity of response is a vital part of the poet's intention and of the greatness of his poem. I shall not argue here the case for believing that the *Aeneid* is more than the straightforward glorification of Augustus, Rome, and imperialism which no doubt Augustus himself hoped to get. The Roman hero is forced by his hard destiny to turn away from the attractions of philosophy and art: others, Anchises tells Aeneas, will excel in the arts, while for the

Roman there remains the self-denying role of the conqueror and leg-
islator (6.847–53). The triumph of Aeneas and of Rome is willed by
heaven, it is the end and meaning of history; and yet Aeneas must
lose home and wife, Dido and Pallas, while L. Brutus must slay his
own sons for the republic, and Rome must be deprived of the most
wonderful Roman of them all, Marcellus. The heavy cost of imperialism is not underrated by Virgil, and that is not the least of the reasons why his epic is so great. Whereas other Roman writers, even of
the rank of Horace, were content to assert in separate places both
that Roman conquest was splendid and admirable, and also that aggressive war was wrong and greedy and that only pleasure and
beauty mattered, Virgil alone faced the real problems and attempted
to solve them. The *Aeneid* was to show both the greatness of Rome
and also its human cost, not denying or minimizing either of them
nor separating them off into compartments in which each one could
be developed without mentioning the other, but doing full justice to
both and looking both steadily in the eye. Not the least powerful of
Virgil's devices for achieving this is the way he exploits our familiarity with his literary predecessors and our emotional response to
them.

Because we have felt for Dido a complex of emotions evoked by
Nausicaa and Calypso and Medea and Cleopatra, our response to her
destruction must also be complex. The opponent of destiny and the
enemy of Rome must yield to the inevitable, and must indeed have
brought her ruin on herself, but the beautiful and loving heroine
must win our sympathy in her suffering and death. The complex
harmony is not to be resolved into its simple elements. The doom of
Dido is fundamentally complex and meant to be felt as such. This
was the price of Rome: the hero does right to sail away and let her
die, but he does so in the wake of too many mythological seducers
for us not to feel that his hands, like theirs, are dirty. The death of
Turnus, dashing and brave yet wrongheaded and impossible, repeats
the same bitter lesson. As Achilles standing over the dying Hector
rejects his prayer for burial and kills him without mercy, so Aeneas
standing over the helpless Turnus rejects his prayer for life and kills
him when he might have let him live. The belt of Pallas on Turnus'
armor justifies his killing, but our sympathy for Hector helps Virgil
to force on us the tragedy of Turnus' death. That too was part of the
price. Aeneas would have preferred to avoid paying it and to let him
live, and we too in a way would have preferred to see him spared, but
empire is not won without such tragedies.

In conclusion, I should like to make three points in a form necessarily summary. First, if what I have been saying makes sense then

the idea of typology is fundamentally inapplicable to the *Aeneid*. No typological exegesis sets out to show that events in the Old Testament place events in the New Testament in a morally dubious or complex light, and conversely the *Aeneid* does not represent Rome as simply the triumph and justification of Troy. Rome remains a morally complex phenomenon, and the devices we have been considering help to make it so. Rather than talk in the language of Biblical exposition it will be better to stick to such cautious terms as those of R. Syme: "The poem is not an allegory, but no contemporary could fail to detect in Aeneas a foreshadowing of Augustus."[43] There is a relationship, a foreshadowing, but it is not to be reduced to an identity, even a typological one.

Second, we see again from another angle the vital importance to Virgil of his learning. What might have been a mere burden of decorative or insignificant *doctrina* is put to work in the service of the central purposes of the poem. We do not simply enjoy the pleasure of recognition of a source, but we are guided in our emotional response by Virgil's use of that recognition. He does so in a way that helps him with the task, which must have seemed almost impossible, of developing throughout the poem both sides of the Roman destiny of imperialism.

Third and finally, we see again that even the most highly poetical devices of Roman poetry do not exist in isolation from the realities of ordinary life. The poetry of love is intimately linked with the facts of the life of pleasure and does not exist in a separate world of literary genres and conventions.[44] Virgil, too, in his brilliant exploitation of the device of presenting characters in the light of other characters, of seeing through his Aeneas at one moment Achilles, at another Menelaus, at another Augustus, was following up not an exotic and special borrowing from Judea but a habit familiar in the law courts, in proverbs, in religion, in politics. Even when he looks through complex vistas of history and mythology, Virgil still belongs to his own world. That was what gave him the power to be its truest interpreter.

NOTES

1. D. L. Drew, *The Allegory of the Aeneid*, p. 83.
2. A. A. Barrett, "Dido's Child: A Note on *Aeneid* 4.327–30," *Maia* 25 (1973): 51–53.
3. Drew, *The Allegory of the Aeneid*, p. 53.
4. E. Kraggerud, *Aeneisstudien, Symb. Oslo.* Suppl. 22: 128.

5. G. Binder, *Aeneas und Augustus: Interpretationen zum 8. Buch der Aeneis*; V. Buchheit, *Der Anspruch des Dichters in Vergils Georgika*, p. 85; K. W. Gransden, *Aeneid Book VIII*, pp. 14 ff.; G. N. Knauer, *Die Aeneis und Homer*, pp. 354 ff.; J. Perret, "Du nouveau sur Homère et Virgile, Review of G. N. Knauer, *Die Aeneis und Homer*," *REL* 43 (1965): 128; M. von Albrecht, "Die Kunst der Spiegelung in Vergils *Aeneis*," *Hermes* 93 (1965): 55; E. Zinn, "Nachwort zu V's *Aeneis*," in *Vergil-Horaz*, trans. R. A. Schröder, vol. 5, p. 320. Programmatically, von Albrecht, "Vergils Geschichtsauffassung in der 'Heldenschau,'" *WS* 80 (1967): 182: "Vergils Weg durch die römische Geschichte steht im Zeichen typologischer Zusammenschau. . . ."

6. See N. Nakagawa, "Typologie im NT," p. 1095.

7. Ibid.

8. Gregory of Nyssa *Vita Moysis* 140 and 131.

9. Eus. *Dem. Evang.* 5, *Praef.* 20–24.

10. *Patristic Greek Lexicon*, ed. Lampe, s.v. τύπος, D.

11. Knauer, *Die Aeneis und Homer*, p. 352. Cf. Buchheit, *Der Anspruch des Dichters*, p. 85, on Octavian as "Steigerung und Endpunkt."

12. D. Thompson, "Allegory and Typology in the *Aeneid*," *Arethusa* 3 (1971): 151.

13. See Conington's remark on *Ecl.* 9.7: "There are no hills or beeches in the Mantuan territory" (J. Conington and H. Nettleship, *The Works of Virgil*, vol. 1, p. 106).

14. F. Leo, "Virgil und die *Ciris*," *Hermes* 37 (1902): 18.

15. See W. Meincke, *Untersuchungen zu den enkomiastischen Gedichten Theokrits*, pp. 175 ff., rather than the commentary by G. R. McLennan, *Callimachus. Hymn to Zeus: Introduction and Commentary*, p. 99.

16. Dion. Hal. 1.2.2.

17. V. Ehrenberg, *Alexander and the Greeks*, p. 55. "Die Gestalt, die für ihn zum zentralen Erlebnis geworden war, war Achilleus": F. Taeger, *Charisma: Studien zur Geschichte des antiken Herrscherkultes*, vol. 2, p. 185. Lysimachus: R. Lane Fox, *Alexander the Great*, p. 59. Cf. Arrian 7.14.4: κατὰ ζῆλον τὸν Ἀχιλλέως, πρὸς ὅντινα ἐκ παιδὸς φιλοτιμία αὐτῷ ἦν. Heracles: F. Schachermeyr, *Alexander der Grosse: Das Problem seiner Persönlichkeit und seines Wirkens*, p. 408: "Alexander glaubte ja allen Ernstes, ein zweiter Herakles zu werden, ja zu sein. . . ." The helmet: Lane Fox, p. 443. Dionysus: Schachermeyr, p. 411, Lane Fox, p. 399, U. Wilcken, *Alexander der Grosse*, pp. 167 ff., but cf. A. D. Nock, "Notes on Ruler-Cult, I–V," *JHS* 48 (1928): 20 ff. See also J. Perret, *Les origines de la légende troyenne de Rome*, pp. 419–30.

18. E.g. A. Heuss, "Alexander der Grosse und die politische Ideologie des Altertums," *A&A* 4 (1954): 65–104, D. Michel, *Alexander als Vorbild für Pompeius, Caesar und M. Antonius*, O. Wippert, *Alexander-Imitatio und röm. Politik in der rep. Zeit.* Sallust *H.* 3.88M: "Pompeius a prima adulescentia sermone fautorum similem fore se credens Alexandro regi, facta consultaque eius quidem aemulatus erat."

19. S. Weinstock, *Divus Julius*, p. 188.

20. "Deutlicher als durch diesen Akt konnte sich Oktavian gar nicht in die Nachfolge Alexanders stellen," D. Kienast, "Augustus und Alexander," *Gymn.* 76 (1969): 451.

21. F. Blumenthal, "Autobiographie des Augustus," *WS* 35 (1913): 122.

22. E. Norden, *Kleine Schriften zum klassischen Altertum*, ed. B. Kytzler, pp. 422 ff.

23. K. Scott, "The Identification of Augustus with Romulus-Quirinus," *TAPA* 56 (1925): 82–105. G. K. Galinsky, *The Herakles Theme*, pp. 138–41.

24. Dio Cass. 56.34.2; H. T. Rowell, "The Forum and Funeral Images of Augustus," *MAAR* 17 (1940): 132 ff.

25. E. Bethe, *Ahnenbild und Familiengeschichte bei Römern und Griechen*, pp. 39 ff., 85.

26. J. Boardman, "Herakles, Peisistratos and Sons," *RA* (1972): 59, and "Herakles, Peisistratos and Eleusis," *JRS* 95 (1975): 1–12; cf. also C. Sourvinou-Inwood, "Theseus Lifting the Rock and a Cup near the Pithos Painter," *JHS* 91 (1971): 98 ff., and references there; K. Schefold, "Antwort klassischer Sagenbilder auf politisches Geschehen," *GB* 4 (1975): 231–42.

27. Cato: Polyb. 35.6.4. Scipio: Polyb. 38.22.2.

28. For instance, E. Skard, "Zu Horaz, *Ep.* 1.11," *Symb. Oslo.* 40 (1965): 57 ff., V. Buchheit, "Vergilische Geschichtsdeutung," *GB* 1 (1973): 38, Cic. *De Or.* 1.201, *Orat.* 120, *Mur.* 66, *Sest.* 130, *Prov. Cons.* 21, *Rab. Post.* 2, *Phil.* 2.26.

29. Suet. *Aug.* 31; A. Degrassi, "Virgilio e il foro di Augusto," *Epigrafica* 7 (1945): 88–103.

30. Cf. Cic. *Sest.* 37 with the note of H. A. Holden; *Har. Resp.* 41 with the note of J. O. Lenaghan; V. Buchheit, "Ciceros Triumph des Geistes," *Gymn.* 76 (1969): 232 and 245.

31. Cic. *Dom.* 72, *Verr.* 3.31, *Prov. Cons.* 9, *Pis.* 20, *Phil.* 11.11, *Phil.* 13.25, *Verr.* 5.146, *Sest.* 50.

32. Cic. *Leg. Agr.* 2.93.

33. διδεῖν ἐκ τῆς ἱστορίας, a phrase of Gregory of Nyssa, *Vita Moysis* 14b.

34. Ov. *Tr.* 4.10.51–54; Prop. 4.1.64.

35. Pericles: cf. O. Weinreich, *Menekrates Zeus und Salmoneus*, p. 82; Ptolemy II: cf. Callim. *H.*1, Theoc. 17; Ptolemy III: F. Taeger, *Charisma*, vol. 2, p. 300; Mithradates Eupator: Cic. *Flac.* 60; Antony: e.g., L. R. Taylor, *Divinity of the Roman Emperor*, p. 109; Lunatics: Weinreich, op. cit.; Plautus: E. Fraenkel, *Elementi Plautini in Plauto*, pp. 89 ff.; maenadism: A. Henrichs, "Greek Maenadism from Olympias to Messalina," *HSCP* 82 (1978): 121–60; p. 144, "The Greeks understood maenadism as a reenactment of myth." Ovidian passages where *Iuppiter* stands for Augustus are listed by P. Riewald, *De imperatorum Romanorum cum certis dis . . . aequatione*, pp. 274 ff.

36. P. Grimal, *L'Amour à Rome*, p. 194; cf. also J.-P. Boucher, *Etudes sur Properce*, C. W. Macleod, "A Use of Myth in Ancient Poetry," *CQ* 24 (1974): 82–93.

37. See, for instance, E. Simon, *Ara Pacis Augustae*, pp. 22–29, A. Boëthius, *The Golden House of Nero: Some Aspects of Roman Architecture*, p. 89.

38. Galinsky, *The Herakles Theme*, p. 132.

39. "Urbem praeclaram statui, mea moenia vidi, / ulta virum poenas inimico a fratre recepi." On this passage see E. Fraenkel, *Kleine Beiträge zur klassischen Philologie*, vol. 2, pp. 73, 141, 223. I regard as too flimsy the associations of Dido with Scribonia (Drew, *The Allegory of the Aeneid*, p. 82) and with Pasiphaë (Kraggerud, *Aeneisstudien*, p. 60).

40. Knauer, *Die Aeneis und Homer*.

41. Perret, "Du nouveau sur Homère et Virgile."

42. Thus, for instance, W. S. Anderson, "Vergil's Second *Iliad*," *TAPA* 88 (1957): 27, calls Aeneas "the true Achilles of this *Iliad*," whereas V. Pöschl, *The Art of Vergil: Image and Symbol in the Aeneid*, p. 115, believes that "all that is significant about (Turnus) comes from Achilles"; cf. also p. 127, where he insists "It is not Hector . . . who is the real model for Turnus, as has always been assumed, but Achilles." The flatness of such a contradiction—and arguments can be offered on both sides—ought to suggest that something is seriously amiss with the procedures that produce it.

43. R. Syme, *The Roman Revolution*, p. 463.

44. J. Griffin, "Augustan Poetry and the Life of Luxury," *JRS* 56 (1976): 87–105.

Patrons, Painters, and Patterns: The Anonymity of Romano-Campanian Painting and the Transition from the Second to the Third Style

ELEANOR WINSOR LEACH

The direction to be taken in the study of patronage in Romano-Campanian painting has been dictated by those accidents of survival that have left us a large number of paintings located almost entirely in houses, while almost all paintings in public buildings have been lost. Where our interest in literary patronage centers primarily upon the author's career and his work, here it is less the painter than the patron we want to investigate. To what extent did the decorations of his house reflect his social standing, the rituals of his life, the level of his culture, or even his private fantasies? [1]

Fragments of painted plaster from the archaic houses on the Via Sacra suggest that the custom of painting interiors is very old,[2] although our literary evidence is generally thought to describe only those traditions of the Pompeian first style which may have begun some time in the second century B.C. Similarly, scraps of literary evidence suggest that the public tradition may be even older than the domestic, but we are even less able to trace this tradition back to its beginnings or to follow it very accurately in its development.[3] No more can we be certain how patronage first began to become involved in either private or public painting, in spite of a legendary tradition that made Demaratus of Corinth, father of Tarquin, the first to import a painter into Italy (Pliny *HN* 35.16). Our understanding of Roman traditions is faced with the virtual anonymity of patrons and painters alike. Although in public Roman art the anonymity of the artist may be a true reflection of the dominant shaping purpose of the patron, in private art the traditions established by the painters render the patrons anonymous.

The few remarks made by Pliny the Elder on the history of Roman painting suggest that its public and private traditions stood apart not so much on account of patronage or the artistic merit of the productions or even the difference between painted walls and *tabulae*, but rather because of their orientation toward either the domestic or civic sphere.[4] We have reason to assume that a public tradition still flourished under patronage in the late republic and early empire alongside the many Greek paintings then on display, but we must also assume that this tradition differed considerably from those of the domestic painting that we know.

If we were able to approach the interpretation of painting within the private tradition through our knowledge of patronage in the public world, we would naturally feel more secure, but these efforts would probably be misdirected even if the necessary information could be gathered.[5] In the essay "Roman Art in Modern Perspective," Otto Brendel emphasizes the distance between the imagery of those public monuments that give us the core of Roman art history and of decorative painting in the private sphere. In no period is the total artistic production uniform, but always the official art of Rome is isolated as a special class. Such a division, Brendel notes, "was itself typically Roman, but so were the two kinds of art that followed from this dualism, representing not only two separate strains of tradition, but also two sides of an identical historical situation that produced them both."[6] Neither is more Roman than the other.

We can make an approximation of such a distinction between the two types of art by contrasting two works executed in different media: the landscape designs of the sculptured end walls of the Ara Pacis and a wall painting from the Villa at Boscotrecase of a roughly contemporary date. Although each presents problems of interpretation, the problems are different in a manner that reflects the differing concerns of public and private patronage, even if the understandable urge to find links between the works of a period has led some to find their common inspiration in the optimistic spirit of Augustan Rome.[7] The Ara Pacis panels are not in fact landscapes but allegorical and historical compositions employing abstract elements of natural symbolism. The great maternal figure sits surrounded by emblems of abundance. Behind the children in her lap are poppies and grain that do not grow out of any solid base of earth but hang suspended in air. The upturned urn by her side pouring forth a stream of water is likewise iconographical. In spite of the token animals in the foreground, this is not a pastoral scene but a well-balanced gathering of figures outside of space and time. In the panel representing a sacrifice (fig. 1), the rough altar of piled stones that provides an organizing center for the action vaguely suggests primitive times. The rocky background supporting a small temple at an ambiguous distance from the foreground is no doubt equally primitive, but it is only from the figures and their action that we draw such conclusions about

1. Ara Pacis Augusti, Rome, 9 B.C. Sacrifice panel. Alinari/Editorial Photocolor Archives.

these elements. In themselves, they are no more than compositional props for the ritual scene.

The painted landscape also presents an image of ritual (fig. 2), but one that is both in composition and idea wholly unrelated to the Ara Pacis scene. Both allegory and narrative are absent; we appreciate this piece on compositional principles alone, observing its spatial juxtapositions and contrasts of forms within a symmetrical order that produces an impression of great tranquillity. This calm atmosphere is nonetheless neither archaic nor timeless, for the elegant background buildings invoke the contemporary world. At the same time that this is a more coherent landscape, however, it is harder to interpret than the Ara Pacis panels. If the specific identity of the maternal figure raises questions,[8] her appropriateness to the contextual theme of Pax remains self-evident. Likewise the sacrificer has an understandable place in the rites of the state religion, his gesture representing a significant moment in Rome's legendary his-

2. Villa of Agrippa Postumus at Boscotrecase. Sacral-idyllic landscape from the north wall of the Red Room. Deutsches Archaeologisches Institut Neg. 59.1973.

tory that merges present and past. But the rural shrine with its villa background may be seen in mutually contradictory ways—as an elicitation of pristine *pietas* in full Augustan moral dress or as a fashionably sentimental fantasy of the lure of the countryside.[9] Should we think of eighty-two temples rebuilt in accordance with senatorial decree, or of Horace's and Tibullus' exploitation of the ethic of simplicity in the service of the self-satisfied private life? In precisely such efforts at interpretation we crave a missing knowledge of the communication between patron and painter to supply us with the equivalent of a poetic context.

Not only are accounts of such communication lacking in our ancient literary discussions of painting, but also the tradition that has governed scholarship on Roman painting since the late nineteenth century has fixed its attention upon the study of painters and the evolution, almost *sua sponte*, of their work. Out of the chronological system of the four styles has developed an interest in refining the internal chronology of each style in such a manner as to give each house in Rome or Campania its relative position within a theoretical history of artistic evolution. In first developing his four stylistic categories, August Mau proceeded upon the assumption that the patterns for each style—and thus the shape of the entire chronology—had their backgrounds in Eastern cities from where, step by step, they migrated to Rome.[10] His pioneering discussion left virtually no place for the taste of a patron in determining the decoration of his house. Although succeeding scholars have refined Mau's theories, and the issue of indigenous origins for or influences upon the designs has been continually debated, the assumptions underlying our interpretations of painting have remained evolutionary. We are left with the fact that a system based primarily upon a self-generating progress in style does not fully account for the role of the decorated wall in shaping the environment of Roman domestic life, nor fully exploit the potential significance of Roman themes in Roman art.

Toward an investigation of these matters, the literary evidence has perhaps one contribution to offer. Where it touches upon the periods of the second and early third style, our stylistic chronology corresponds with the testimony of Vitruvius, a writer of Augustan date whose *Decem libri de architectura* provides our only extensive description of the appearance of paintings. Within the context of animadversions against contemporary taste and judgment, Vitruvius drops what may well be our best hints of the influence of patron upon painter, even if his account leaves many questions unanswered and the information to be gleaned comes as much from grammatical inference as from direct statement.

The ancients (*antiqui*), Vitruvius observes, painted walls in imitation of marble revetments and went on to place stones and cornices in varied arrangements. Throughout his brief outline of the decorative modes we identify as the first and second styles he makes no mention of patrons, but rather his verbs in the third person plural refer to the painters and to their productions (7.5.1–3). The artists progressed, as he puts it (*ingressi sunt*), to the point of rendering architectonic forms or projecting columns and gables along with a number of popular topics: landscapes in *exedrae*, stage fronts, megalographic deities, and heroic scenes. Although this range of possibilities might seem to have offered some choice to patrons, what Vitruvius emphasizes instead is the suitability of some topics to the spaces afforded by particular kinds of rooms. Commending all these subjects for their preservation of fidelity to natural appearances, he then goes on to expostulate: "haec quae ex veris rebus exemplis sumebantur, nunc iniquis moribus improbantur." With this last word, spectators enter whose fickle disregard of natural truth plays an active role in influencing art. There follows a list of monstrous images defying probability: reeds set up in place of columns, candelabra supporting pediments, calyxes sporting figures of men and beasts—"things that never are, nor could be, nor have been." The fault, Vitruvius continues, lies with judges whose poor taste has defeated the virtues of art: "at haec falsa videntes homines non reprehendunt, sed delectantur, neque animadvertant si quid eorum fieri potest nec ne." Although there is no hint of the sources from which painters might have derived their new fancy for unnatural innovations, their persistence through encouragement is clear.

Vitruvius' standards are conservative and his analysis of contemporary decoration, as I shall later show, reveals an almost perverse blindness to the nature and function of its ornamental components. All the same his indication of an alteration in taste accompanied by a new reciprocity between patron and painter in establishing the representational trend of decoration is in agreement with the evidence offered both by Rome and by Pompeii, and makes it possible to piece together more than he tells us when we turn to the evidence itself. The rich period of the late republic and early Augustan age that his remarks encompass is one in which the subjects represented in paintings can be read very clearly, and where our ability to read them has been greatly enhanced by recent discoveries that give a new order to the corpus. Although the variety of the second style is considerable, we can sort out two major subjects that constituted, I believe, the basis for competition between workshops. These subjects were so well adapted to the needs and desires of their purchasers as to provide apt settings for the rituals of Roman life. Within this context, the transition from second to third style is less an evolution than a revolution, one based upon the widespread appeal of a single subject. One forerunner of third-style painting can be seen among the productions of second-style workshops in Pompeii. Although the emergence into popularity of this type cannot be traced, once it had reached its ascendency it dominated Romano-Campanian mural painting for sixty years. The popularity of the new style can be explained by its capacity for balancing the interests of painters and patrons; it was a format that offered choices to the patron yet gave the painter full opportunity for innovation. The one major revolution that took place within the traditions of Romano-Campanian painting was fully Roman in character and, at its inception, wholly in keeping with the social disposition of the Augustan age.

To understand the significance of recent discovery, we must first go back to a room that has long been at the center of all controversy surrounding the meaning and development of the second style: the familiar room from the villa of P. Fannius Sinistor at Boscoreale now in the possession of the New York Metropolitan Museum of Art (fig. 3). Of the several painted rooms of a rather substantial villa on the slopes of Vesuvius excavated in the 1920s, this is the only one now to be seen in its complete form, the two walls of the stylistically related "summer triclinium" having been divided between the Museo Nazionale in Naples and the Chateau de Mariemont in Belgium. Along with the paintings in the Pompeian Villa dei Misteri, the Casa del Labirinto, and the Casa del Criptoportico, Boscoreale has, until recently, constituted our largest single portion of the corpus of the second style.

Among these examples the complexity of the New York room is unique. The decoration divides the walls into an antechamber and alcove, each part distinguished by a symmetrically ordered set of three panels. On the side walls forming the antechamber, a great gate standing before a statue within a *syzygia* is flanked by matching panels with a panorama of doors and balconies, while the side panels of the alcove show hollow pediments framing a tholos. The design of the rear wall is that of a grotto and arbor. This room, commonly called a cubiculum, has been assigned its chronological place at the climax of second-style evolution marking the stage at which the architectonic design achieves its greatest degree of openness and its

3. Villa of P. Fannius Sinistor at Boscoreale. Cubiculum in the Metropolitan Museum of Art, New York. Deutsches Archaeologisches Institut
Neg. 56.937.

greatest depth of spatial illusion.[11] Before this, the stylistic march is
said to have progressed gradually from the representation of projecting columns standing out before a series of elongated orthostats to
half glimpses of an illusionistic architecture seen through openings
in the upper zone of the wall. Succeeding to this movement toward
openness is a reversal of sorts effected by the reclosing of the lateral
parts of the wall until its central aedicula remains the only open
area, and thus the high point of its symmetry. The entire history of
these stages of second-style decoration is conventionally given a
chronological range from about 65 to 30 B.C., and within this span
the openness of the Boscoreale wall with its complete immersion of
the spectator within its fictive prospects has been matched until recently by only one other example: that of a Corinthian oecus in the
Casa del Labirinto whose right wall centers about the tholos motif

4. Casa del Labirinto, Pompeii. Corinthian oecus. Deutsches Archaeologisches Institut Neg. 56.1235.

(fig. 4), while its rear wall, although faded, shows traces of a gateway and balcony panorama almost identical with that of Boscoreale.

In itself, the position of Boscoreale within the program of second-style evolution has never been considered controversial; rather, controversy has focused upon conflicting interpretations of the subjects imitated by its designs. Shortly after the discovery of the paintings, scholars proposed that their megalographic architecture must be based upon, indeed quite directly copied from, the decorations of the Hellenistic stage.[12] This theory rests upon the testimony of several ancient references to stage paintings, including comments that seem to indicate its realization of a form of single vanishing-point perspective, but especially upon passages in Vitruvius. As I have already mentioned, his descriptions of paintings representing the forms of buildings or of projecting columns and pediments fit the conspicuous features of the second style (7.5.1–2). Along with this description goes mention of several specific subjects such as spacious *exedrae* decorated "tragico aut comico aut satirico more." For the meaning of these terms we turn back to the chapters on the theater where Vitruvius defines the tragic mode as a decoration formed of columns, pediments, statues, and other objects suited to kings; the comic as a composition of balconies and views representing rows of windows such as those in everyday houses; and the satiric as a landscape of trees, caverns, mountains, and other rustic features represented in a topographical manner (5.6.9). This passage led scholars to propose that the New York room with its gateway, balconies, and grotto might be interpreted as a compendium of the three dramatic settings, with additional proof given by the series of Silenus masks hanging suspended in the centers of the panels. When expanded to encompass the architectonic features of the Boscoreale summer triclinium with its more homogeneous decorations of doors and columns, as well as similar motifs in other contemporaneous paintings, this theory has made theatrical imitation the basis for the entire second style. Thus H. G. Beyen's comprehensive study of the evolution of this style, which remains the standard point of reference, is accompanied by a number of reconstruction drawings that abstract from second-style paintings several hypothetical schemes for the architecture of the *scaenae frons*.[13] In keeping with general concepts of chronological evolution, the stages that follow after Boscoreale's open walls are represented by a panel of unknown provenience in the Naples museum whose closed lateral areas set off an open aedicula framing the view of a tholos, by a room on the Palatine excavated in the 1950s by Carettoni whose architecture includes projecting gables and porches (fig. 5), and finally by the com-

5. Ambiente delle Maschere, Palatine, Rome. Gabinetto Fotografico Nazionale Neg. E47767.

plex, double-storied balcony patterns to be seen in the bath quarters of the Casa del Criptoportico.[14]

While the stage decoration theory thus encompasses the greater part of the second-style corpus, the alternative theory developed to explain the Boscoreale paintings includes only the rooms of the villa and their counterparts in the Casa del Labirinto. Challenging the identification of these designs with stage settings in large part on the grounds that Vitruvius never says that the tragic, comic, and satiric modes were combined in single rooms, Phyllis Williams Lehmann argues instead that the scenes are illusionary views of the grounds of a Roman villa, a villa not unlike this Boscoreale residence yet somewhat grander in keeping with the owner's dream of what an ideal villa might be.[15] Within the context of her identification, the great gate becomes the entrance to a villa sanctuary; the flanking doors are the actual entrance portals while the towers and balconies approximate dovecotes and other traditional buildings of the farmstead. The tholos is a temple of Aphrodite presiding over the fertility of the farm, and the grotto on the rear wall is a feature of a landscaped garden complete with its fountain and a trellis that demonstrates a traditional Italian method of yoking vines. The wider implications of this theory are to make the paintings neither copied nor derivative from Hellenistic models, but wholly Roman in subject and conception. Because of its attractive common sense, this theory has not gone without support and further development,[16] but still has never wholly triumphed over the stage decoration theory. As the situation has stood, neither is more capable of conclusive proof than the other, since we have no better evidence for the actual buildings of a Roman farm villa than we have for the structure and decoration of the Hellenistic *scaenae frons*. Insofar as the two theories touch upon the question of patronage, their implications are precisely opposite, for the *scaenae frons* theory, involving as it does the notion of pictures copied from patterns, places the second-style tradition wholly within the hands of the painters, while Lehmann's villa theory assigns the conceptual genesis of the paintings to the patron.

The only way of resolving such a conflict of rival interpretations is by the introduction of new evidence. In this respect the study of Pompeian painting has had in the past decade the dramatic good fortune of Alfonso de Franciscis' excavation of a large seaside villa at Torre Annuziata, three miles northeast of Pompeii, to which he has given the name Oplontis. The villa has a core of five fully decorated rooms that can be attributed to the mid first century.[17] The question one might ask in the abstract of any addition to the second-style corpus is whether it would so completely repeat known designs as to demonstrate an absolute lack of originality among the painters, or conversely whether it would differ so radically from familiar material as to disprove the whole stylistic order of the period. The Oplontis paintings do neither, but in fact give us further parallels for the Boscoreale motifs within compositional formats that are still unique unto themselves. In a large triclinium we find the familiar tholos, the garden statue, the majestic gateway, and the jewel-inlaid columns of Boscoreale not simply juxtaposed in contiguous panels but interrelated within a spacious and coherent design that fills its entire wall (sala 14). In a second, even larger oecus (fig. 6) is a variation upon this design in a double-tiered "porticus" of truly regal proportions seen through the apertures of a grandiose propylon whose central arch frames a great tripod (sala 15). It is a new set of motifs, yet one that fits the familiar repertoire. To these rooms, however, the house adds something new by way of a very large atrium, our first surviving example of atrium decorations in the high second style. This room alone breaks the rules hitherto formulated for the style in such a manner as to cast new light upon its decorative intentions as a whole. Such a unique combination of the formulaic and unprecedented makes Oplontis the key to second-style workshops.

Both the illusion of spatial openness and the centrally oriented symmetry of other walls are missing in the atrium, whose mode of decoration is demonstrably appropriate to the nature of the room (fig. 7). The function of the atrium in the daily rituals of the Roman man of affairs is well known. With its adjoining tablinum and laterally placed *alae* to the rear, it forms the spatial and practical framework of the morning *salutatio*, chief ceremony of the patron-client relationship.[18] Formal atria in the houses of the Pompeian tufa and limestone periods follow a standard pattern that visually demonstrates their function: they are at once the principal rooms of the house, surrounded by small side chambers for sleeping and storage, and the grand reception room exhibiting the status of the master. The atrium of the second-century Casa di Sallustio exemplifies the traditional plan. But in the decorated Oplontis atrium, which forms a laterally closed rectangle at the core of the house, these functional aspects of the room survive only in visual fiction.

The patterns of the two side walls echo each other with only small variations in detail. In the places where real doors customarily open are painted facsimiles flanked by projecting columns and set within recessed alcoves.[19] While the architectural framework of the door closer to the impluvium is symmetrical, in the case of the second pair of doors this order is broken in a peculiar way. Although three columns flank this door on either side, their placement is un-

6. Villa Romana di Oplontis, Torre Annunziata. Sala 15. Deutsches Archaeologisches Institut Neg. 74.2689.

even since the inside left column actually overhangs and obscures a part of the door while that on the right is spatially separated from it. Furthermore the door itself, although set back within its alcove on the left side, projects into open space on its right. The surface of the right hand wall is located behind the door, and the three columns form a line that recedes backwards and continues beyond the free-standing corner of the wall. When viewed from a vantage point opposite the first door, it gives the impression of a wall ending abruptly before a transverse passageway.[20] This illusionary lateral expansion

7. Villa Romana di Oplontis, Torre Annunziata. Portion of the atrium wall. Deutsches Archaeologisches Institut Neg. 74.2692.

of the room occupies the position of the traditional *alae,* and one may assume that these are what it is intended to represent. Quite clearly the decorations of the room re-create the architectural pattern of an atrium, but this atrium is intended less for practical business than for show.

At the same time this fictive decoration is one of the greatest opulence. The doors are of ivory inlaid with tortoise shell, such doors as Virgil mentions in *G.* 2.461–64 to symbolize wealth and power. The corridor columns are of alabaster; the others of *giallo antico.*[21] There were of course no rooms so luxurious in the Pompeii of the late republic, nor does Rome itself offer remains of any such houses from the period, and yet literary sources suggest that they did indeed exist. In 95 B.C. the orator Licinius Crassus had columns of Hymettian marble originally bought to decorate a theater installed in his Palatine house (Pliny *HN* 36.2.7–8). Although there were only 6 columns, and these a modest twelve feet high, his showiness won him the nickname "Palatine Venus." In 78 B.C. Marcus Lepidus built his doorframes of Numidian *giallo antico.* According to Pliny (36.34.109), there was no house in the Rome of that day more beautiful than Lepidus', but thirty-five years later a hundred houses were rated higher. Among these must have been the house of Marcus Scaurus who, as aedile in 58 B.C., created a scandal by decking the stage of a temporary theater with 360 columns of dark Melian marble, the largest of which he later set up in his atrium (36.2.5–6). Finally, the notorious Mamurra of Catullan fame was by Pliny's account (36.7.48) the first Roman to cover walls throughout his whole house with marble revetments and to have all his columns of marble. Surely it is to such showplaces that Horace refers in the disclaimer that closes *Odes* 3.1:

> Cur invidendis portibus et novo
>   sublime ritu moliar atrium.

Although no description supplies such precise details as how and where marble columns were incorporated into these lofty atria, the elaboration of the traditional pattern at Oplontis would suggest that its decorators had taken their inspiration from the fabled luxury of contemporary Rome.

Second only to the atrium in the unusual nature of the decoration and also in its appropriateness to its physical context is a double alcove room at the western corner of the building with a door and a window opening onto an ambulacrum. Both the Villa dei Misteri and the Casa del Labirinto have rooms of this shape, which Lawrence Richardson has identified as one typical of women's dining rooms.[22] The alcoves, he proposes, were meant for couches on which the women dined seated. Such rooms always have their counterparts in larger dining rooms with reclining couches for men. Women probably joined their husbands in these for the entertainment that followed the meal. The Villa dei Misteri has four such pairs of rooms in accordance with the Roman need for different exposures for different seasons. The Oplontis room also has a larger counterpart, although its second-style decoration has been painted over.[23]

All previously known examples of the double alcove room have modest decorations of orthostat walls well suited to their shape and size with apertures only in their upper zones, but at Oplontis the rear walls of both alcoves are fully opened by illusionistic prospects.[24] That of the left-hand alcove offers a view through a broken pediment into a colonnaded courtyard with a *syzygia* at its center, while the side walls are pierced by framed windows opening onto massed foliage that screens any further view. The stone-and-metal balustrades that finish these apertures give them the appearance of balcony windows. Within the right-hand alcove an interrupted architrave that appears to be located beyond the surface of the wall is framed by the arch of a grotto farther on. Its ledgelike rocks are clearly rendered with sharp angles and strong highlights. Both in shape and in surface they are similar to the rocks of the Boscoreale grotto, even if this very symmetrical cavern is less interesting than the other with its fountain and its arbor above. The combination of this topographical feature with the elegant architrave clearly indicates that this grotto forms no part of a setting for a satyr drama, but rather belongs to a stylized garden landscape. The two real openings into the ambulacrum on two sides of the room are matched by fictional apertures giving onto more sumptuous illusionary gardens. The decoration of the room has been closely coordinated with its setting to create a partially walled enclosure, half out of doors, half within—a shell of space pierced by apertures linking the interior with its exterior environment.

Turning back from Oplontis to Boscoreale and its contemporary analogues, we can recognize sufficient similarities and repetitions of motif to be certain that we are dealing with four houses decorated by the same workshop, and it is logical to assume further that the significance of the designs should in all cases be analogous. If the Oplontis atrium has a Roman pattern and theme, the remainder of the rooms may be interpreted accordingly. What Oplontis demonstrates is that Lehmann was essentially correct in her identification of the Boscoreale paintings as fictional views of a villa, and yet the grandeur of their designs far exceeds the utilitarian model she had in mind.[25] One thinks perhaps of the palaces of Hellenistic kings, but there are Roman possibilities closer at hand, and for these we may look again to our fullest source of information on late republican villas in Varro's book on farming.

In addition to its practical observations on agricultural method, *De re rustica* tells us much about several kinds of country houses and their surroundings. A running theme of banter among the speakers has to do with the limits to which luxurious accommodation in the country may be pressed without perverting the serious agricultural character of a farm. In the first two books, the sentiment for utilitarian simplicity prevails. The speakers agree upon a distinction between farms whose well-ordered cultivation is their main source of beauty and the "regie polita aedificia" of the rich (*Rust.* 1.2.10). A truly worthy villa is one whose visitors admire the *oporothecae,* or fruit rooms, and not, as in the villas of Lucullus, the *pinacothecae,* or picture galleries. By this allusion Varro indicates that class of pleasure villas built by the great fortune gatherers of the late republic for relaxation away from the heat and public business of Rome. It is a semimoral distinction that he draws, coloring it with an aesthetic utilitarianism that places his remarks within the Catonian tradition of personal dedication to agriculture.

In the third book, however, once the traditional crops and animals have been firmly established as the philosophical and economic basis of villa life, Varro gives his discourse a more playful and self-indulgent tone. The new topic introduced is that of making the most of the space of the farmstead. Although the speakers keep sight of the laudable Roman aims of productivity and profit, the crops and animals they mention belong to a sphere of use quite different from common grain, grapes, and cattle. They are in fact the provisions of the refined table: rabbits, dormice, fowl of all kinds from doves to peahens, fish, and flowers for garlands. Such luxury products extend the purposes of farming beyond sober productivity and accordingly greater attention is given to a more elegant and complex kind of villa farm. Not only do we hear some defenses of fine interiors for villas but also more detailed mention of architecture of exterior landscaping (3.2.3–11). The keeping of small animals necessitates a variety of specialized buildings. Especially the breeding of birds contributes its own architecture of towers and dovecotes to the areas around the house. In her discussion of the Boscoreale paintings, Lehmann has cited some of Varro's descriptions, but one passage she omits seems pertinent to the buildings here. This is a lengthy, digressive account of an aviary that Varro locates on his own property in Casinum (3.8–17). In describing his own landscape architecture with obvious pride in its originality and ingenuity, Varro somewhat undermines his professed allegiance to the spare and utilitarian farm. His construction centers about a stream running through the grounds of the villa that he has bordered with a walk leading to a colonnade. Nets of hemp suspended between the columns keep the birds inside. At the far end is a round building with an exterior circle of stone columns and an interior circle of wooden ones—a version of course of the tholos, that ubiquitous building type that seems quite indiscriminately to have been used for temples, tombs, and even in such commercial contexts as the centers of the *macella* of Pompeii and Puteoli. A wood surrounds Varro's tholos, but is screened off from it to keep the birds from the interior of the enclosure. This space appears to serve as an open-air dining room with a platform surrounded by a balustrade and a duck pond.[26] All in all, it is a most elegantly extravagant piece of topographical construction, even to a planisphere inside the building.

The striking combination of tholos and colonnade is the very combination to be seen in the fictive courtyards of so many Pompeian walls. Varro himself supplies a point of reference in admitting that his buildings surpass the creations of Lucullus at Tusculum. Such elegant structures belong to the villas of the most prosperous Romans and are in all probability to be associated with one of the chief of Roman social rituals, that of dining. Among the Tusculan extravagances Plutarch attributes to the scandalously rich Lucullus, otherwise notorious for his fishponds and water channels at Baiae, are open-air dining rooms fronting upon great porticoes (*Luc.* 38). When Pompey questioned the practicality of these rooms, Lucullus answered that he, like the birds, could move his habitation with the seasons. The splendor of Lucullus' porticoes was doubtless no less than what is represented here—the models being the great parks of the Ptolemies and Eastern kings but the showmanship indigenously Roman. What we see then at Oplontis in the Boscoreale rooms, in the Casa del Labirinto, and in the Villa dei Misteri is, I propose, a Lucullan "porticus" style flamboyantly imitating the extravagance of boundless wealth as it displayed itself on Italian soil. The decorations of the Oplontis rooms, more palatial than those of Boscoreale, are of a piece with the atrium in their creation of an atmosphere far beyond the means and circumstances of even this ample villa. Such fantasies of identification with a fabled stratum of society were, I believe, the commodity that one Campanian workshop of the mid first century B.C. sold to its middle-class patrons.

Whatever the level of Roman society, the ceremonies of hospitality and dining were of the greatest importance and understandably to be staged with great formality and show. Several subordinate motifs in these second-style rooms may also be explained by an association with dining. Most obvious are the bowls, baskets, or casually placed clusters of fruit on shelves or architraves. In explaining the handsome glass bowl on the rear wall of the New York Boscoreale room, scholars have referred to a passage in Vitruvius describing the Greek custom of sending *xenia*, or painted representations of items of uncooked food, to guests by way of an invitation (6.10).[27] While there is some argument for the logic of incorporating such symbols of hospitality into a cubiculum, there is still more for their inclusion among the decorations of a dining room (which, in accordance with the arguments of Richardson I have mentioned earlier, is the role that should be assigned to the Boscoreale room).[28] A very similar glass bowl of pomegranates in one of the rooms at Oplontis is among the details in which these two productions of one workshop are most similar. The room on the eastern side of the Oplontis atrium has not only the most abundantly filled basket of fruit in Campanian painting, but also a small table on which is a kind of sweetmeat that one of the custodians informs me is still prized in contemporary Italy, and it is surely only as a *xenium* that we can explain the vulgarly large fresh fish suspended on the half wall of the Naples panel. The persistence of fruit, fish, fowl, and such delicacies within the traditions of Pompeian painting up through the fourth style would seem to confirm their possessing a symbolism of their own quite independent of other changing fashions in the decoration of dining room walls.

Closely analogous to the *xenia* in their association with the rituals of Roman hospitality are, I believe, the masks which have often figured as evidence to support the stage decoration theory. In the greater number of second-style rooms these are satyr masks. As Agnes Allroggen-Bedel has shown in a recent study, there is little evidence for that kind of correspondence between the choice of tragic, comic, or satyr masks and the presence of doors, columns, balconies, grottos, and other such supposedly thematic motifs which one would have to expect were the stage decoration theory to be carried to its logical conclusion.[29] But in fact there is no reason why masks should be out of place in a Roman dining room decorated in any thematic mode, since the ritual of the dinner consisted not only in a leisurely service of formal courses but also in the host's planned after-dinner entertainment of a literary, musical, or theatrical nature. Augustus was well known for his provision in this line, giving very formal dinner parties enlivened, as Suetonius records, "with performances by musicians, actors or even men who gave turns at the circus, but most often by professional storytellers" (*Aug.* 74). Such entertainment ranged from a host's reading of his own writings (perhaps not always a pleasure) to troupes of trained actors, especially comic actors, or musicians. In this context the masks might well figure as a promise that the niceties of hospitality will be maintained. Although the allusions cannot be pressed too far, the prevalence of satyr masks perhaps indicates a preference for lighter entertainment. In any event, the persistence of masks alongside the *xenia* in numerous rooms long after the disappearance of second-style megalography would seem to indicate that they too possess their own traditional symbolic value.

Thus I have disassociated this particular group of second-style paintings to which Oplontis belongs, both in motif and execution, from specific dependence upon the decorations of the theater only to restore theatricality to the walls as a metaphor. But such self-conscious dramatization, even beyond the provisions for formal entertainment, is also indigenously Roman. In literature we find more than one suggestion of the meal as a staged performance. Varro refers to his tholos-formed aviary as a *theatridion avium* (*Rust.* 3.5.13), ostensibly describing its rows of perches but possibly implying that the spectacles here offered by feathered performers are equal to shows of other kinds. In Hor. *Sat.* 2.8, Fundanius' snobbish account of the elaborate dinner given by the socially anxious Nasidienus is full of stage business, planned and unplanned, which culminates in the accident of a falling curtain—such a curtain, we may guess, as was frequently seen in painted dining rooms. Although the guests make their hasty excuses before the time for after-dinner entertainment, Horace's own comment on the spectacle seems thematic: "nullos his mallem ludos spectasse" (79). Finally, Trimalchio's self-conscious hospitality complete with dancers, musicians, and a recital by the host is the ultimate in the ritual theatricality of dining.

Within this context, then, Roman dining rooms decorated with stage designs would scarcely be out of place, and in the fourth style they were recognizably a part of the fashion. Likewise I think they existed in the second-style period; it remains only to distinguish them from the "porticus" rooms I have identified. The mural designs of Carettoni's Palatine Ambiente delle Maschere are conspicuously unlike those of these Campanian rooms. Their architecture is not composed of monumental portals and gateways, but rather of wings and gables projecting forward in such a manner as to enclose, instead of open, the interior space of the room. The prospect of a colonnaded exterior courtyard is lacking; the architectonic structure seems rather to be built outwards from a solid wall while the gabled side pediments meet at the corners in a curiously unfinished angle (fig. 5).[30] Similar projecting structures appear in a series of adjoining rooms in the Casa del Criptoportico. The complex north wall of the frigidarium is double-storied, a projecting aedicula with columniated wings forming its lower level while a loggia is built into the upper tier. Although this room has apertures revealing glimpses of columns and balconies, they seem less like exterior prospects than backward extensions of the large ornamental structure itself. Unlike the "porticus" walls, these include human figures. The ones placed in alcoves flanking the aedicula on the first story are clearly statues while those above are ambiguous enough to be taken for real figures. The structure and ornamentation of this wall are far more complex than ones we see in the Ambiente delle Maschere, but a more recently discovered room in the Palatine excavation, still unpublished, shows the form of a double-storied construction very similar to those of the Criptoportico walls.[31] Although equally elaborate in their patterns, walls of this type appear somewhat less opulent in their furnishings than those of Oplontis and Boscoreale. Their squared columns imitate painted wood instead of alabaster and marble. Here then we are likely to have our real imitations of the *scaenae frons*. Even so the designs are probably not, as Allroggen-Bedel has sensibly suggested, copies of full stages but rather abstractions from the common repertoire of stage motifs recombined at the painters' fancy.[32] Perhaps they are most reminiscent of the temporary sets used when wooden theaters were put up for their limited periods of Roman festival days. Thus they do not carry the house into the sphere of the theater, but rather reconstitute the theater within the house.

On the basis then of their compositional patterns and motifs, the most dramatically architectonic of second-style walls can be divided into two quite coherent groups. Since the masonry construction of late republican walls gives slim grounds for chronological distinction between these groups, there is no real evidence to argue against the possible contemporaneity or near contemporaneity of their two modes of design. Thus I propose that the stage pattern did not evolve out of the "porticus" pattern but that it existed in contradistinction to it, the dominant factor in the development of the period being the competition of workshops for patronage. Rooms were decorated in a manner thematically appropriate to their use, but each workshop had its own repertoire to offer. Some overlapping of details suggests that the workshops were not beyond borrowing from each other. There is, for instance, a tripod in the upper story of the Criptoportico frigidarium, and the *thymateria* that figure heavily in the Oplontis and Boscoreale decorations appear also in one room of the Criptoportico. These common details might also reflect such common grounds between the trappings of lavish houses and those of the stage as are suggested by accounts of the theater of

Scaurus. Whatever their exact sources, the workshops must have been known by their repertoires. No matter whether the motifs were recorded in pattern books or merely in the minds of the painters, one may assume that the patron was able to choose the motif for which he contracted, the particular kind of illusion he wanted his house to display. The many variations among the houses belonging to the "porticus" group suggest that the painters did not copy their designs exactly, but rather adapted them freely to the nature of the spaces given them to fill. The illusionistically open walls of the Oplontis double-alcove room should thus appear as an experimental approach to the handling of areas rigidly defined by a conventional architecture, while the plenitude of motifs crowded into the New York Boscoreale room may simply betray a patron's wanting his money's worth in variety. With such possibilities of combination and recombination, I see little value in attempting to establish a relative chronology for the productions of this one workshop, since the determining factor in its execution of any design must have been the guidelines that patron and architect had laid down for the painter.[33]

Such impressive megalographics appear suited to the temper of the late republic with its still surviving concepts of personal power, its jostlings for influence and strong alliances of political interest. Still one wants to know the kinds of patrons these designs were created for, and again there is the chance that Oplontis may eventually provide an answer, although the evidence remains far from complete. To the best of our knowledge, the "porticus" style displayed here is restricted to Pompeii and its environs, and employed only in very large houses where we may assume its appropriateness to the pretensions of the owners. It does not automatically follow that these owners were members of the Roman aristocracy. As John D'Arms reminds us in a recent study of Vesuvian villas, there is not one piece of secure evidence to link any of the fifteen Romans whose proprietorship in the area is attested to by literary sources with a single one of our excavated houses.[34] Rather, D'Arms' analysis of the evidence for the economic function of the villas points to ownership by the prosperous commercial middle-class. Not only does the Villa Oplontis include its own extensive rustic quarter, but also it is located not far to the west of a large, rustic wine-producing establishment of late second- or early first-century date just now in the process of excavation. Quite possibly some definite association between the elegant residence and the commercial property will appear with time.[35] The Villa dei Misteri, if we accept Richardson's analysis of its history, was constructed in the mid first century as a fine residence with space and apparatus for producing large quantities of wine.

Boscoreale was likewise a vineyard villa. The fortunes that built the Pompeian amphitheater and *odeon* in the Sullan period were made in wine;[36] one can scarcely believe that Roman aristocrats were alone in appreciating views of the sea. The probability of ownership by local citizens gives a rationale for the popularity of the "porticus" style in Pompeii. If not the most prized resort of the luxury-loving urban aristocracy, this fertile Vesuvian land which made its cultivators prosperous still lay in the shadow of the *crater delicatus*, the picturesque Baian region where Lucullus and his peers had built their fabled villas. To that region we may attribute either the original ideas or the patterns for decorations to lend elegance to the self-importance of provincial men. In Pompeii political competition and family alliances were always strong, and so must have been the accompanying rituals of hospitality. After the Roman domination of the Sullan period, the balance of power slowly adjusted itself by alliances among Roman and Campanian families.[37] When asked by a friend to procure a kinsman's entry into the Pompeian *ordo decurionum*, Cicero replied, "Romae, si vis habes; Pompeiis difficile est."[38]

That the rival style of *scaenae frons* decoration which Vitruvius knew should have been more widely disseminated is also not difficult to understand. Although the Roman and Campanian examples need scarcely be products of the same workshop, their general outlines are not dissimilar. Naturally, in the event that the attribution of the Palatine rooms to Augustus himself should ever be definitively proven,[39] we might find here Vitruvius' source and think also of the well-known love of the *princeps* for the stage; even so we would have to admit that the style of his decorations was not unique but represented only one of many commissions in a popular mode.

Within this general framework, explanations for other versions of the second style can be found. The contemporaneous use of orthostat walls and architectonic illusions within a single house would seem to confirm that there was never any step-by-step evolution of designs.[40] Among the variants I have not before mentioned is a paratactically ordered wall decorated with ornamental herm figures common to the Casa del Criptoportico and Casa di Caesio Blando,[41] whose factual prototype might be identified by a Lucretian reference to houses adorned with golden images holding lamps in their hands (2.23–26). Most significant among alternative patterns in its bearing upon the later history of painting is one unique to a small room off the peristyle of the Pompeian Casa degli Epigrammi— a room that gives the house its name (fig. 8).[42] Like the Oplontis atrium, this room lacks the spatial openness generally associated with the high second style, but the nature of its decoration is not hard to identify. The room is fitted out as a gallery for the display of pictures. Five separate figured panels comprise the chief furnishings: three closely juxtaposed on the rear wall and one centered on each side wall. These bordered panels are separated by a series of scale pattern columns in variegated colors set forward on a projecting dado. On the side walls the dado forms a podium beneath each panel while the columns continue above to support gabled aediculae framing each picture. On either side these aediculae are flanked by statues set upon small square pedestals within recessed niches. Above the niches the decoration continues with a molding in the egg-and-dart pattern and a series of figured friezes.

Neither motif nor technique leads me to place this room within the repertoires of the Oplontis or Casa del Criptoportico workshops, and yet I would venture to suggest that the background for these decorations lies within the same general context as that of the "porticus" style, for in fact the *pinacotheca* is the one kind of room prominently associated with the lavish establishments of the rich that second-style painters have not elsewhere imitated.[43] This Pompeian adaptation has a definite plan and theme. All five of its panels illustrate epigrams similar to Hellenistic epigrams of the Greek anthology. The room has an artistic unity as well. The three juxtaposed compositions on the rear wall resemble one another in their organization of graceful monuments and slender forms. Much smaller than any room previously mentioned, the room of the epigrams scarcely offers the space for comfortable dining, not even for the women, but its literary flavor suggests instead a small reading room so decorated as to exhibit its owner's cultivation and taste—such a room as Cicero in a letter to M. Fabius Gallus mentions wanting to decorate with pictures (*Fam.* 7.23.1–3).

When next we encounter a stately example of the *pinacotheca* mode in the Palatine Casa di Livia its appearance is quite changed from that of the diminutive Pompeian oecus (fig. 9).[44] The symmetrical centering traditional within Romano-Campanian wall schemes has taken over so that the picture panels are now framed within imposing central aediculae that dominate their walls. To these have been added small shuttered boxes for the display of additional *pinakes*. Although the design of the wall contains elements akin to those of the second style—ornamental columns, elaborate architraves, molded cornices, brackets, and acroteria—the new room is at once less extravagantly showy and less firmly architectonic in character than second-style walls we have seen. It is in fact not a structured but a surface-ornamented wall whose purpose is to set off

8. Casa degli Epigrammi, Pompeii. Room of the Epigrams. Deutsches Archaeologisches Institut Neg. 56.1218.

9. Casa di Livia, Palatine, Rome. Mythological Landscapes Room. Alinari/Editorial Photocolor Archives.

to advantage its mythological panels; on the short rear wall Polyphemus and Galatea, on the long wall a representation of the nymph Io, guarded by Argus as she sits beneath a statue of her rival Juno on a pedestal. That this panel is an adaptation from some earlier Greek composition is suggested both by parallel versions in Pompeii and by the iconography of Greek pottery, but the painter has certainly added touches of his own, especially in the landscape background.[45]

No clear intermediary steps link the small Pompeian gallery with this grand chamber. There is even reason to look to a different model or frame of reference for this new version of the *pinacotheca* mode. While private collections had been the chief repositories of works of art brought into Italy before the mid first century, later years saw the beginnings of the public museum in such showplaces as the Theater of Pompey with its great porticoes. Asinius Pollio is credited with establishing one of the first museums of the Augustan age in his library (Pliny *HN* 35.9), but soon afterward a great part of the propagandistic building program of Augustus and Agrippa took the form of "porticus" buildings furnished as galleries. To call attention to this munificence, as Pliny records (35.26–28), Agrippa delivered his famous oration recommending that collectors should not retain their imported statues and paintings for private delectation in their country villas but place them on public display. Naturally such an imitation of a *pinacotheca* as this of the Casa di Livia would be in accordance with Agrippa's recommendation (no matter whether its organization resembled that of a private or of a public gallery), but the corollary notion that it might represent a compensatory kind of picture room invented within the bosom of the Augustan family is probably no more than a pretty fantasy. What seems likely is that the development of public displays of art made the imitative *pinacotheca* popular as house owners began to discover that such creations lay within their painters' illusionary skills. A more certain feature of the decoration is its incorporation of those unreal structures and improbable ornaments deplored by Vitruvius which, however fantastic they may sound in the abstract, explain themselves perfectly in context as the elements of an appropriately rich setting for the display of pictures.

Such elements are even more notable among the smaller scale furnishings of another room of the same species painted perhaps ten years later that displays the style at its most elegant. Here along with the central paintings in their ornamental frames are heavy candelabra shaped to represent Diana as *potnia theron* and the goddess Fortuna that may be counted as works of art in their own right (fig. 10).[46] *Pinakes* again appear in subordinate positions at the sides

10. Villa alla Farnesina, Museo Nazionale delle Terme, Rome. Cubiculum B, rear wall. Alinari/Editorial Photocolor Archives.

of the central panels while the representation on the rear wall of Dionysus and his nurses in a landscape setting is flanked by statues of figures supporting small line drawings (fig. 11). The flat surfaces of the walls are varied by elegant panels imitating patterns inlaid in stone whose fine detail is carried out with meticulous brushwork. A fine line drawing of a seated Aphrodite must have a fifth-century

Greek painting for its original; both in style and in execution it differs from the Dionysus landscape. Unlike the Livia room, this is not
a thematically organized gallery but rather an eclectic gathering of
works to display the organizer's personal taste.

The question of taste brings us back to the specifics of patronage
and its role in historical Rome. In interpreters' attempts to forge
links between the private world of painting and the facts and Roman
personalities we know, these rooms from the Villa alla Farnesina
have been of great interest since Beyen, on the basis of the villa's location by the Tiber just above the Pons Agrippae, assigned its ownership to Julia and Marcus Agrippa.[47] But the ownership of these
choice pieces of Tiber property is by no means certain, and the area
deserves another look. In a recent article reinvestigating the course
of the Agrippan Aqua Virgo and Euripus, Robert Lloyd has called attention to the *sepulchrum C. Platorini* of late Augustan date which
was located on the right bank by the terminal of the Pons.[48] He suggests that the A. Crispinus Caepio also buried in the tomb was the
first proprietor of the *Figlinae Caepionis* whose bricks bear the
stamp *ab euripo*, a factory that under imperial patronage flourished
for well over two centuries. Although we are again in the realm of
speculation, the presence of this tomb, no doubt located on family
property, in the area of the Tiber villa suggests the perfect kind of
commissioner for the paintings: a prosperous patron of the equestrian order eager to display at an affordable cost his ability to share in
a contemporary enthusiasm for art or in the cultivated tastes of great
aristocratic collectors.

Like the "porticus" pattern of the second style, the Augustan
pinacotheca bears, I believe, the mark of middle-class imitation of
the creations of wealth and power. Its emphases are nonetheless
quite different from those of the flamboyant republican style. Instead of the social importance of the house owner, the interconnec-
tion of his public and his domestic life, or the extravagance of his
hospitality, the picture gallery style attests the refinement and comfortable well-being of the private man. The fantastic elements that
ornament the gallery wall (and it is strange that Vitruvius did not
allow it) are the fantasies created by the decorative arts, while their
sudden popularity, for which Vitruvius may give us quite accurate
witness, is a consequence of their belonging to a new mode that offered each patron the opportunity to place a personal stamp on his
environment through his selection of pictures or myths. With their
delicately executed details, many of which are imperceptible to the
spectator at a distance, these are designs to be looked at carefully
and at leisure within the framework of that comfortable materialis-

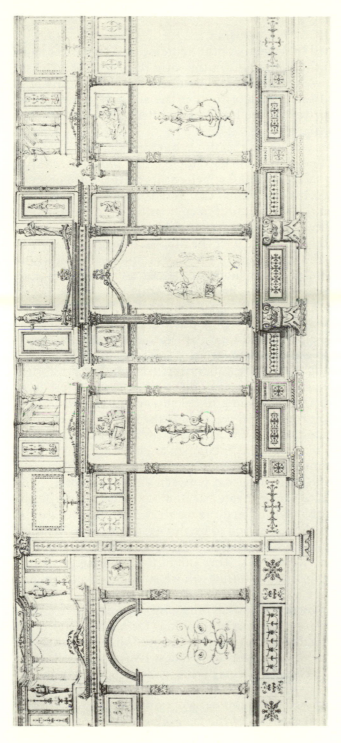

11. Villa alla Farnesina, Museo Nazionale delle Terme, Rome. Cubiculum B, drawing of the side wall. Deutsches Archae-ologisches Institut Neg. 56.318.

tic world inhabited by so many of the addressees of Horace's second book of *Odes*. In the subtle tone of the early third style we may see reflected the changed temper of the Augustan world where the *princeps* championed the virtues of solid citizens in whose lives quiet prosperity and dutiful service had replaced the republican passions for honor and display.

The accidents of survival that direct our attention from Pompeii to Rome for the first fully formed example of the *pinacotheca* style cause us to look back again to Pompeii for its further development. It is perhaps scarcely coincidental that Augustan associations were growing strong in the municipium in company with Augustan middle-class prosperity.[49] Once the picture gallery had come into vogue here, it was scarcely displaced over the next sixty years. During that time it survived the mutations of the background wall from third-style solidity to the stagy architectural fantasies of the fourth style and was challenged only in the final, Vespasianic years of the city by a new and far more literal rendering of the *scaenae frons* in full dress with actors standing in place to play their roles. The reason for the dominance of the *pinacotheca* appears to me quite simply the equality of its appeal to painters and patrons.

To the painter the picture gallery must have offered a format easily adaptable to the proportions of any given space; there is no more of the occasional crowding of designs found in second-style rooms. As the pictures themselves become the focal points of mural composition, the marks of the workshop grow less evident. No two of the third-style *pinacothecae* in Pompeii are identical, nor do even the banded columns that frame the central aediculae show identical patterns of detail. Colors repeated between the ornamental members and the picture panels create harmonious unities within each room. Above all, the style offered the painters new opportunities to put their hands to the adaptation of mythological pictures. Very few it appears were content to copy exactly from sources or models, and their free disposition both of setting and of figures brought about a genuinely Roman brand of painting whose substance was the integration of landscape and myth.

To the house owners likewise *pinacothecae* must have offered new opportunities for individualism. With its format so easily adaptable to large or small spaces, the style was one that cut across the boundaries of prosperity, and many a modest house, not to mention commercial establishment, has its picture gallery rooms. Unlike the eclectic Farnesina rooms, the mythological orientation of Pompeian *pinacothecae* may well place emphasis upon the display of acquired learning rather than the taste of the connoisseur collector. As there are many levels of prosperity in houses, or of quality in painting, so also we see hints of varied levels of learning from houses that seem to announce an intimate familiarity with Greek or Latin literature to those whose standard, endlessly repetitive subjects may show simple pride in the acquisition of any culture at all. From among the ranks of such citizens we acquire our best literary portrait of a patron, one whose taste is never quite paralleled in Pompeii and yet is perhaps only slightly exaggerated.[50] As we enter Trimalchio's vestibulum, we see illustrations of the *Iliad*, the *Odyssey*, and a local gladiatorial contest. Where else in the ancient world do art and literature join more closely with life? What better testimony is found of the patron's wish to reflect his personality in his surroundings and of the painter's compliance in executing his desire?

NOTES

1. The greater part of the research on which this essay is based was made possible by a Fellowship awarded by the John Simon Guggenheim Memorial Foundation in 1976. I wish to acknowledge the kindness of the several scholars who granted me permissions for my work: Professor Alfonso de Franciscis, Dottore Fausto Zevi, Soprintendente delle Antichità delle Province di Napoli e Caserta, Dottoressa Giuseppina Cerulli-Irelli, Professore Adriano La Regina, Soprintendente delle Antichità di Roma, and Herr Professor Doktor Hellmut Sichtermann of the Deutsches Archaeologisches Institut, who has allowed me to publish the following photographs: D.A.I. negatives 56.937, 74.2692, 56.318, 59.1973, 56.1235, 56.1218, 74.2689, 66.1845.

2. E. Gjerstadt, *Early Rome*, vol. 4:2, p. 406.

3. M. Borda, *La pittura Romana*, pp. 145–63, discusses the written and visual evidence.

4. The somewhat self-contradictory nature of Pliny's several remarks pertinent to patronage betrays this point. In praising the Augustan "inventor" of mural landscapes who might seem to have offered patrons some opportunities for choice in painting "qualia quis optaret," he takes occasion to remark on the superiority of *tabulae* over mural paintings and romanticizes the civic currency of Greek paintings (*HN* 35.117–18). Consistent with this prejudice is his selection of Fabius Pictor and Pacuvius, who worked in temples probably without the support or dictates of patronage, as the most honorable of Roman painters (35.18–19), but we cannot be certain that these artists did not paint directly on walls. Following this mention (35.22) Pliny adds that the importance of painting in Rome gained much from a series of painters (unnamed) who created narrative battle posters for triumphing generals. While we can be sure that these took directions from patrons, one cannot imagine that their productions were of the highest quality.

5. Such an approach is exemplified by the discussion of M.-Th. Picard Schmitter, "Bétyles hellenistiques," *Mon. Piot.* 57 (1971): 43–88, who constructs an Augustan iconography for the second-style paintings of the Palatine Ambiente delle Maschere from the evidence of coins and monuments.

6. O. J. Brendel, *Prolegomena to the Study of Roman Art* (expanded from "Prolegomena to a Book on Roman Art" with a foreword by J. J. Pollitt), pp. 153–56.

7. Interpreters of the Ara Pacis reliefs are accustomed to invoke Augustan literature: the *Aeneid* for the sacrifice panel; the *Georgics* and Horace's *Carmen saeculare* for the "Tellus" (e.g., E. Simon, *Ara Pacis Augustae*, pp. 23–24, 26–29), while observing that the handling of the natural elements owes its form to the conventions of Hellenistic art. Comparisons between the altar and Augustan landscape painting are thus most frequently made by scholars who, unlike Brendel, attribute the character of all Augustan public and private art to Hellenistic influence, e.g., R. Bianchi Bandinelli, *Rome: The Center of Power, 500 B.C. to A.D. 200*, trans. P. Green, pp. 189–93, and R. Brilliant, *Roman Art from the Republic to Constantine*, pp. 239–40.

8. In discussing such problems for the "Tellus" panel, G. K. Galinsky, *Aeneas, Sicily, and Rome*, pp. 191–241, very appropriately stresses the compositional structure of the design as the basis on which its symbols should be interpreted.

9. P. H. von Blanckenhagen, *The Paintings from Boscotrecase, MDAI(R)* Suppl. 6, pp. 30–35, uses his observations on the "unreal" perspective of the landscape to argue for the latter point of view.

10. A. Mau, *Pompeii: Its Life and Art*, trans. F. W. Kelset, pp. 456–84.

11. A complete and chronologically categorized presentation of the corpus up until the discoveries of the past two decades is provided by H. G. Beyen, *Die Pompejanische Wanddekoration von zweiten bis zum vierten Stil*, vols. 1 and 2.

12. A history of scholarship on this point is provided by P. W. Lehmann, *Roman Wall Paintings from Boscoreale in the Metropolitan Museum of Art in New York*, p. 91 n. 23, and is updated by G. C. Picard, "Origine et signification des fresques architectoniques dites de Second Style," *RA* (1977): 231–52.

13. Beyen, *Wanddekoration*, vol. 1, illustrations 28–33, 51–55, 59, 70–71b, 74–76.

14. G. Carettoni, "Due nuovi ambienti dipinti sul Palatino," *BA* 46 (1961): 189–99. V. Spinazzola, *Pompei alla luce degli scavi nuovi de Via dell'Abbondanza (Anni 1910–1923)*, vol. 1, pp. 462–88.

15. Lehmann, *Paintings from Boscoreale*, pp. 82–131.

16. Especially important for its modification of Lehmann's theories is the study by J. Engemann, *Architekturdarstellungen des frühen zweiten Stils: Illusionistiche römische Wandmalerei der ersten Phase und ihre Vorbilder in der realen Architektur, MDAI(R)* Suppl. 12, which argues that the paintings were of a wholly indigenous origin developing step by step in company with the painters' mastery of the perspective techniques necessary to

represent possible interior extensions of the house. Picard, "Fresques archi-tectoniques," pp. 234–40, emphasizes the importance of Engemann's con-tribution to arguments against the *scaenae frons* theory, but while he him-self rejects this theory as too narrow to encompass the entire meaning of the second style, he still argues that the whole corpus must have a single theme: to his mind, a religious one.

17. A. de Franciscis, "La Villa Romana di Oplontis," in *Neue For-schungen in Pompeii*, ed. B. Andreae and H. Kyrieleis, pp. 7–38. Aside from de Franciscis' initial statement, the one specific attempt to give the paint-ings a date and a place in second-style chronology is that of K. Schefold, "Zur Geschichte der Wandmalerei Campaniens," *Antike Kunst* 19 (1976): 118, who has assigned them to the years 40–30 B.C., placing them after Boscoreale but still before the Casa del Criptoportico, and at the high point of the second style.

18. See the discussion in A. G. McKay, *Houses, Villas, and Palaces in the Roman World*, pp. 32–34, but also T. P. Wiseman's historically docu-mented description in this volume.

19. A somewhat analogous situation appears in the atrium of the Villa dei Misteri where the two pair of blocked doors on either side of the room were apparently covered by wooden or painted facsimiles. The place of these mock doors in the decorative scheme is discussed by K. Fittschen, "Zur Herkunft und Entstehung des 2. Stils," in *Hellenismus in Mittelitalien: Kolloquium in Göttingen 1974*, ed. P. Zanker, pp. 539–57, who holds to the common opinion that the doors, originally functional, were blocked when the room received a second-style decoration.

20. Fittschen, "Herkunft und Entstehung," p. 548, attributes this lack of symmetry to the painter's having worked with a pattern that did not fit the wall, but this is to overlook the marked differences between the two sides of the door and the deliberate positioning of the corridor that leads off behind. One may notice that the *imagines clupeati* (shield portraits) hung in the alcove of the first door are thematically appropriate to the decoration of an atrium in their double association with the public and private life. Pliny (*HN* 35.13) records that M. Aemilius Lepidus (consul 78 B.C.) set up such portraits both in the basilica Aemilia and in his own house.

21. Fittschen, "Herkunft und Entstehung," pp. 549–56, provides a de-tailed analysis of such imitations both at Oplontis and in other second-style paintings. Although he reviews the evidence for the employment of lux-urious building materials in Roman houses, he attributes their appearance in the paintings wholly to a Hellenistic background. P. Zanker, "Die Villa als Vorbild des späten pompejanischen Wohngeschmacks," *Jahrbuch des Deutschen Archäologischen Instituts* 94 (1979): 460–523, follows Fitt-schen in attributing the architectonic character of second-style painting to Hellenistic sources, finding evidence for indigenous influence only in later periods.

22. This theory which I owe to discussions with Lawrence Richard-son, jr., will be published by him in a forthcoming issue of *Chronache Pompeiane*.

23. De Franciscis, "Villa di Oplontis," p. 11, fig. 1. The room numbered 12 on the plan is connected with room 11 by a door cut through the rear wall of the left hand alcove. It is a somewhat larger room which has been redecorated in the third style.

24. De Franciscis, "Villa di Oplontis," pls. 14–16.

25. Lehmann herself, *Paintings from Boscoreale*, pp. 157–61, does not identify all the details of the paintings from Roman sources but attributes several to Hellenistic prototypes (and these the most luxurious), referring especially to Athenaeus' accounts of the pavilion of Ptolemy II and the boats of Ptolemy IV and Hieron. K. Schefold, "Der zweite Stil als Zeugnis alexandrinischer Architektur," in *Neue Forschungen in Pompeii*, ed. B. Andreae and H. Kyrieleis, pp. 53–60, believes that the paintings came directly from Hellenistic patterns, as does Fittschen, "Herkunft und Entstehung," pp. 549–56, but Zanker, "Die Villa als Vorbild," pp. 462–68, while again stressing the significance of villas themselves as a symptom of Roman response to the attractions of Hellenistic culture, does interpose a mention of the luxury villas in Italy as a reason for the popularity of the "porticus" designs.

26. For a discussion and hypothetical plan of the aviary, see G. Fuchs, "Varros Vogelhaus bei Casinum," *MDAI(R)* 69 (1962): 96–105.

27. Vitr. 6.7.4. Beyen, *Wanddekoration*, vol. 1, p. 315; Lehmann, *Paintings from Boscoreale*, p. 159. The background and use of *xenia* are discussed by J. M. Croisille, *Les natures mortes campaniennes, Collection Latomus* 76, pp. 11–16. Since Lehmann's discussion is based upon the assumption that the cubiculum was that of the master's personal use, the *xenium* is only marginally appropriate in context.

28. In the first full publication of the villa, F. Barnabei, *La villa pompeiana di P. Fannio Sinistore scoperto presso Boscoreale*, pp. 77 ff., did identify the room as a triclinium, but Beyen, *Wanddekoration*, vol. 1, p. 141, sees the division into anteroom, or "procoeton," and alcove as that of a cubiculum, although admitting (n. 2) that this pattern came to be seen as better suited to triclinia. Lehmann, *Paintings from Boscoreale*, p. 15 n. 39, completely dismisses the possibility of its being a triclinium, and says the same of the contiguous second-style room *N*, but the juxtaposition of these two rooms of different sizes is quite in accordance with Richardson's observations on triclinia in pairs.

29. A. Allroggen-Bedel, *Maskendarstellungen in der römische-kampanische Wandmalerei*, pp. 28–30. She finds the closest apparent link in the Boscoreale summer triclinium where tragic masks might seem to accompany a decoration of doors and columns *tragico more* on the Naples wall, but the Mariemont wall is only a simpler version of this one and yet has comic masks. Her emphasis upon the importance of understanding the place and function of the masks within the total context of their decorative surroundings is well taken, but her ultimate conclusion (pp. 68–72) that masks exist as symbols of the *mimus vitae* is broader than it need be.

30. Carettoni, "Due nuovi ambienti," pp. 191–94, first characterized these as representations of wooden stage decorations, incomplete for want

of space, on the rear wall. One should notice a strong similarity between the architecture of this construction and that of the rear wall of Room 23 of the Oplontis Villa, de Franciscis, "Villa di Oplontis," p. 24, pl. 13. In contrast with the variations in the "porticus" rooms, we seem here to be dealing with a standard pattern that the painters reproduced in its exact lineaments, altering only the superficial ornamentation to their taste. My own explanation for the parallel is that Room 23 at Oplontis was painted later than the rooms in the west wing, perhaps in the attempt to bring the decoration of the house up to date by inclusion of a new style of theatrical room.

31. I wish to thank Gianfilipo Carettoni for his kindness in showing and discussing these newly excavated rooms in October 1976.

32. Allroggen-Bedel, *Maskendarstellungen*, p. 33. The possible link with temporary stage sets was suggested to me by Lawrence Richardson. Like the "porticus" paintings, the "theatrical" walls of the Casa del Criptoportico include colonnades in receding perspective. They do not, however, extend backwards so deeply, nor do they define an enclosed space beyond the wall. A theatrical explanation may be available for these structures if we consider a passage where Vitruvius (5.9.1) mentions the need for *porticus* behind the *scaena* to offer playgoers shelter from a sudden rain as well as space for preparing the apparatus of the stage. Although the view of these spaces was in the real theater presumably blocked by the *scaena*, there is no reason why the painters of fictional stages should not have chosen to open these prospects to give depth to their designs since the illusion of depth was clearly one of the attractive features of the rival "porticus" style.

33. I cannot in any case agree with Schefold, "Geschichte," p. 118, that Oplontis follows after Boscoreale, if only because the grotto motif in Room 11 is so much less fully developed than that in the New York room. As for the Villa dei Misteri, even though its scheme of predominantly orthostat walls has led scholars to assign it an early place in their evolutionary chronologies, its full complement of second-style decoration may have included at least one illusionistically open wall. The *L*-shaped triclinium at the northwest corner, whose second-style paintings were destroyed by a later remodeling, still shows remnants of a grandiose second-style pediment comparable to one in the Casa del Labirinto above the cornice line of a false vault constructed when the shape of the room was changed.

34. J. H. D'Arms, "Ville rustiche e Ville d'*otium*," in *Pompeii 79*, ed. F. Zevi, pp. 78–79.

35. D'Arms, ibid., p. 76. A locational map showing the two excavation sites now appears in W. Jashemski, *The Gardens of Pompeii*, p. 322, fig. 497.

36. P. Castrén, "*Ordo Populusque Pompeianus*": Polity and Society in Roman Pompeii, pp. 88–91.

37. Castrén, ibid., p. 85.

38. Macrob. *Sat.* 2.3.12; cited by Castrén, "*Ordo Populusque*," p. 62.

39. Carettoni's arguments on the basis of a location close to the Temple of Apollo are in *London Illustrated News*, September 20, 1969, pp. 24 ff. The painted terracotta metope plaques which he considers the best evidence to confirm the identification of the temple site are in "Nuova serie di

grandi 'lastre fittili' Campana," *BA* 58 (1973): 75–87, and "Terracotte 'Campana' dallo scavo del Tempio di Apollo Palatino," *RPAA* 44 (1971–72): 123 ff.

40. Remarking on the coincidence of illusionistic and paratactic orthostat walls within the same houses, Fittschen, "Herkunft und Entstehung," pp. 543–44, reaches the conclusion that architectural illusion and the opening of space need not be considered the primary aims of the second style.

41. Spinazzola, *Via dell' Abbondanza*, pp. 488–503.

42. C. Dilthey, "Dipinti pompeiani accompagnati d'epigrammi greci," *Ann. Inst.* 48 (1876): 294–314, describes the paintings and provides a text of the inscribed epigrams, none of which is exactly identical with its counterpart in the *Anthology*. Allroggen-Bedel, *Maskendarstellungen*, pp. 24–25, dates this room later than the Casa del Criptoportico on account of the "vegetative" nature of the columns, which she sees as forerunners of the candelabra style.

43. A. W. van Buren, "*Pinacothecae* with Especial Reference to Pompeii," *MAAR* 15 (1938): 70–81, deals with forms of *pinakes* and with *pinacothecae* as a class, but follows Vitr. 6.5.2 in regarding them as gallery rooms existing solely for their picture displays and not as rooms whose primary purpose might have been utilitarian. He quite rightly identifies the large oecus in the Casa di Obellio Firmo as one of this mode (for which see Allroggen-Bedel, *Maskendarstellungen*, pp. 26–28). This room in fact combines elements of the "porticus" and "pinacotheca" styles, and the unusual nature of its brushwork which defines almost all details by the use of single lines might suggest that it is the product of still a different workshop. K. Schefold, *La Peinture pompéienne: Essai sur l'évolution et de sa signification*, pp. 50–52, discusses *pinacothecae* in the third and fourth style but finds none in the second, identifying "cubiculum B" of the Villa alla Farnesina as the earliest example.

44. G. E. Rizzo, *Monumenti della pittura antica scoperti in Italia III.3: Le pitture della Casa di Livia.*

45. J. M. Moret, *L'Ilioupersis dans la céramique italiote: Les mythes et leur expression figurée au IV Siecle*, p. 285, mentions two south Italian vases that have the same iconography but depict a different moment in the unfolding of the action.

46. J. Lessing and A. Mau, *Wand und Deckenschmuck eines römischen Hauses aus der Zeit des Augustus.*

47. H. G. Beyen, "Les domini de la Villa de la Farnésine," *Studia varia Carolo Guilielmo Vollgraf a discipulis oblata* (1948): 3–21.

48. R. B. Lloyd, "The Aqua Virgo, Euripus, and Pons Agrippa," *AJA* 83 (1979): 193–204.

49. Castrén, "*Ordo Populusque*," pp. 92–103. In this context one should take account of D'Arms' questioning, pp. 66–67, of the evidence for imperial proprietorship of the "first" notable Campanian third-style villa, commonly called the Villa of Agrippa Postumus, at Boscotrecase, which is famed for the high quality of its mythological panels. The excavations, as

D'Arms points out, were interrupted by the Vesuvian eruption of 1906; there is no evidence that this was strictly a resort villa, and much argument from the size of its slave quarters and from the terrain itself, that it was not.

50. A gladiatorial scene in the *fauces* of the Casa di Fabio Amando is shown and described by Borda, *Pittura Romana*, p. 159, who attributes the taste to the Samnite strain in Pompeian culture. Pliny (*HN* 35.52) makes mention of the first gladiatorial painting displayed in Rome in the mid second century, but the piece was commissioned by the sponsor of the games rather than by a fan.

Notes on Contributors

BARRY BALDWIN is professor of classics and history and chairman of classics at the University of Calgary.

BARBARA K. GOLD is assistant professor of classics and comparative literature at the University of Texas at Austin.

JASPER GRIFFIN is lecturer in Latin at Balliol College, Oxford University.

ELEANOR WINSOR LEACH is professor and chair of classical languages at Indiana University.

PETER WHITE is professor of classics at the University of Chicago.

GORDON WILLIAMS is professor of classics at Yale University.

T. P. WISEMAN is professor of Latin at the University of Exeter.

JAMES E. G. ZETZEL is associate professor of classics at Princeton University.

Abbreviations

Mon. Piot   *Monuments et Mémoires publiés par l'Aca-*
             démie des Inscriptions et Belles-Lettres
             (Fondation Piot)
NJKA   *Neue Jahrbücher für das klassische Altertum*
PP   *La Parola del Passato*
RA   *Revue Archéologique*
RE   *Paulys Real-Encyclopädie der classischen*
             Altertumswissenschaft
REL   *Revue des Études Latines*
RFIC   *Rivista di Filologia e di Istruzione Classica*
RhM   *Rheinisches Museum*
RPAA   *Rendiconti della Pontificia Accademia di*
             Archeologia
Symb. Oslo. *Symbolae Osloenses*
TAPA   *Transactions and Proceedings of the Ameri-*
             can Philological Association
WS   *Wiener Studien*

Bibliography

Africa, T. W. "The Opium Addiction of Marcus Aurelius." *Journal of the History of Ideas* 22 (1961): 97–102.

Allen, Walter, Jr. "On the Friendship of Lucretius with Memmius." *CP* 33 (1938): 167–81.

Allroggen-Bedel, Agnes. *Maskendarstellungen in der römische-kampanische Wandmalerei*. Munich: Fink, 1974.

Altaner, Berthold, and Stuiber, Alfred. *Patrologie*. 7th ed. Freiburg: Herder, 1966.

Anderson, R. D., Parsons, P. J., and Nisbet, R. G. M. "Elegiacs by Gallus from Qaṣr Ibrîm." *JRS* 69 (1979): 125–55.

Anderson, William S. "Vergil's Second *Iliad*." *TAPA* 88 (1957): 17–30.

Arnott, W. G. "The Praenomen of Archias." *Hermes* 99 (1971): 254–55.

Badian, E. Review of M. Gelzer, *Kleine Schriften*. *JRS* 57 (1967): 216–22.

————. Review of A. Degrassi, ed., *ILLRP: Imagines (CIL Auctarium)*. *JRS* 58 (1968): 240–49.

Baldwin, Barry. "An Anonymous Latin Poem in Gellius." *Arctos* 13 (1979): 5–13.

————. "The *Caesares* of Julian." *Klio* 60 (1978): 449–66.

————. "Executions, Trials, and Punishment in the Reign of Nero." *PP* 117 (1967): 425–39.

————. "Hadrian's Farewell to Life: Some Arguments for Authenticity." *CQ* 20 (1970): 372–74.

————. "The Minor Characters of Athenaeus." *Acta Classica* 20 (1977): 37–48.

————. *Studies in Aulus Gellius*. Lawrence: University of Kansas Press, 1975.

————. "Turnus the Satirist." *Eranos* 77 (1979): 57–60.

Bardon, Henry. *La littérature latine inconnue*. 2 vols. Paris: Klincksieck, 1952.

Barnabei, Felice. *La villa pompeiana di P. Fannio Sinistore scoperto presso Boscoreale*. Rome: Reale Accademia dei Lincei, 1901.

Barnes, T. D. "Hadrian's Farewell to Life." *CQ* 18 (1968): 384–86.

————. "The Lost *Kaisergeschichte* and the Latin Historical Tradition." In

Bonner Historia Augusta-Colloquium 1968–69, pp. 13–29. Bonn: Habelt, 1970.

———. *Tertullian: A Historical and Literary Study*. Oxford: Clarendon Press, 1971.

Barrett, A. A. "Dido's Child: A Note on *Aeneid* 4.327–30." *Maia* 25 (1973): 51–53.

Bennett, A. W. "*Sententia* and Catalogue in Propertius (3.9.1–20)." *Hermes* 95 (1967): 222–43.

Bergk, Theodor. "Philologische Thesen." *Philologus* 12 (1857): 578–81.

Bethe, Erich. *Ahnenbild und Familiengeschichte bei Römern und Griechen*. Munich: Beck, 1935.

Beulé, C. E. *Auguste, sa famille et ses amis*. 3rd ed. Paris: M. Lévy Frères, 1868.

Beyen, Hendrik G. "Les domini de la Villa de la Farnésine." *Studia varia Carolo Guilielmo Vollgraf a discipulis oblata*, pp. 3–21. Amsterdam: Noord-Holland Uitgevers Maatschappij, 1948.

———. *Die pompejanische Wanddekoration von zweiten bis zum vierten Stil*. Vol. 1. The Hague: Nijhoff, 1938. Vol. 2. The Hague: Nijhoff, 1960.

Bianchi Bandinelli, Ranuccio. *Rome: The Center of Power, 500 B.C. to A.D. 200*. Translated by Peter Green. New York: G. Braziller, 1970.

Biers, William R., and Geagan, Daniel J. "A New List of Victors in the Caesarea at Isthmia." *Hesperia* 39 (1970): 79–93.

Binder, Gerhard. *Aeneas und Augustus: Interpretationen zum 8. Buch der Aeneis*. Meisenheim am Glan: Hain, 1971.

Birley, A. R. *Marcus Aurelius*. Boston: Little, Brown, 1966.

Birt, Theodor. *Kritik und Hermeneutik nebst Abrisse des antiken Buchwesens*. Munich: Beck, 1913.

———. "Verlag und Schriftstellereinnahmen im Altertum." *RhM* 72 (1917–18): 311–16.

Blumenthal, F. "Autobiographie des Augustus." *WS* 35 (1913): 113–30, 267–88.

Boardman, John. "Herakles, Peisistratos and Eleusis." *JRS* 95 (1975): 1–12.

———. "Herakles, Peisistratos and Sons." *RA* (1972): 57–72.

Boëthius, Axel. *The Golden House of Nero: Some Aspects of Roman Architecture*. Ann Arbor: University of Michigan Press, 1960.

Borda, Maurizio. *La pittura Romana*. Milan: Società editrice libraria, 1958.

Boucher, Jean-Paul. *Etudes sur Properce. Problèmes d'inspiration et d'art*. Paris: de Boccard, 1965.

Bowersock, G. W. *Augustus and the Greek World*. Oxford: Clarendon Press, 1965.

———. *Greek Sophists in the Roman Empire*. Oxford: Clarendon Press, 1969.

Brendel, Otto J. *Prolegomena to the Study of Roman Art*. New Haven: Yale University Press, 1979.

Brilliant, Richard. *Roman Art from the Republic to Constantine*. London: Phaidon, 1974.

Browning, R. "Literacy in the Byzantine World." *BMGS* 4 (1978): 39–54.

Buchheit, Vinzenz. *Der Anspruch des Dichters in Vergils Georgika.* Darmstadt: Wissenschaftliche Buchgesellschaft, 1972.

———. "Ciceros Triumph des Geistes." *Gymn.* 76 (1969): 232–53.

———. "Vergilische Geschichtsdeutung." *GB* 1 (1973): 23–50.

Butler, H. E., and Barber, E. A., eds. *The Elegies of Propertius.* Oxford: Clarendon Press, 1933. Reprinted Hildesheim: Olms, 1969.

Cagnat, P. "Praeda." In *Dictionnaire des antiquités,* edited by C. Daremberg and E. Saglio, vol. 4, pp. 610–11. 5 vols. Paris: Librarie Hachette, 1877.

Cairns, Francis. *Generic Composition in Greek and Roman Poetry.* Edinburgh: Edinburgh University Press, 1972.

Cameron, Alan. "Wandering Poets: A Literary Movement in Byzantine Egypt." *Historia* 14 (1965): 470–509.

Camps, W. A., ed. *Propertius: Elegies, Book II.* Cambridge: Cambridge University Press, 1967.

———, ed. *Propertius: Elegies, Book III.* Cambridge: Cambridge University Press, 1966.

Carettoni, Gianfilipo. "Due nuovi ambienti dipinti sul Palatino." *BA* 46 (1961): 189–99.

———. "The House of Augustus-I." *London Illustrated News,* September 20, 1969, 24–25.

———. "Nuova serie di grandi 'lastre fittili' Campana." *BA* 58 (1973): 75–87.

———. "Terracotte 'Campana' dallo scavo del Tempio di Apollo Palatino." *RPAA* 44 (1971–72): 123–39.

Castrén, Paavo. *"Ordo Populusque Pompeianus": Polity and Society in Roman Pompeii. Acta Instituti Romani Finlandiae* 8. Rome, 1975.

Cavenaile, R., ed. *Corpus Papyrorum Latinarum.* Wiesbaden: Harrassowitz, 1958.

Cellini, Benvenuto. *The Life of Benvenuto Cellini.* Translated by J. A. Symonds. 5th ed. New York: Charles Scribner's Sons, 1927.

Champlin, Edward. "The Life and Times of Calpurnius Siculus." *JRS* 68 (1978): 95–110.

Clausen, Wendell. "Ariadne's Leave-taking: Catullus 64.116–120." *Illinois Classical Studies* 2 (1977): 219–23.

Coarelli, Filippo. "Il Comizio dalle origini alle fine della Repubblica." *PP* 174 (1977): 166–238.

———. "Sperlonga e Tiberio, Review of R. Hampe, *Sperlonga und Vergil.*" *Dial. Arch.* 7 (1973): 97–122.

Commager, Steele. *A Prolegomenon to Propertius.* Norman: University of Oklahoma Press, 1974.

Conington, J., and Nettleship, H. *The Works of Virgil.* 5th ed. Revised by F. Haverfield. 3 vols. London: G. Bell and Sons, 1898.

Corbett, P. B. "The *scurra* in Plautus." *Eranos* 66 (1968): 118–31.

Croisille, Jean Michel. *Les natures mortes campaniennes. Collection Latomus* 76. Brussels, 1965.

Crook, John. *Consilium Principis.* Cambridge: Cambridge University Press, 1955.

D'Arms, John H. *Romans on the Bay of Naples*. Cambridge, Mass.: Harvard University Press, 1970.

———. "Ville rustiche e Ville d'*otium*." In *Pompeii 79*, edited by Fausto Zevi, pp. 65–90. Naples, 1979.

Davies, Ceri. "Poetry in the 'Circle' of Messalla." *Greece and Rome* 20 (1973): 25–35.

de Franciscis, Alfonso. "La Villa Romana di Oplontis." In *Neue Forschungen in Pompeii*, edited by B. Andreae and H. Kyrieleis, pp. 7–38. Recklinghausen: Bongers, 1975.

Degrassi, A. "Virgilio e il foro di Augusto." *Epigrafica* 7 (1945): 88–103.

———, ed. *Inscriptiones Latinae Liberae Rei Publicae*. 2 vols. Florence: La nuova Italia, 1957–63.

Dilthey, C. "Dipinti pompeiani accompagnati d'epigrammi greci." *Ann. Inst.* 48 (1876): 294–314.

Doblhofer, Ernst. *Die Augustuspanegyrik des Horaz in formalhistorischer Sicht*. Heidelberg: Winter, 1966.

Drew, D. L. *The Allegory of the Aeneid*. Oxford: Blackwell, 1927.

Dziatzko, Karl. "Autor- und Verlagsrecht im Alterthum." *RhM* 49 (1894): 559–76.

———. "Buchhandel." *RE* 3 (1897): 973–85.

Ehrenberg, Victor. *Alexander and the Greeks*. Translated by Ruth Fraenkel von Velsen. Oxford: Blackwell, 1938.

Elder, J. P. "Catullus 1, His Poetic Creed, and Nepos." *HSCP* 71 (1966): 143–49.

Engemann, Josef. *Architekturdarstellungen des frühen zweiten Stils: Illusionistiche römische Wandmalerei der ersten Phase und ihre Vorbilder in der realen Architektur*. *MDAI(R)* Suppl. 12. Heidelberg, 1967.

Farquharson, A. S. L., ed., trans. *The Meditations of the Emperor Marcus Antoninus*. 2 vols. Oxford: Clarendon Press, 1944.

Fiechter, E. R. "Römisches Haus," *RE* 1A (1914): 961–95.

Fittschen, Klaus. "Zur Herkunft und Entstehung des 2. Stils." In *Hellenismus in Mittelitalien: Kolloquium in Göttingen, 1974*, edited by Paul Zanker, pp. 539–57. 2 vols. Göttingen: Vandenhoeck und Ruprecht, 1976.

Fordyce, C. J. *Catullus: A Commentary*. Oxford: Clarendon Press, 1961.

Fowler, H. W., and Fowler, F. G., trans. *The Works of Lucian of Samosata*. 4 vols. Oxford: Clarendon Press, 1905.

Fraenkel, Eduard. "Catulls Trostgedicht für Calvus." *WS* 69 (1956): 278–88.

———. *Elementi Plautini in Plauto*. Translated by Franco Munari. Florence: La nuova Italia, 1960.

———. *Horace*. Oxford: Clarendon Press, 1957.

———. *Kleine Beiträge zur klassischen Philologie*. 2 vols. Rome: Edizione di Storia e Letteratura, 1964.

Frederiksen, M. W. "Caesar, Cicero and the Problem of Debt." *JRS* 56 (1966): 128–41.

Friedländer, Ludwig. *Roman Life and Manners under the Early Empire*. Translated by A. B. Gough. 4 vols. London: Routledge, 1908–13.

Fuchs, Günter. "Varros Vogelhaus bei Casinum." *MDAI(R)* 69 (1962): 96–105.

Funaioli, G., ed. *Grammaticae Romanae Fragmenta*. Stuttgart: Teubner, 1969.

Galinsky, G. Karl. *Aeneas, Sicily, and Rome*. Princeton: Princeton University Press, 1969.

———. *The Herakles Theme*. Oxford: Blackwell, 1972.

Gjerstad, Einar. *Early Rome*. 4 vols. *Acta Instituti Romani Regni Sueciae* 17. Lund, 1953–66.

Glucker, John. *Antiochus and the Late Academy*. Göttingen: Vandenhoeck und Ruprecht, 1978.

Goold, G. P. *Interpreting Catullus*. London: Lewis, 1974.

———. "O Patrona Virgo." In *Polis and Imperium: Studies in Honor of Edward Togo Salmon*, edited by J. A. S. Evans, pp. 253–64. Toronto: Hakkert, 1974.

Gow, A. S. F., and Page, D. L., eds. *The Greek Anthology: The Garland of Philip and Some Contemporary Epigrams*. 2 vols. Cambridge: Cambridge University Press, 1968.

Gransden, K. W., ed. *Aeneid Book VIII*. Cambridge: Cambridge University Press, 1976.

Green, Peter. "The Penumbra of Power: Review of T. P. Wiseman, *Cinna the Poet and Other Roman Essays*." *Times Literary Supplement*, May 2, 1975, p. 478.

Griffin, Jasper. "Augustan Poetry and the Life of Luxury." *JRS* 56 (1976): 87–105.

Grimal, P. *L'Amour à Rome*. Paris: Librarie Hachette, 1963.

———. "Le quatrième livre des 'Elégies' de Properce et la politique d'Auguste." *Comptes Rendus de l'Académie des Inscriptions et Belles-Lettres* (1952): 258–61.

Hanslik, R. "Der Dichterkreis des Messalla." *Anzeiger der österreichische Akad. d. Wiss.: Phil.-Hist. Kl.* 89 (1953): 22–38.

Heitsch, Ernst, ed. *Die griechischen Dichterfragmente der römischen Kaiserzeit*. 2 vols. Göttingen: Vandenhoeck und Ruprecht, 1963–64.

Hellegouarc'h, J. *Le vocabulaire latin des relations et des partis politiques sous la république*. Paris: "Les Belles Lettres," 1963.

Henrichs, A. "Greek Maenadism from Olympias to Messalina." *HSCP* 82 (1978): 121–60.

Heuss, A. "Alexander der Grosse und die politische Ideologie des Altertums." *A&A* 4 (1954): 65–104.

Highet, Gilbert. *Juvenal the Satirist*. Oxford: Clarendon Press, 1954.

Hillard, T. W. *The Claudii Pulchri, 76–48 B.C.: Studies in Their Political Cohesion*. Ph.D. dissertation, Macquarie University, 1976.

Hillscher, Alfredus. "Hominum litteratorum Graecorum ante Tiberii mortem in urbe Roma commoratorum historia critica." *Jahrb. f. cl. Phil.* Suppl. 18 (1892): 353–444.

Holden, Hubert A., ed. *M. Tulli Ciceronis Pro Publio Sestio Oratio*. London: Macmillan, 1924.

Horsfall, Nicholas. "The Collegium Poetarum." *BICS* 23 (1976): 79–95.

Hubbard, Margaret. *Propertius.* London: Duckworth, 1974.

Innes, D. C. "Gigantomachy and Natural Philosophy." *CQ* 29 (1979): 165–71.

Jashemski, Wilhelmina. *The Gardens of Pompeii.* New Rochelle: Caratzas Bros., 1979.

Jory, E. J. "P. Cornelius P. L. Surus: An Epigraphical Note." *BICS* 15 (1968): 125–26.

Kaibel, G., ed. *Epigrammata Graeca.* Berlin: Reimer, 1878.

Keil, H., ed. *Grammatici Latini.* 7 vols. Leipzig: Teubner, 1857–80.

Kenney, E. J. *Lucretius. Greece and Rome: New Surveys in the Classics* 11. Oxford: Oxford University Press, 1977.

Kienast, D. "Augustus und Alexander." *Gymn.* 76 (1969): 430–56.

Knauer, G. N. *Die Aeneis und Homer.* Göttingen: Vandenhoeck und Ruprecht, 1964.

Kraggerud, Egil. *Aeneisstudien. Symb. Oslo.*, Suppl. 22. Oslo, 1968.

Lane Fox, Robin. *Alexander the Great.* New York: Dial Press, 1974.

Lehmann, Phyllis Williams. *Roman Wall Paintings from Boscoreale in the Metropolitan Museum of Art in New York.* Cambridge, Mass.: Archeological Institute of America, 1953.

Lemerle, Paul. *Le premier humanisme byzantin.* Paris: Presses universitaires de France, 1971.

Lenaghan, John O. *A Commentary on Cicero's Oration "De haruspicum responso."* The Hague: Mouton, 1969.

Leo, Friedrich. *Plautinische Forschungen.* 2d ed. Berlin: Weidmannsche, 1912.

———. "Virgil und die *Ciris.*" *Hermes* 37 (1902): 14–55.

Lessing, J., and Mau, August. *Wand und Deckenschmuck eines römischen Hauses aus der Zeit des Augustus.* Berlin, 1891.

Lintott, A. W. *Violence in Republican Rome.* Oxford: Clarendon Press, 1968.

Lloyd, Robert B. "The Aqua Virgo, Euripus, and Pons Agrippa." *AJA* 83 (1979): 193–204.

Luck, Georg. *The Latin Love Elegy.* London: Methuen, 1959.

Lucot, R. "Mécène et Properce." *REL* 35 (1957): 195–204.

Lyne, R. O. A. M., ed. *Ciris: A Poem Attributed to Vergil.* Cambridge: Cambridge University Press, 1978.

McKay, A. G. *Houses, Villas, and Palaces in the Roman World.* Ithaca: Cornell University Press, 1975.

McLennan, G. R. *Callimachus. "Hymn to Zeus": Introduction and Commentary.* Rome: Edizione dell'Ateneo e Bizzarri, 1977.

Macleod, C. W. "A Use of Myth in Ancient Poetry." *CQ* 24 (1974): 82–93.

MacMullen, Ramsay. *Roman Government's Response to Crisis: A.D. 235–337.* New Haven: Yale University Press, 1976.

Magie, David. *Roman Rule in Asia Minor.* Princeton: Princeton University Press, 1950.

————, ed., trans. *Scriptores Historiae Augustae.* 3 vols. London: Heine-
mann, 1922–32.

Marache, R. "La révolte d'Ovide exilé contre Auguste." In *Ovidiana*, edited
by N. I. Herescu, pp. 412–19. Paris: "Les Belles Lettres," 1958.

Mariotti, Italo. *Studi Luciliani.* Florence: La nuova Italia, 1960.

Marshall, A. J. "Library Resources and Creative Writing at Rome." *Phoenix*
30 (1976): 252–64.

Marx, Friedrich. "Der Dichter Lucretius." *NJKA* 3 (1899): 532–48.

Mattingly, Harold, Sydenham, Edward, et al., eds. *The Roman Imperial
Coinage.* 9 vols. London: Spink and Son, 1923–67.

Mau, August. *Pompeii: Its Life and Art.* Translated by F. W. Kelset. Rev. ed.
New York: Macmillan, 1902.

Meincke, W. *Untersuchungen zu den enkomiastischen Gedichten Theokrits.* Ph.D. dissertation, Kiel University, 1965.

Michel, D. *Alexander als Vorbild für Pompeius, Caesar und M. Antonius.*
Collection Latomus 94. Brussels, 1967.

Michels, Agnes K. *The Calendar of the Roman Republic.* Princeton: Princeton University Press, 1967.

Millar, Fergus. *The Emperor in the Roman World.* London: Duckworth,
1977.

Momigliano, Arnaldo. "Literary Chronology of the Neronian Age." *CQ* 38
(1944): 96–100.

Morel, W., ed. *Fragmenta Poetarum Latinorum epicorum et lyricorum.* 2d
ed. Leipzig: Teubner, 1927.

Moret, Jean Marc. *L'Ilioupersis dans la céramique italiote: Les mythes et
leur expression figurée au IV siecle. Bibl. Helvetica Rom.* 14. Geneva,
1975.

Munro, H. A. J. *Criticisms and Elucidations of Catullus.* Cambridge: Deigh-
ton, Bell, 1878.

Münzer, F. "Ticida." *RE* 6A (1936): 844–46.

Nakagawa, N. "Typologie im NT." In *Die Religion in Geschichte und Gegenwart*, edited by H. v. Campenhausen, et al., vol. 6, p. 1095. 3rd ed. 6
vols. Tübingen: J. C. B. Mohr (Paul Siebeck), 1962. Cited in C. K. Bar-
ret, "The Interpretation of the Old Testament in the New." *Cambridge
History of the Bible, I: From the Beginning to Jerome*, edited by P. R.
Ackroyd and C. F. Evans, p. 410. Cambridge: Cambridge University
Press, 1970.

Nash, Ernest. *Pictorial Dictionary of Ancient Rome.* 2d ed. 2 vols. New
York: Praeger, 1968.

Nethercut, William R. "The σφραγίς of the *Monobiblos.*" *AJP* 92 (1971):
464–72.

Nicolet, Claude. "*Amicissimi Catilinae*: A propos du *Commentariolum petitionis.*" *REL* 50 (1972): 163–86.

————. *L'Ordre équestre à l'époque républicaine.* 2 vols. Paris: de Boccard,
1966.

Nisbet, R. G. M., ed. *M. Tulli Ciceronis in L. Calpurnium Pisonem Oratio.*
Oxford: Clarendon Press, 1961.

Nock, A. D. "Notes on Ruler-Cult, I-V." *JHS* 48 (1928): 21–43.

Norden, Eduard. *Kleine Schriften zum klassischen Altertum,* edited by B. Kytzler. Berlin: de Gruyter, 1966.

Palmer, Arthur. "On Ellis's Catullus." *Hermathena* 3 (1879): 293–363.

Palmer, R. E. A. "Tre lettere in cerca di storico." *RFIC* 99 (1971): 385–409.

Perret, Jacques. "Du nouveau sur Homère et Virgile, Review of G. N. Knauer, *Die Aeneis und Homer." REL* 43 (1965): 125–30.

———. *Les origines de la légende troyenne de Rome.* Paris: "Les Belles Lettres," 1942.

Peter, H. W. G., ed. *Historicorum Romanorum Reliquiae.* Stuttgart: Teubner, 1967.

Phillimore, J. S., trans. *Propertius.* Oxford: Clarendon Press, 1906.

Picard, G. C. "Origine et signification des fresques architectoniques dites de Second Style." *RA* (1977): 231–52.

Picard Schmitter, M.-Th. "Bétyles hellenistiques." *Mon. Piot.* 57 (1971): 43–88.

Pichon, Rene. *De sermone amatorio apud Romanos elegiarum scriptores.* Paris: Librarie Hachette, 1902.

Pillinger, Hugh E. "Some Callimachean Influences on Propertius, Book 4." *HSCP* 73 (1969): 171–99.

Platnauer, Maurice. *Latin Elegiac Verse: A Study of the Metrical Usages of Tibullus, Propertius and Ovid.* Cambridge: Cambridge University Press, 1951.

Pöschl, Viktor. *The Art of Vergil: Image and Symbol in the Aeneid.* Translated by Gerda Seligson. Ann Arbor: University of Michigan Press, 1962.

Postgate, J. P., ed. *Select Elegies of Propertius.* London: Macmillan, 1950.

Puelma Piwonka, Mario. *Lucilius und Kallimachos: Zur Geschichte einer Gattung der hellenistisch-römischen Poesie.* Frankfurt am Main: Klostermann, 1949.

Putnam, M. C. J. "Catullus 11: The Ironies of Integrity." *Ramus* 3 (1974): 70–86.

———. "Horace *c.* 3.30: The Lyricist as Hero." *Ramus* 2 (1973): 1–19.

———. "Propertius' Third Book: Patterns of Cohesion." *Arethusa* 13 (1980): 97–113.

Rawson, Elizabeth. Review of T. P. Wiseman, *Cinna the Poet and Other Roman Essays. JRS* 66 (1976): 266–67.

Reinach, Théodore. *Mithradate Eupator, roi de Pont.* Paris: Firmin-Didot, 1890.

Richardson, John S. "The 'Commentariolum Petitionis.'" *Historia* 20 (1971): 436–42.

Richardson, Lawrence, jr. Article forthcoming in *Chronache Pompeiane.*

———. "The Tribunals of the Praetors of Rome." *MDAI(R)* 80 (1973): 219–33.

———, ed. *Propertius Elegies I–IV.* Norman: University of Oklahoma Press, 1977.

Riewald, P. *De imperatorum Romanorum cum certis dis . . . aequatione*. Ph.D. dissertation, Halle University, 1912.

Rist, J. M. *Plotinus: The Road to Reality*. Cambridge: Cambridge University Press, 1967.

Rizzo, Francesco Paolo. *Le fonti per la storia della conquista pompeiana della Siria*. Palermo: Banco di Sicilia, 1963.

Rizzo, Giulio Emmanuele. *Monumenti della pittura antica scoperti in Italia III.3: Le pitture della Casa di Livia*. Rome: Libreria dello Stato, 1936.

Robert, L. "Deux poètes grecs à l'époque impériale." In *Stele: In Memory of N. Kontoleon*, pp. 10–20. Athens, 1977.

Roberts, C. H. "The Antinoë Fragment of Juvenal." *JEA* 21 (1935): 199–207.

Rose, H. J. *The Eclogues of Virgil*. Berkeley: University of California Press, 1942.

Ross, David O., Jr. *Backgrounds to Augustan Poetry*. Cambridge: Cambridge University Press, 1975.

Rowell, H. T. "The Forum and Funeral Images of Augustus." *MAAR* 17 (1940): 131–43.

Rudd, Niall. *Lines of Enquiry: Studies in Latin Poetry*. Cambridge: Cambridge University Press, 1976.

Sandy, Gerald N. "Indebtedness, *Scurrilitas*, and Composition in Catullus (Cat. 44, 1, 68)." *Phoenix* 32 (1978): 68–80.

Schachermeyr, Fritz. *Alexander der Grosse: Das Problem seiner Persönlichkeit und seines Wirkens*. Sitzungsberichte der österreichischen Akademie der Wissenschaft 285. Vienna, 1973.

Schanz, Martin, and Hosius, Carl. *Geschichte der römischen Literatur bis zum Gesetzgebungwerk des Kaisers Justinian*. 4th ed. 2 vols. Munich: Beck, 1935.

Schefold, Karl. "Antwort klassischer Sagenbilder auf politisches Geschehen." *GB* 4 (1975): 231–42.

———. *La peinture pompéienne: Essai sur l'évolution et de sa signification*. Collection Latomus 108. Brussels, 1972.

———. "Zur Geschichte der Wandmalerei Campaniens." *Antike Kunst* 19 (1976): 118–19.

———. "Der zweite Stils als Zeugnis alexandrinischer Architektur." In *Neue Forschungen in Pompeii*, edited by B. Andreae and H. Kyrieleis, pp. 53–60. Recklinghausen: Bongers, 1975.

Scott, K. "The Identification of Augustus with Romulus-Quirinus." *TAPA* 56 (1925): 82–105.

Shackleton Bailey, D. R. *Propertiana*. Cambridge: Cambridge University Press, 1956.

———. *Two Studies in Roman Nomenclature*. University Park, Pa.: American Philological Association, 1976.

Simon, Erika. *Ara Pacis Augustae*. Tübingen: Wasmuth, 1967.

Skard, E. "Zu Horaz, *Ep*. 1.11." *Symb. Oslo*. 40 (1965): 81–82.

Skutsch, F. "Q. Ennius, der Dichter." *RE* 5 (1905): 2589–628.

Sourvinou-Inwood, Christiane. "Theseus Lifting the Rock and a Cup near the Pithos Painter." *JHS* 91 (1971): 94–109.

Spenser, Edmund. *The Shepherd's Calendar*. Edited by W. L. Renwick. London: Scholartis Press, 1930.

Spinazzola, Vittorio. *Pompei alla luce degli scavi nuovi di Via dell' Abbondanza (anni 1910–1923)*. 2 vols. Rome: Libreria dello Stato, 1953.

Syme, Ronald. *History in Ovid*. Oxford: Clarendon Press, 1978.

———. "The Origin of the Veranii." *CQ* 7 (1957): 123–25.

———. *The Roman Revolution*. Oxford: Clarendon Press, 1939.

———. *Tacitus*. Oxford: Clarendon Press, 1958.

Taeger, Fritz. *Charisma: Studien zur Geschichte des antiken Herrscherkultes*. 2 vols. Stuttgart: Kohlhammer, 1957–60.

Tamm, Birgitta. *Auditorium and Palatium: A Study on Assembly-Rooms in Roman Palaces during the 1st Century B.C. and 1st Century A.D. Stockholm Studies in Classical Archaeology* 2. Translated by Patrick Hort. Stockholm: Almquist and Wiksell, 1963.

Taylor, Lily Ross. "Republican and Augustan Writers Enrolled in the Equestrian Centuries." *TAPA* 99 (1968): 469–86.

———. *The Voting Districts of the Roman Republic. Papers and Monographs of the American Academy at Rome* 20. Rome, 1960.

Thompson, David. "Allegory and Typology in the *Aeneid*." *Arethusa* 3 (1971): 147–53.

Townend, G. B. "The Fading of Memmius." *CQ* 28 (1978): 267–83.

———. "The Literary Substrata to Juvenal's Satires." *JRS* 63 (1973): 148–60.

Tränkle, H. *Die Sprachkunst des Properz und die Tradition der lateinischen Dichtersprache. Hermes Einzelschrift* 15. Wiesbaden, 1960.

Treggiari, Susan M. "Intellectuals, Poets, and Their Patrons in the First Century B.C." *Echos du monde classique: Classical News and Views* 21 (1977): 24–29.

———. *Roman Freedmen during the Late Republic*. Oxford: Clarendon Press, 1969.

Trevor-Roper, Hugh. *Princes and Artists: Patronage and Ideology at Four Habsburg Courts, 1517–1633*. New York: Harper and Row, 1976.

van Buren, A. W. "*Pinacothecae* with Especial Reference to Pompeii." *MAAR* 15 (1938): 70–81.

Vogel, K. H. "Praeda." *RE* 22 (1953): 1200–13.

Voltaire. *Carnet Piccini*, edited by T. Besterman. Geneva: Institut et Musée Voltaire, 1952.

von Albrecht, M. "Die Kunst der Spiegelung in Vergils *Aeneis*." *Hermes* 93 (1965): 54–64.

———. "Vergils Geschichtsauffassung in der 'Heldenschau.'" *WS* 80 (1967): 156–82.

von Blanckenhagen, Peter H. *The Paintings from Boscotrecase. MDAI(R)* Suppl. 6. Heidelberg, 1962.

Weinreich, Otto. *Menekrates Zeus und Salmoneus*. Stuttgart: Kohlhammer, 1933.

Weinstock, Stefan. *Divus Julius*. Oxford: Clarendon Press, 1971.

White, Peter. "*Amicitia* and the Profession of Poetry in Early Imperial Rome." *JRS* 68 (1978): 74–92.

Widmann, Hans. *Geschichte des Buchhandels vom Altertum bis zur Gegenwart.* 2d ed. Wiesbaden: Harrassowitz, 1975.

Wilcken, U. *Alexander der Grosse.* Leipzig: Quelle und Meyer, 1931.

Williams, Gordon. *Change and Decline: Roman Literature in the Early Empire.* Berkeley: University of California Press, 1978.

———. *Figures of Thought in Roman Poetry.* New Haven: Yale University Press, 1980.

———. "Horace *Odes* 1.12 and the Succession to Augustus." *Hermathena* 118 (1974): 147–55.

———. "Poetry in the Moral Climate of Augustan Rome." *JRS* 52 (1962): 28–46.

———. *Tradition and Originality in Roman Poetry.* Oxford: Clarendon Press, 1968.

Wimmel, Walter. *Kallimachos in Rom. Die Nachfolge seines apologetischen Dichtens in der Augusteerzeit. Hermes Einzelschrift* 16. Wiesbaden, 1960.

Wippert, O. *Alexander-Imitatio und röm. Politik in der rep. Zeit.* Ph.D. dissertation, Wurzburg University, 1972.

Wiseman, T. P. *Catullan Questions.* Leicester: Leicester University Press, 1969.

———. "Catullus, His Life and Times, Review of F. Stoessl, *C. Valerius Catullus.*" *JRS* 69 (1979): 161–68.

———. "The Census in the First Century B.C." *JRS* 59 (1969): 59–75.

———. *Cinna the Poet and Other Roman Essays.* Leicester: Leicester University Press, 1974.

———. *Clio's Cosmetics: Three Studies in Greco-Roman Literature.* Leicester: Leicester University Press, 1979.

———. *New Men in the Roman Senate 139 B.C.–A.D. 14.* London: Oxford University Press, 1971.

Youtie, H. C. "Pétaus, fils de Pétaus, ou le scribe qui ne savait pas d'écrire." *Chronique d'Egypte* 41 (1966): 127–43.

Zanker, Paul. "Die Villa als Vorbild des späten pompejanischen Wohngeschmacks." *Jahrbuch des Deutschen Archaeologischen Instituts* 94 (1979): 460–523.

Zetzel, J. E. G. "Horace's *Liber Sermonum:* The Structure of Ambiguity." *Arethusa* 13 (1980): 59–77.

Zinn, E. "Nachwort zu Vergils *Aeneis.*" In *Vergil-Horaz,* translated into German by Rudolf Alexander Schröder, vol. 5. Berlin: Suhrkamp, 1952.